D0597880

Which of the following statements are true?

- All blue-eyed blondes tend to look good in the same colors.

- Heavy women should never wear large prints.

- Colors that "wash you out" when you are pale will look great when you have a suntan.

- There should be one "pure" white blouse in every woman's wardrobe.

- Bright colors are not as "tasteful" as neutral tones.

- Large jewelry looks best on large women and vice versa.

- Women 60 years old and older look prettier wearing soft, dusty, and pastel colors rather than bright or clear or more vibrant colors.

- Coral blush is a basic makeup color that every woman can wear enhancingly.

If you have answered "true" to any of these statements, you may be dressing in a way that does not do justice to your own individual coloring. COLOR WONDERFUL explodes these and other myths, as it shows you how to expand your world of color and make the entire spectrum your personal palette.

JOANNE NICHOLSON AND JUDY LEWIS-CRUM are the co-founders of COLOR 1 ASSOCIATES, INC., the most comprehensive personalized color service in the world, currently offered in all fifty states and many foreign countries by more than four hundred consultants. The authors have combined their professional fashion experience, along with years of color research, consultation, and teaching, to provide the very best color information available. JoAnne Nicholson and Judy Lewis-Crum maintain an active speaking schedule throughout the United States and abroad.

COLOR WONDERFUL

The Revolutionary Color 1 Associates Wardrobe and Makeup Program

by
JoAnne Nicholson and Judy Lewis-Crum
with Jacqueline Thompson

BANTAM BOOKS
TORONTO · NEW YORK · LONDON · SYDNEY · AUCKLAND

*We dedicate this book to
our Color 1 associates and our clients
throughout the world.*

COLOR WONDERFUL
A Bantam Book / February 1986

*The name COLOR 1 ASSOCIATES, INC.® and the logo consisting of
the numeral "1" and the word "COLOR" below are registered trade-
marks of COLOR 1 ASSOCIATES, INC.*
*COLOR WONDERFUL™ is a trademark of COLOR 1 ASSOCI-
ATES, INC. All rights reserved.*
*The models appearing in COLOR WONDERFUL are associates and
clients of COLOR 1 ASSOCIATES, INC.*

*Due to variations in print runs, the color swatches in the insert may
vary slightly from the actual hues.*

All rights reserved.
*Copyright © 1986 by JoAnne Nicholson and Judy Lewis-Crum.
Cover photograph copyright © 1986 by Anthony Loew.
Color insert designed by Art Patrol, NYC.
This book may not be reproduced in whole or in part, by
mimeograph or any other means, without permission.
For information address: Bantam Books, Inc.*

Library of Congress Cataloging-in-Publication Data

Nicholson, JoAnne.
  Color wonderful.

  Includes index.
  1. Beauty, Personal.   2. Color in clothing.
3. Cosmetics.   4. Hairdressing.   I. Lewis-Crum, Judy.
II. Color 1 Associates.   III. Title.
RA778.N724   1986   646.7'2   85-47794
ISBN 0-553-34238-X

Published simultaneously in the United States and Canada

---

*Bantam Books are published by Bantam Books, Inc. Its trademark,
consisting of the words "Bantam Books" and the portrayal of a rooster, is
Registered in U.S. Patent and Trademark Office and in other countries.
Marca Registrada. Bantam Books, Inc., 666 Fifth Avenue, New York,
New York 10103.*

PRINTED IN THE UNITED STATES OF AMERICA

KP   0 9 8 7 6 5 4 3 2 1

Acknowledgments

We would like to acknowledge the contribution of our Color 1 associates to the creation of this book.

You, our consultants throughout the United States and the world, are responsible for the continuing excellence of the Color 1 concept. Your hard work, your personal achievements, and your concern for your clients are a great source of fulfillment to us. You have been the catalysts for unprecedented changes in the lives and looks of tens of thousands of women each year. We applaud you, appreciate you, thank you, and love you.

We could not have brought our Color 1 concept to life without the help of our master photographer, Michael Perham, and our very talented makeup artist and hair stylist, Brenda Perham. The unswerving dedication, understanding, and professionalism they brought to this project are highly appreciated.

Our "models" were our consultants and clients. These women devoted generous portions of their time to the task of helping us show you some of the differences in human coloring that exist around the globe, and we would like to thank them.

We want to acknowledge a debt of gratitude to our clients, men and women whose belief in Color 1 Associates has made us not only the largest, but the most highly respected personal color charting service in the world. It excites us that, by following the Color 1 concept, our clients feel happier, more attractive, and more confident about their look and wardrobe than ever before. Thank you for recommending our concept to so many of your family and friends.

This book is for our clients and for women the world over who want more individualized color wardrobe and makeup knowledge—and want to look fabulous all the time!

Contents

Acknowledgments   v
List of Plates   xii

Introduction: Exploding the Color Myths   1
   The Best You Can Be—with Color 1   6

Part I: Color 1 Color Basics   9

Chapter 1: Your Color 1 Color Type   11
  Determining Your Skin Tone   12
  Determining Your Main Hair Color and
    Highlights   15
  Determining Your Color Type   16
    The Pure White Test   17
    The Woman-Across-the-Room Test 17
    The Judgment Test   20
    Cross-Color Types   21

Chapter 2: Your Color 1 Color Chart   24
  Shades and Clarities   25
  Your Body Colors   26
  Your Complimentary Colors   28
  Your Best White   29
  Your Gray   30
  Your Dark Neutrals   31

Chapter 3: Wardrobe Wizardry   33
  Universal Color Principles   33
  Striking the Right Balance Through
    Contrast Levels   36
  Universally Enhancing Colors—There Are a Few   38
  Color Camouflage: Dealing with Figure Faults   40
  Advice for Women Who Think They're Too Heavy   41

Chapter 4: Makeup and Hair Coloring Magic   45
  Universal Makeup Principles   45
    Choosing the Right Base for Your Complexion   46
    Exceptions to the Rule: If You Have to
      "Correct" Your Complexion   47
    What Difference Does a Tan Make?   48
    Your Skin Tone and Aging   49
    All About Lip Color   50
    Adding Color to Your Cheeks   52
    Glasses and Makeup   53
  Universal Hair Coloring Principles   53
    Do Blonds Have More Fun?   54
    Will I Change Color Types When I
      Color My Hair?   55
    Should I Color My Gray Hair?   56

Part II: Coloramics for Your Color Type   57

Chapter 5: Wardrobe Advice for Muted Coloring   59
  Your Best Color Clarities   60
  Your Best Level of Contrast   61
  Adding an Accent Color   62
  Your Best Neutrals   62
  Fabric Textures and Weights   70
  Patterns, Prints, and Designs   71
  Jewelry   71
  Handbags and Attaché Cases   73
  Shoes   74
  Eyeglass Frames   75
  Evening Wear   75
  Furs   76
  Makeup and Hair Coloring Advice   76
    Makeup Colors   77
    Coordinating Your Makeup and
      Clothing Colors   79
    Hair Coloring   81

Chapter 6: Wardrobe Advice for Gentle Coloring   84
    Your Best Color Clarities   85
    Your Best Level of Contrast   85
    Adding an Accent Color   87
    Your Best Neutrals   87
    Fabric Textures and Weights   94
    Patterns, Prints, and Designs   95
    Jewelry   95
    Handbags and Attaché Cases   97
    Shoes   98
    Eyeglass Frames   98
    Evening Wear   99
    Furs   100
   Makeup and Hair Coloring Advice   100
    Makeup Colors   102
    Coordinating Your Makeup and
       Clothing Colors   104
    Hair Coloring   106

Chapter 7: Wardrobe Advice for Light-Bright Coloring   108
    Your Best Color Clarities   109
    Your Best Level of Contrast   110
    Adding an Accent Color   111
    Your Best Neutrals   112
    Fabric Textures and Weights   120
    Patterns, Prints, and Designs   121
    Jewelry   121
    Handbags and Attaché Cases   122
    Shoes   123
    Eyeglass Frames   124
    Evening Wear   124
    Furs   124
   Makeup and Hair Coloring Advice   125
    Makeup Colors   126
    Coordinating Your Makeup and
       Clothing Colors   129
    Hair Coloring   131

Chapter 8: Wardrobe Advice for Contrast Coloring   132
    Your Best Color Clarities   133
    Your Best Level of Contrast   134
    Adding an Accent Color   135
    Your Best Neutrals   136

Fabric Textures and Weights 142
Patterns, Prints, and Designs 143
Jewelry 145
Handbags and Attaché Cases 146
Shoes 147
Eyeglass Frames 148
Evening Wear 148
Furs 149
Makeup and Hair Coloring Advice 149
Makeup Colors 150
Coordinating Your Makeup and
Clothing Colors 153
Hair Coloring 155

Part III: Cast a Color Spell 157

Chapter 9: Color Chic 159
The Color 1 Capsule Wardrobe Concept 160
Capsule Wardrobes for Muted Color Types 165
Capsule Wardrobes for Gentle Color Types 166
Capsule Wardrobes for Light-Bright
Color Types 167
Capsule Wardrobes for Contrast Color Types 168
Alice—A Case Study 169
The Color 1 Capsule Coat Wardrobe 171
The Color 1 Capsule Casual Wardrobe 174

Chapter 10: Color Charisma 175
Color—the Great Self-Motivator 176
Color—Its Impact on Others 176
Mood Dressing and Other Special Effects 179
The Ethereal or Fragile Look 179
Earthy Looks 180
Showstopper Looks 182
Power Dressing 185
A Final Note About Your Get-Ahead Wardrobe 189

Chapter 11: Color Budgeting 190
Wardrobe Errata 191
The Conglomeration Collection 191
Bargain Bare 192
The Neutral Niche 192
The Uniform Dresser 193
The Headless Person 193

Ms. Insignificant 194
Salvaging Some of the Clothes You Already Own 195
Deploying the "Color Break" as a Salvage Tool 195
The Cost of Your Wardrobe Salvage Operation 197
Shopping with a Color Chart 197

Glossary 199
Color 1 Associates in the United States
    and Abroad 202

Index 209

List of Plates

1 Muted Color Type
2 Gentle Color Type
3 Light-Bright Color Type
4 Contrast Color Type
5 Skin Tones
6 Caucasian Skin Tones
7 Black Skin Tones
8 Lip Colors
9 Muted Coloring and Color Chart
10 Gentle Coloring and Color Chart
11 Light-Bright Coloring and Color Chart
12 Contrast Coloring and Color Chart
13 Muted Coloring with Gray Hair
14 Gentle Coloring with Gray Hair
15 Light-Bright Coloring with Gray Hair
16 Contrast Coloring with Gray Hair
17 Black Muted Coloring
18 Black Gentle Coloring
19 Black Light-Bright Coloring
20 Black Contrast Coloring
21 Clarities of Green
22 Clarities of Red
23 Clarities of Blue
24 Color Value

25 Contrast Levels and Print Sizes
26 Fabrics for Muted Coloring
27 Wrong Muted Wardrobe Look
28 Right Muted Wardrobe Look
29 Fabrics for Gentle Coloring
30 Wrong Gentle Wardrobe Look
31 Right Gentle Wardrobe Look
32 Fabrics for Light-Bright Coloring
33 Wrong Light-Bright Wardrobe Look
34 Right Light-Bright Wardrobe Look
35 Fabrics for Contrast Coloring
36 Wrong Contrast Wardrobe Look
37 Right Contrast Wardrobe Look
38 Wrong Muted Makeup Look
39 Right Muted Makeup Look
40 Wrong Gentle Makeup Look
41 Right Gentle Makeup Look
42 Wrong Light-Bright Makeup Look
43 Right Light-Bright Makeup Look
44 Wrong Contrast Makeup Look
45 Right Contrast Makeup Look
46 Jennifer Ho
47 Jennifer Ho's Color Chart

Introduction

Exploding the Color Myths

Color. It's Mother Nature's siren call, luring the bee to the blossom, his mate to the peacock—indeed, Adam to that bright red apple. Color is one of nature's greatest gifts to humankind. It's a universal language to which we all respond. But how many of us think of color in this way?

Color is also the quintessential element in dressing successfully. It's certainly the least costly. But it's also probably the most overlooked.

Why? Because the majority of adults are suffering from color phobia. Most of us were born with a glorious, *instinctive* sense of color that was systematically bred out of us as we matured. As children, we absorbed our teachers' clichéd opinions about color in school and our parents' color biases at home. As we grew up, we lost that awesome, wondrous sensation we experienced as kids munching popcorn and watching Walt Disney's Technicolor marvel *Fantasia* for the first time.

Gradually, instead of following our own color instincts, we succumbed to the color expectations of others: "You can't wear red. Red is too flashy." "Black is for funerals." "Brown, how dull! It's for people with no pizazz."

Once we were open and adventurous; then we became timid and insecure.

Through the Color 1 concept, we want to restore your lost sense of color magic and teach you how to showcase your own best self through the medium of color. We want to instill in you the belief that your color horizons are bounded only by the limits of your own imagination—and no one else's. Let us liberate you from the prevailing color mythology that is imprisoning so many contemporary women.

The Color 1 concept works for everybody everywhere, for Color 1 Associates Inc. is a highly personalized *international* color and image consulting company whose concept has been helping women and men look terrific since 1968. Ours is the first color firm to train a far-flung network of consultants, now numbering 429 women—and some men—who chart thirty to forty thousand clients a year in fifty states as well as in the Philippines, Japan, Indonesia, Thailand, Singapore, Australia, England, France, Germany, Israel, and Canada.

We—Judy Lewis-Crum and JoAnne Nicholson—began researching the subject of coloring in the 1960s. Our mutual interest in it grew out of our experience as working professionals in the fields of art and fashion. This book embodies our color discoveries—not only truths we stumbled upon back in the late 1960s when we, as individuals, first began color-charting clients, but what we've learned more recently by listening to the feedback from our thousands of Color 1 Associates clients.

Our color insights will surprise you because all you'll need to perform color sorcery are many of the clothing and makeup items you already possess, a few well-chosen additional purchases, and a thorough knowledge of how to combine them effectively to look your most radiant.

Prepare yourself for a second shock. The Color 1 principles we are about to enunciate in *Color Wonderful* are going to widen, not narrow, your wardrobe and makeup choices. They are going to make it simpler, not more difficult, for you to mix and match your outfits every morning. Rather than locking you into a rigid color "formula," the Color 1 concept is designed to liberate you from color prison.

The five tenets that form the cornerstone of the Color 1 concept are definitive and easy to grasp:

1. All women fall into one of four basic color types (see Plates 1–4, 9–20); some fall in between in what we call cross-color types.
2. You have a unique body color scheme, which determines your color category and your best colors as well. In deciding which color shades are most enhancing, skin tone is the most important factor, but *all* of your natural body colors must be taken into consideration.
3. *You can wear every color*—provided you select the shade, clarity, and intensity of that color most becoming to you.
4. You have at least fourteen best color families in your personal color spectrum and possibly as many as twenty-eight. Mixing them in a wardrobe is a snap since nearly every color coordinates with all the others.
5. To dress effectively, you must know the shades, clarities, and values of colors that look best on you in addition to following the color coordination rules that apply to your specific color type.

Once you have determined your color type, you will be able to use the universal principles for all color types in Part I. Then you will also be able to use the specific rules in the separate chapter on your color type in Part II to find your best level of color contrast, your best print sizes and levels of contrast within the prints, your best fabric weights and textures, your best jewelry size and metallic finishes, your best fur colors, your best colors, sizes, and materials for purses, your best color and materials for shoes, your best colors for eyeglass frames, and your best evening wear colors in line with expected lighting conditions. The universal principles in Part I and the specific rules in your chapter of Part II will also tell you how to select the right makeup, nail polish, and hair coloring shades to compliment your natural coloring.

Don't be surprised if some or all of the five Color 1 tenets strike you as heresy. They are heresy. They represent a revolt against the Neanderthal thinking that has turned America, in our opinion, into a nation of color illiterates. And not only America.

How did people arrive at this advanced state of color confusion? By listening to their mothers, their teachers, and their friends. By reading information in magazines and books that was either wrong or far too general to be helpful (like the magazine article that advised its readers: "Screaming, can't-miss-it *red* is everybody's best bet!").

Some unfortunate women are still valiantly trying to build their wardrobes around traditional color conventions they should have discarded twenty years ago. Many of these women still believe, for example, that their hair color dictates what colors look good on them. Redheads should stuff their closets with greens and other earth tones and eschew any form of the heinous red. (But see how fabulous our red-haired model in Plate 28 looks in her best red.) Blonds should envelop themselves in pastels, while the lucky brunettes can bask in all the vibrant colors of the spectrum.

They still believe the shibboleth, "Certain colors for certain seasons." To be fashionably dressed, a woman should pack away her whites and other light and bright-colored clothes in winter and don the deeper, somber shades of black, gray, and burgundy. She should choose pastels and navy-red-white combinations (with patent leather accessories) for spring, flaunt vivid, tropical colors and/or pale pastels all summer, and retire to the muted colors of the autumn leaves throughout the fall.

And when their hair finally turns to gray, many of these women still believe they're automatically doomed to a narrow range of "old lady colors"—lavender, dove gray, black (worn with pearls, of course), navy, rose beige, and similar neutrals. At all costs, they must avoid loud prints and large geometrical patterns and forever after live in solids or subdued florals. (But note how vibrant our gray-haired models look in their best shades, clarities, and levels of contrast in Plates 13–16.)

While many of the over-forty half of the adult female population remain color starved because of such old wives' tales, many of the under-forty generation adhere to an equally restrictive color diet for an entirely different set of reasons. They're held in check by the rigid color rules of the "dress for success" crowd. The theory is this:

In order to succeed in the working world, women must wear suits ("the business uniform") in dark "authority" colors, ranging from black to steel gray, dark brown (but only in the Midwest), navy, deep maroon, and beige (but only in the Sunbelt in the summer). In addition, women should avoid suits in pastels, most shades of green, or any color that is bright or exotic.

Blouses, like suits, should be solid-colored or have such a subdued pattern that they look solid at a distance. Finally, there must be high contrast between the colors of a woman's suit and her blouse. All this adds up to what is called the "power look."

Obviously, this has everything to do with symbols and nothing at all to do with women's natural coloring. That kind of uniform can hardly be expected to flatter more than a very few women. (You can see how our model in Photo 6.3 is being overpowered by the navy-and-white "success" look. The level of contrast in Photo 6.4 is far more flattering, when the model wears a pale coral blouse with the navy suit.)

As if the damage inflicted on women's wardrobes by the "dress for success" proponents wasn't bad enough, along came a battery of so-called image consultants and color experts in the early 1980s to confuse women even further. One divides the whole universe of women according to the medieval concept of the four humors (sanguine, melancholy, choleric, and phlegmatic).

Others claim that all women fall into one of four seasonal categories. All "winters," for example, get the same *prepackaged* set of colors to match when they are choosing clothes and makeup. They also claim a woman's "season" indicates her "clothing personality"—whether she's the dramatic, sporty/natural, romantic, or ingenue type.

We loudly disagree!

You can't lump all women into four categories and expect each woman to be equally enhanced by one of four identical, prepackaged sets of colors.

Moreover, it's a myth that only a limited number of colors is appropriate for a basic wardrobe, formal wear, resort, and leisure wear, or for certain seasons or regions of the country. It's a myth that women must select colors based solely on their hair color or personality type or age. Only *some* business attire is excepted, and we hope to eliminate this one remaining taboo in the near future.

If your goal is to look sensational all the time, the Color 1 concept will tell you how. Whether you're a high-powered professional woman or a housewife and mother, our advice to you is the same: To look and feel like that proverbial million dollars, you must find the shades and color intensities that compliment your unique natural coloring—*and stick with those colors as closely as possible no matter what.* Once you discover your own special rainbow of colors, sticking with them won't be hard because you'll never have looked better in your life! Suddenly your skin will look clear and radiant, your hair will shine, your eyes will sparkle, your teeth will look whiter, your smile will be warmer—and you'll see people gasping as you walk into a room.

The difference is *color.* Perhaps for the first time in your life, you'll be dressing in a way that will enhance rather than detract from your natural body coloring.

Think of it this way. Color is the most important factor in dressing effectively. Color can not only completely change your appearance and mood but can exert a powerful, though subliminal, impact on the mood of each and every person coming into contact with you. Why? Because *color creates your first visual impact.* Make no mistake about it, color attracts the eye more quickly than any style or silhouette ever will. The color or colors you're wearing—and how well they work with your natural body colors—will dominate the viewer's first impression more than any other aspect of your attire.

It is our goal to teach you to use color like a precision instrument. We want to free you from all those inhibiting color myths. We want to teach you not only how to dress in the right shades to enhance your coloring, but how to use color therapeutically, to lift your own and other people's spirits. And we want you to learn how to use color to achieve the kind of effect on others that will help you realize your personal and career goals.

Finding your own color type—Muted, Gentle, Light-Bright, or Contrast—is the first step in making color work for you. And it's a big step. It's not always easy to clear your mind of old self-images and give yourself a good hard look. That's one of the reasons why our Color 1 associates are so good at what they do—they can look at you with objectivity and experience behind them. But if you're ready to be honest with yourself, you too can take that hard, objective look.

First of all, then, use the next chapter to determine your own color type. You might also take a peek at the individual chapters on color types in Part II to make sure you're on the right track.

Then go to Chapter 2. Walk through each body color, taking notes on Your Color 1 Color Chart (page 23) as you go. You will add to these notes as you read the chapter on your color type in Part II.

The rest is fun and easy.

Read about Wardrobe Wizardry (Chapter 3) and Makeup and Hair Coloring Magic (Chapter 4), and then go directly to your own Coloramics chapter in Part II. Make it all come together!

Finally, learn how to cast a color spell in Part III. Find out how to mix and match for color chic (Chapter 9), how to dress for effect (Chapter 10), and how to use color magic to unclutter your closet and spare your pocketbook (Chapter 11).

Our greatest hope is that reading this book and studying the photographs will make you perceive color in a new way, as a kind of magic that can transform you from what you are into what you aspire to be. By following the Color 1 principles, which are anything but restrictive, you can prove to yourself that color is a magic wand. Utilized correctly, they can make you look healthier, slimmer, younger, more vivacious, and generally more exciting and interesting.

Basing all your wardrobe and makeup decisions on color first and foremost is the smartest aesthetic and financial move you'll ever make. Why? Because your best colors are one of the few things that never go out of style.

Part I

Color 1 Color Basics

Chapter 1

Your Color 1 Color Type

Finding your own Color 1 color type is the first step to breaking out of color prison and discovering just how terrific the Color 1 concept can make you look.

No matter what your nationality or ethnicity, chances are you fall into one of Color 1's four main color types: Muted, Gentle, Light-Bright, or Contrast. (Some people are "cross-color types," but more on that later.) But remember, these are only broad classifications. A multitude of people, all quite different-looking, coexist under each color type.

Remember, too, that your color type is based on your natural body coloring, particularly the coloring in and around your face. *Most important in determining your color type is the shade of your skin; your natural hair color is only a secondary indicator.*

Because your body contains more of your skin color than any other, your skin works as a background for every other color you wear, whether it's the color of your clothes, makeup, or jewelry. Any color that makes your skin look dulled, sallow, grayish, or muddy is the wrong color for you. The right color, on the other hand, will make your skin look clear and glowing at all times. In fact, that's the ultimate test in deciding whether a particular shade fits into your color spectrum.

Women sometimes complain that their skin looks pale and blah. Or sallow and uninteresting. They may be right, but not because their genes dealt them a poor hand. It's because their closets and makeup shelves are jammed with colors that give their skin a negative cast.

Mother Nature never errs in her color schemes. Your skin is the *right* color to compliment the rest of your natural-born look. Color 1 coloramics will show you how to make the most of nature's gifts.

To get a feel for the four color types, look at the color plates 1–4, which give you classic examples of each, Plate 5, which displays the range of skin tones, and Plates 6 and 7, which show Caucasian and black skin tones, respectively.

The four color types and their personal color charts are illustrated further in Plates 9–12. Each chart is based on the model's body coloring—skin tone, hair, eye, and lip colors. Remember, though, even if you are the same color type as one of those models, the colors on your own color chart will vary, since it's rare to find two people who have identical coloring. In fact, when you stop and consider all the variables, it has to be a million-to-one shot that you and another woman will ever arrive on this earth with precisely the same natural color scheme.

Determining Your Skin Tone

Ascertaining the shade of your skin is the first order of business in finding your color type.

There is only one way to assess color accurately, whether it's the color of your skin or a piece of fabric, and that's to view it in daylight (although you should not stand directly in the sun).

Obviously, to discover your skin's true color, it must be free of any makeup. Incidentally, don't try to judge the color of your complexion right after removing your makeup. Cleansing can cause pinkness or redness. Wait until that flush has subsided and the natural color of your skin has had a chance to reassert itself.

Now, makeup off? Are you standing in natural light? Then take a good hard look at your skin tone in your face and neck area and compare what you see with the sample skin-tone shades illustrated in Plates 5–7 and with the Universal Skin-Tone Chart below.

Once you've decided which skin-tone shade best describes you, make a note of it on Your Color 1 Color Chart at the beginning of Chapter 2.

We can't overemphasize the importance of knowing your skin tone for choosing appropriate colors. We're reminded of a client of ours who purchased a beautiful brown designer suit, exquisitely styled in a lovely fabric. Soon after buying it, though, she realized the suit didn't look quite right on her but couldn't figure out why.

"How can something that has everything going for it look so wrong on me!" she complained. The suit was a great disappointment because she'd spent a mint on it. We were able to tell her what went wrong:

This woman has pink-beige skin, which means she needs to wear beiges and browns with a *pinkish* cast to them. Unfortunately, her designer suit was *golden* brown. Neither her skin nor her hair have any golden tone in them. As a consequence, the golden brown suit didn't relate in any way to her natural coloring. The suit hung on her body, calling attention to itself rather than to her own good looks, because it didn't pick up any of her inherent color assets.

Universal Skin-Tone Chart

Skin Tone	Race			
	Caucasian	Oriental	Black	American Indian
Porcelain (very light ivory)	X	X		
Ivory (little or no pink or gold)	X	X	X	X
Clear camel (little or no pink or gold)	X	X	X	X
Clear golden (light, medium, dark)	X	X	X	X
Clear golden olive (light, medium, dark)	X	X		
Olive (light, medium, dark)	X	X		
Clear golden beige (light, medium, dark)	X	X	X	X
Pink-beige (light, medium, dark)	X		X	X
Pink-brown beige (light, medium, dark)	X		X	X
Brown-beige (light, medium, dark)	X		X	X
Golden brown-beige (light, medium, dark)	X	X	X	X
Pink (light, medium, dark)	X		X	X
Red-brown (light, medium, dark)			X	X
Brown (light, medium, dark)			X	X
Golden brown (light, medium, dark)			X	X

The popular myth that your skin tone changes as you grow older or when you tan is just that—a myth. Once you reach adulthood your skin tone is set for life. The only time it might change is as a consequence of illness, chemotherapy, or similar medical treatment. Hormonal or nutritional imbalance, various skin disorders, and constant exposure to the sun, resulting in severe skin damage, might also alter your complexion, but these situations are relatively uncommon.

When you tan, you may look different, but the basic shade of your skin has only darkened, not changed. You may go from a clear, light golden beige in the spring, say, to a golden camel at the end of the summer, or from a pink-beige to a pink-camel. That is, of course, unless you overdo it. But your *basic* skin-tone shade stays the same (as seen on the chart).

Determining Your Main Hair Color and Highlights

Now take the same close look at your hair that you did at your skin.

Hair color is never simply blond, red, brown, gray, black, or white. Everyone's hair contains at least one highlight color: lighter or darker tones of your main hair color; or perhaps totally different colors such as gold, camel, bronze, or rust.

Your hair color will always be one of the best colors to repeat in your clothing or accessories because your natural hair color is never unflattering. If you think it is, that's because you haven't learned to match or showcase it properly.

It's important to be specific about the colors in your hair. If you're a blond, for example, you may be golden blond, reddish blond ("strawberry"), dark blond, ash blond, beige-blond, "champagne" blond, or white-blond ("platinum"). (Brenda, in Plate 3, is a golden blond.)

While it's true that all heads of hair, upon close examination, often have several shades of color, you should pay attention to the shade that predominates. If you're a blond, for example, do not study the hair near your scalp to decide your true color. Instead, look at the outer layer of hair. Ask yourself, "What shade is most apparent to people who look at me?" (In Plate 10, Myrt has ash brown hair with slight golden highlights.)

Red hair, too, comes in a multitude of shades: auburn, bronze, cinnamon, copper, rust, pinkish rust, amber, and red-gold. (Plate 28 offers a good example in JoAnn's red hair.)

And then there's the ubiquitous brown. Are you ash brown, which is brown with grayish highlights? Chocolate brown, best described as a dark shade lacking apparent ash, golden, or red highlights? Chocolate brown is actually the color many think of as a "true" dark brown. How about golden brown, which is just what the name implies? Perhaps your hair color could be termed "warm" brown because of its slight red cast? Or is it a more intense reddish brown with its unmistakable red highlights? (In Plate 1, Lin has medium brown hair with strong caramel highlights. Patti, in Plate 2, has somewhat lighter brown hair with highly apparent golden camel highlights.)

Those of you with blackish-looking hair might actually have black-brown hair—hair that is such a deep brown that it often looks black. (Dolly, Plate 4, has black-brown hair.) Or does your black hair have reddish, golden, bronze, camel, or even navy highlights?

Gray hair also comes in many shades: silver (see Plate 16), pearl (Plate 14), slate (Plate 13), brownish, blondish, to name some. When all or nearly all the pigment is gone, your hair looks white.

You can see that those natural glints and streaks of second and sometimes third colors that run through your hair can range from blue-black to blond and from bronze, rust, and red to shades of gold and camel. Sometimes these highlights in your hair actually match your skin tone; for example, a golden-skinned woman who has medium brown hair with light golden blond highlights.

Once you've discovered not only your basic hair color but your highlights, make a note of them on Your Color 1 Color Chart. Then look at the survey of the Four Basic Color Types at the end of the chapter to see where you might fit in.

Determining Your Color Type

By now you're probably starting to get a feel for which color type you are. You may even be quite certain. Just to make sure you're on the right track—or to get you going if you're still puzzled—we want you to perform a few tests using yourself as the model. Fortunately, these tests are as much fun as they are revealing. And when you're all finished, you'll *know* your color type and be all set to fill in your color spectrum and find out how to apply Color 1 color basics to keep you looking Color 1-derful all the time!

The Pure White Test

Find an example of pure white—a stark white piece of paper or a very white swatch of fabric. A sheet, blouse, or some other top will suffice for this experiment. Place the pure white under your chin so that it covers your shoulders completely. Frame your face in the mirror so that you can only see your face and hair and the pure white.

Close your eyes for a moment, then open them. Now, what do you see?

Perhaps you see a woman on whom the pure white looks overly bright, harsh, and garish? If so, your coloring is either Muted or Gentle. Women with Muted coloring can never wear pure white. Those with Gentle coloring can only wear it sparingly in a small print or as tiny trim. (To understand this even better, look at Plate 27. Close your eyes, then open them. Notice that your eyes keep going to the pure white in this Muted model's outfit. Then look at Photo 6.3. Even in this black-and-white photo, you can see that the white blouse is too white for this Gentle color type.)

Or do you see a woman who looks enhanced with such a large amount of pure white next to her face (as in Plate 3)? If so, you have either Light-Bright or Contrast coloring. Keep in mind that to look absolutely superb, even some women with Light-Bright or Contrast coloring need to augment such a large splash of pure white next to their face with a touch of a second bright color (as in Plate 43).

The Woman-Across-the-Room Test

This is actually a series of tests. Your props are a full-length mirror in a well-lighted room and various wardrobe items, which we will describe.

Here is what we want you to do:

Wearing the designated outfit, stand with your back to the full-length mirror. Walk four to six paces away from it and turn around. Glance at yourself quickly in the mirror as if you are looking at a stranger who has just entered the room. Savor that first impression. Ask yourself . . .

Do I see a whole woman in the mirror or just an outfit?
Does the outfit seem to be wearing me rather than vice versa?
Does my face fade out in comparison to the outfit?
Does the outfit appear too overpowering—too strong or too bright—for my coloring?

Or, at the other extreme . . .

Does the outfit make me look drab or washed out from head to toe?
Does my face seem absolutely vibrant compared to the toned-down colors of the outfit?
Does the outfit appear weak and insignificant on me?
Is my natural coloring visually stronger than the outfit?

- The first outfit you test should be a dark suit of black or navy worn with matching black or navy shoes and a *pure white* blouse.

  When you glance at yourself in this color combination, does the stark white jump out at you?

  Do your eyes become riveted to this strong-contrast outfit to the detriment of everything else?

  If the outfit is prominent here and you fade to insignificance in comparison, you have Muted or Gentle coloring. On the other hand, when you look in the mirror you may see a woman who can carry off this highly contrasting outfit. Women with Light-Bright and Contrast coloring can.

- If your hair is fairly dark but has golden tones in it, you may still be wondering if you are a Light-Bright or a Contrast color type. To find out, put on a jacket or shirt with a large, red-and-black lumberjack check and black slacks or a black skirt.

  If the mirror test convinces you this outfit is too overpowering for your coloring (giving you the headless-person look), you are a Light-Bright, not a Contrast, color type. (Check against Photos 7.3 and 8.6.)

• For those of you who can't decide whether you have Light-Bright or Gentle coloring, here's a test:

Don a blouse or some other item of clothing with a pattern or stripe comprised of lots of pure white accented with a bright second color (as in Photo 7.2).

As you turn to glance in the mirror, does the pure white jump out at you? Does the garment make you look a little—or very—washed-out?

If so, you are a Gentle color type. On the other hand, you may have the opposite reaction and feel the top makes you look alive and sparkling. In that case, you are a Light-Bright color type.

• Perhaps you've got your color type narrowed down to Gentle or Muted but you can't decide which. Try this:

Put on a blouse or dress with a small print. The print should have a combination of a small amount of pure white and toned-down pastel colors. (By toned-down, we mean colors that have a touch of gray or brown in them. The opposite of toned-down clarities are clear and bright clarities of colors. Look at the clarities of green, red, and blue shown in Plates 21–23 to get an idea of what we mean.)

If the mirror test shows the pure white jumping out at you and the print looking washed out, you have Muted coloring. If the pure white is fine and the print does *not* look washed out, you have Gentle coloring.

• Because your hair is fairly dark, you may be stumped: Do I have Muted or Contrast coloring?

To find out, try on a garment with a large black-and-soft white pattern, or a large print combining pure white with a second clear, bright color.

If this color combo wears you (as it does the model in Photo 5.1) instead of you wearing it, then you have Muted coloring.

To crystallize what you've already discovered about your coloring, take the following three tests:

• Put on a candy-striped blouse in which the bright red and pure white stripes are on the small side (see Photo 7.2). If you're a Light-Bright color type, this blouse will look super on you. It will look all right with Contrast coloring; too bright with Gentle coloring; and most unflattering with Muted coloring.

- Slip into a small floral print of pastel blue, yellow, pink, and a touch of pure white. A woman with Gentle coloring will look smashing in this. Women with Light-Bright or Muted coloring will look washed-out. And women with Contrast coloring will look dulled—the ultimate in drab.
- Finally, find a medium-scale batik print comprised of medium and dark *toned-down* colors, say, blue, rust, brown, and/or green. Such a print will look great on a woman with Muted coloring, too heavy and dark on a woman with Gentle or Light-Bright coloring, and a touch too subdued on a woman with Contrast coloring.

The Judgment Test

This time, without any props, let your best judgment and common sense be the guide to your color type.

Answer the following series of questions:

Overall, is my coloring dark and light, medium, or light?

If you select *dark and light,* ask yourself,

Does my coloring present a strong contrast because of my very dark hair and lighter skin?

If the answer is yes and you can wear large-pattern black-and-white clothes, you have Contrast coloring.

If you select *medium* because of your medium-tone hair of either red or brown, ask yourself,

Do I have a brown-on-beige or red-on-beige look?

If the answer is yes to either of these questions *and* you cannot wear pure white in any way, you have Muted coloring.

Do I have golden glints in my hair picking up on the golden tones in my skin, giving me a somewhat bright but medium look?

If the answer is yes *and* you can wear pure white, you are a Light-Bright color type. Even if you have medium brown hair now, many of you had much lighter brown or blond hair as a child. If you have the same golden glints in your hair and a golden brown-beige skin but are *not* enhanced by pure white, you have Muted coloring.

If you select *light* because of the light color of your hair and your light to medium-light skin, ask yourself,

> *Do I have a gold-on-gold aura about me because of my golden skin and golden blond hair?*

If the answer is yes *and* you can wear a lot of pure white, you have Light-Bright coloring.

> *Is my hair more ash or beige blond and my skin more ivory or pinkish in cast?*

If the answer is yes *and* you can wear a little pure white in a smaller print, you are a Gentle color type.

By now, most of you know into which of the four basic color types you belong. To help you further, an overview is offered in Color 1's Four Basic Color Types below.

Cross-Color Types

Perhaps you've reached this point in our narrative and you're still not positive that you've identified your color type. If this is the case, you may be one of a group of people who are cross-color types—that is, your skin tone falls into one of the four basic color types and your hair color into another.

For example, suppose you have golden-brown beige skin and black-brown hair with rust highlights. This natural color scheme would indicate you may be a Muted/Contrast color type. Suppose, on the other hand, you have very slightly pink-toned skin and golden blond hair. Then you may have Gentle/Light-Bright coloring. Pink-beige skin and medium brown hair with bronze highlights may indicate that you are a Gentle/Muted color type.

What does it mean if you are one of those women who are cross-color types? It means you will need to use a level of contrast pertaining to one color type and the clarity of colors associated with another color type. We will cover these two concepts in depth in Chapter 3.

Of course, knowing your color type is only a stepping-stone. As you regularly arrive at crossroads in the decision-making process about how best to select and combine colors, your color type and the universal wardrobe principles we describe in Chapter 3 will serve as your guide to looking fabulous 100 percent of the time.

The Four Basic Color Types

Color Type	Skin Tone (without makeup)*	Natural Hair Color	Overall Look
MUTED (white)	ivory beige, brown beige, or golden brown-beige	redhead; caramel, red, or bronze highlights in blond or light to dark brown hair	beige-on-brown, brown-on-brown, or red-on-brown appearance medium to strong coloring
MUTED (black)	light to dark golden brown to brown	brown to black	brown-on-brown, brown-on-black medium to strong coloring
GENTLE (white)	ivory or pink-beige	ash blond, ash brown, or red	soft, subtle appearance delicate coloring
GENTLE (black)	light pink beige to dark pink brown	brown to black	same as above
LIGHT-BRIGHT (white)	ivory or clear golden beige	golden blond or golden light to medium brown	true light and bright appearance delicate coloring
LIGHT-BRIGHT (black)	clear golden	brown to black	same as above
CONTRAST (white)	ivory, olive, or clear beige	dark brown or black	definite dark-light appearance strong coloring
CONTRAST (black)	light to dark very clear tones with little or no pink or golden tones	brown to black	dark-light appearance *or* dark-on-dark strong coloring

*For a detailed chart categorizing skin tones by color type, see the Universal Skin-Tone Chart on p. 14

Your Color 1 Color Chart (for taking notes)

Color Type:

Body Colors:

Skin:_____

Hair:_____

   Highlights:_____

Eyes:_____

   Secondary Eye Colors:_____

Lips (Your Red):_____

Your Dark Neutrals:

Your Best White:_____

_____

Your Gray:_____

_____

Your Complimentary Colors:_____

_____

_____

_____

_____

Chapter 2

Your Color 1 Color Chart

Your personal color spectrum contains at least fourteen best color families and perhaps as many as twenty-eight. Seven to ten of them are the colors of your skin, hair, eyes, lips, and fingertips—your natural color scheme. We refer to these as "body colors."

The remainder of your best colors are your complimen-tary colors, your dark neutrals, your white, and your gray. These are missing from a woman's natural body coloring. They are equally important, though, because they compliment—or enhance—all her body colors and round out her personal color spectrum. Your complimentary colors look just as flattering as your body colors. And combining your body and complimentary colors, dark neutrals, white, and gray widens your color horizons, creating a rainbow of new and exciting color combinations and adding new variety to your looks and clothing.

Altogether, then, your color chart will contain up to twenty-eight best color families, all the shades and clarities most enhancing to you (more on this below and in Chapter 3).

For an example of a very full color chart, look at the last two color plates (Plates 46–47), which show Jennifer Ho, one of our San Francisco associates, and her actual color chart. Note that Jennifer's Personal Color Harmony Chart contains seven body colors and fourteen complimentary colors, three values of white, a gray, and three dark neutral colors. Thus, her chart contains twenty-eight colors in all.

Before you go ahead and take notes on the rest of your colors, you should know something about shades and clarities, two important color concepts we'll be using a lot.

Shades and Clarities

Every color comes in a myriad of *shades*. Red, for example, can be brick red, fire engine red, Chinese red, raspberry, burgundy, rose, orange-red, and so on.

In addition, each shade of red comes in a variety of *clarities*. Clarity refers to the clearness or lucidity or purity of a color—how distinctly "red" it really is. A bright red would fall at one end of the clarity spectrum, for instance, and a toned-down or muted red containing a lot of brown or gray pigment would fall at the other. (To see examples of several different colors in a range of clarities, turn to Plates 21, 22, and 23.)

How often have you said, or heard someone say, "I love red but I can't wear it because it doesn't look good on me." This is not true. You *can* wear red! What you are really saying is, "The shade and clarity of red that I picture in my mind as true red does not happen to be the one that looks good on me."

Think about it a moment. The term "red" actually covers a lot of territory on the color spectrum. The old stereotypic notion that, as Gertrude Stein might have said, "red is red is red" is just not true.

The fact is that there is a red, in a very specific shade and clarity, that looks fabulous on you. This is the basic tenet of all of Color 1's coloramics. (See Plate 28 for an example of a toned-down coral red and Plate 15 for an example of a bright "true" red.)

Here is another example: Not everyone looks good in kelly green. If you are someone who has worn that green shade and realized that it didn't do anything for you, you might have jumped to the incorrect conclusion: "Green isn't my color." Not so! You *can* wear green—as well as red, yellow, blue, blue-green, rust, coral, orange, purple, brown, gray, beige, white, and navy—provided all these colors are in the specific *shades* and *clarity* most flattering to your natural coloring.

Color is an individual matter. Black is one color that definitely does not enhance everyone, it's true. Still, there are many blonds, redheads, and brunettes who look glorious in black.

Viva la difference!

Your Body Colors

In Chapter 1 you determined your skin color, hair color, and hair highlights and made a note of them on Your Color 1 Color Chart. So you already know at least three of your body colors—more if you were able to detect extra highlights. Your other body colors will be your red—matching your inner lip color or that of your gently squeezed fingertip—and your eye colors.

Your best shade of red is your body's natural blood color, the color you turn when you blush or flush. You can see a very light form of this red in the palms of your hands, your fingertips after you squeeze them, and your lips. That shade could range anywhere from a very orange-red at one extreme to a more blue-red at the other. Compare your lip color to those on Plate 8, and add the matching color to Your Color 1 Color Chart. Whatever shade it is, this red is one of your very best colors. It's *the* shade you wear as your most basic lipstick, nail, and blush color and as a major staple of your wardrobe.

One of our Washington, D. C., clients has very gentle coloring and was dismayed when she first saw the red on her color chart. Her best red is a soft, dusty rose. "I can't be a devil in *that* color," she complained. Our reply was, "Oh yes you can! And this red will be even more effective because no one will suspect you."

A bright red outfit would visually overwhelm this woman's gentle coloring. The bright red outfit would be the only thing people would see. But by wearing the soft rose red shade on her color chart she remains in control and looks beautifully devilish.

Eye colors are terrific colors to pick up in your clothing and makeup shades. And when you take a good look, you'll be surprised at all the color you see. It's the rare human being whose eyes contain only the light and dark values of one color. More typically, the irises of an individual's eyes are the repository for several colors. The average person has anywhere from two to four colors. Some have as many as six. (Note how many eye colors appear on Jennifer's chart in Plate 47.)

Move over to the window with a hand mirror and take a good, long look at your eyes. Those of you who think you have brown eyes may find that your irises are actually a rust color, with yellow, gold, and orange glints. Or perhaps they're rust with navy blue streaks running through the iris and a navy or purple-blue rim running around it. Your so-called brown eyes could also contain various shades of green, purple, and plum.

The eye color known as "hazel" is really a combination of green, yellow, rust, brown, and sometimes blue, blue-green, or bronze brown. The shade of green varies from person to person. It could be a jade, emerald, lime, mint, moss, or sage. Secondary colors in a hazel eye are various shades of blue, blue-green, yellow, orange-yellow, bronze-orange, rust-orange, reddish rust, brownish rust, or bronze-brown.

Women with blue eyes often have a lot of yellow in them as well. That yellow could range from a cream yellow to a lemon yellow to an apricot. If you have blue-green eyes—a teal blue or turquoise blue—the secondary colors in your irises are probably other shades of blue or green and yellow. Your blue eyes could also have purple or rust flecks or streaks in them.

Even though the irises of your eyes may only contain trace amounts of these secondary colors, it is important to know what they are because certain shades of these colors will look extremely attractive on you when worn as items of clothing or as eye shadow. Take a good look, and make notes of those colors on your chart.

Most human eyes have some form of yellow in them. Include your best shade of yellow in your basic wardrobe. Not only will it enhance your skin tone, it will bring out the yellow glints in your eyes, making them absolutely sparkle. You'll love how alive you'll look wearing it!

Your Complimentary Colors

Complimentary colors are the shades of colors other than your body colors that are most enhancing to you. And since each of your complimentary colors coordinate with your specific coloring, they all coordinate with each other and with the other colors on your chart, as we explain in full in Chapter 3. If you hesitate to combine the colors in your spectrum, consider it a failure of imagination—a lack of color daring on your part. It is not that almost all those glorious colors on your chart can't be worn together in handsome and, in some cases, exotic and unusual combinations.

The number of complimentary colors on your chart depends on two factors: (1) the variety of shades that are already included in your body's natural color scheme (for example, Jennifer Ho's chart in Plate 47 shows yellow in her second eye color section. If there were no yellow in Jennifer's eyes, her best shade of yellow would appear in the complimentary color section); and (2) whether two different shades of the same color—a grass green and an emerald, for instance—are flattering next to your skin. If both of these shades keep your skin looking clear, make your eyes sparkle, and keep your hair looking alive, never dull, they will both appear on your color chart.

For example, some of you will look great in as many as five different shades of purple, perhaps a blued one, a grape, iris, lilac, and a plum which is a reddish purple. (Note how many purples appear on Jennifer's chart in Plate 47.) If so, these colors should be on your chart.

As you think about all of the colors that may be complimentary to you, keep in mind the terms "shade" and "clarity." Orange is often a complimentary color, but not necessarily in the *shade* you may be picturing. To work well with your natural body coloring, the orange shade generally must show a hint of pink when placed next to your skin (for example, a salmon color in the orange family). This helps keep your skin glowing. Choosing a shade of orange that has too much of a yellow orange or pumpkin orange quality can sallow or gray your skin. The clarity of the color must be your best as well.

Since all of your colors are unique to your coloring, you can understand why your best green or blue or purple might be a totally different shade than the best shade for someone else in your same color type. An illustration of this: our Contrast models in Plates 4, 12, and 46 each have completely different skin tones. Because of this, their "best" shades of any color may be entirely different.

To help determine *your* complimentary colors, hold a garment or piece of fabric up to your face in natural daylight. (Use only material in your best clarities.) Then ask yourself the following questions:

1. Does the shade sallow, gray, or muddy my skin?

2. Do I look alive and glowing, fresh, and radiant?

3. Does the shade compete with or dull my hair color or eye color?

4. Does the shade relate to my natural body coloring— does it look as if I could wear it forever and look great?

If you can answer yes to #2 and #4, you are bound to receive a lot of "compliments" when you wear that shade—and that's what "complimentary colors" are all about!

Your Best White

Every woman can wear white—but not necessarily stark, pure white. On some women, slightly off-white is the right "white" for them. On others, the absolute whitest of whites looks striking in the best sense of the word.

Again, it depends on your body's inherent color scheme.

Two factors determine the best white for you: your skin tone and your teeth color. Your best white will never be so bright that it looks glaring next to your skin. It is too bright if it appears to "jump off" the skin. (See Photos 5.1, 5.3, 6.3, and Plate 27.) There is a delicate balance here. If you wear a white next to your face that is too bright, your teeth will look dull or yellowed and your skin will be anything but enhanced. Every woman's white shade, whether it be almost pure white or an off-white tone, looks "white" on her, not a creamy or light beige look, but white.

All the off-whites that fall between your best white and your best lightest beige color are excellent colors for you to wear as long as they are not too yellowish, brownish, or grayed for your skin color. You should choose off-whites that are progressively deeper tones of the white on your chart and progressively lighter tones of your best beige.

Your Gray

The best gray on your color chart does not necessarily match the gray your hair will turn. Why? Because when your hair turns gray, the color is a mixture of white hairs and your remaining brown, red, black, or blond ones. Your best gray is the shade that enhances your skin color, hair colors, and eye colors. Enhancing grays make your skin look clear and vibrant, keep your eyes bright, and will never appear to dull your hair. Grays that take on a brownish cast when placed next to your skin are to be avoided, as they will muddy and dull your complexion. Grays that appear to have a hint of a blue-gray quality will keep your skin clearer and more radiant-looking. Your best gray shade, however, should not look like a dusty blue on you.

The color gray is a controversial one. Many women feel it is drab and unexciting. Others see it as a basic neutral shade that they couldn't do without.

While it's true gray doesn't have any "color power" or brightness, it can be subtly enhancing on all women as long as it's worn in the right shade for them. If nothing else, gray affords an excellent backdrop for showcasing your other best colors. For example, your best shade of gray combined with your best shades of green, blue, blue-green, yellow, red, coral, and purple can create a wonderfully handsome outfit. (See Plates 15 and 31.) Your best gray also works well with other neutral shades— brown, beige, camel, rust, white, and navy—*provided* they, too, are worn in the best shades and clarities for you.

The chapter on your color type in Part II will tell you more about your best gray.

Your Dark Neutrals

Dark neutrals are the shades of navy, rust, dark greens, dark plums, wine, and burgundies that are enhancing to you. If black looks great on you, make a note of it, along with your other dark neutrals on your chart.

To be enhancing, your dark neutrals should not look too heavy or dark on you. Many people feel that black is an extremely useful neutral color. However, black is *not* becoming to every complexion. It can sallow or gray or dull some skin tones. If that is the case, there are other dark neutral colors that are more flattering, such as black-brown, deep plum or grape, deep blue-green, deep green, burgundy or wine, and navy. (For an example of a deep grape dark neutral, see Plate 13.) A few of you will look attractive in all of these dark neutral shades, including black. Others will look super in just one or two.

How can you tell if black isn't one of your best colors? By paying close attention to how you look in varying amounts of black: black with a color accent at the neck; black mixed in a print with other colors; black with a lot of skin showing at the neck (a black V-neck sweater as opposed to a black turtleneck, for instance). As you try black in these various ways, ask yourself if you look smashing, or just so-so. Are you being overwhelmed, buried by the garment? Does your skin look clear and glowing? Does a print that has your best colors as well as black look as great on you as a print without any black in it?

If you can't wear black, don't try to fake it by wearing a white accent—a string of pearls, let's say—near your face, thinking that will solve the problem. It won't. The fact of the matter remains: Black doesn't look great on you! It doesn't enhance you or relate to your overall natural body coloring, and there's nothing you can do to change that.

On the other hand, a complexion might be flattered by some black, even if too much black is overpowering. How do you know if a lot of black is overpowering? Hold up a black garment or piece of black fabric to your face and look in a mirror. If your eye goes immediately to the black because it looks overwhelmingly strong, heavy, and dark, and your skin looks washed out, you know a lot of black is not flattering. For you, it will be necessary to use black in sparing and delicate amounts. For example, some women can wear pure black only with a touch of one of their other colors near their face. Others need to have a lot of skin showing for black to be effective.

Suppose your color chart does not have black as a dark neutral and features instead navy, dark green, wine, burgundy, or a dark teal. No matter what your dark neutral colors are, you too might need to accent them with a light or bright color near the face. This might be especially true at night. Otherwise, you may look dulled or visually overpowered.

Again, some of you will find you look best using your dark neutral colors sparingly, perhaps with neck and shoulder skin showing so the dark color is not right next to your face. Or you might combine it with your other best colors. For example, you might wear a dark neutral skirt, pants, or suit, or a garment in a patterned fabric of that dark neutral and your other best colors.

Find out more about black and all the other neutrals and how they fit into your color spectrum by reading the chapter on your color type in Part II.

Chapter 3

Wardrobe Wizardry

Universal Color Principles

In this chapter we will introduce you to the color concepts that are crucial to looking smashing in the clothes you wear. You will note there is nothing occult or gimmicky about our Color 1 principles. Our personal enhancement program is based on objective principles of aesthetics, not unlike those associated with various other art forms.

There are three color concepts you will be using over and over again in putting together sensational outfits: shade, clarity, and value.

The first of these, *shade*, you already know about. Shade refers to the various versions of a single color. For example, there is fire engine red and there is cherry red. These are two different shades of the single color red. As we've already said more than once—and as we'll repeat again before this book is through—every woman can wear every color, providing she chooses a flattering shade. (Go back to Chapter 2 for a quick refresher on this.)

Filling in your color spectrum is a matter of finding the right shade of each color for you. Many women will find more than one shade of a color that clicks with their coloring.

By *clarity* we mean the purity of a color, how distinctly red or blue or yellow or green it is. There are four levels of clarity: intense, bright, toned-down, and subdued. Your skin color will determine which clarities are right for you.

Every woman has her own set of "bright" colors on her chart, whether they are intense, bright, toned-down, or subdued. For example, a toned-down red on Muted color types gives a "bright red" appearance when worn, looking just as bright on a Muted color type as an intense red clarity does on a Contrast color type.

To get an idea of *intense clarity*, picture the strongest reds, yellows, blues, greens you've ever seen. Sometimes these are called pure pigment colors. Sometimes they're called garish. But garish they are not *provided* they are worn by women with the right coloring.

On most women with Contrast coloring, intense clarities look fabulous. There are a few women with Muted/Contrast and Light-Bright/Contrast coloring who can also wear them. (Note the intensity of the colors in Plate 35.)

Bright clarity describes the vibrant colors. Picture jewel tones—clear and vivid, but not overly strong. Technically these are pure pigment colors with a little white added to lighten them just a bit, keeping them vibrant but taking the edge off their intensity.

Light-Bright and Contrast color types revel in bright clarity. Muted/Contrast and Gentle/Light-Bright color types are also enhanced by them. (Note the brightness of the colors in Plate 32.)

Toned-down clarity appears neither bright nor very subdued. Think of it as middle-of-the-road. Any color that has a small touch of brown or gray is a toned-down clarity.

Needless to say, all color types can safely wear this level of clarity and still look good. However, Gentle and Muted color types find them most enhancing. (Note the slightly toned-down quality of the colors in Plates 9 and 18.)

Subdued clarity does not just mean pastels. Picture a pure pigment color that has enough brown or gray pigment added to completely remove its intense or bright quality.

Given the right background, one thing a subdued clarity is not is dull. In fact, worn on the right person, this clarity level is lovely and alluring—the exact opposite of dull and drab!

Many women with Muted and Gentle coloring wear this clarity effectively. Light-Bright and Contrast color types generally look washed-out when they don these softened tones. (Note the subdued quality of the colors in Plates 13, 14, and 31.)

For illustrations of all the clarity levels, review Plates 21, 22, and 23, which show three distinct clarities of green, blue, and red.

Every woman, no matter what her color type, needs a certain amount of clarity in the colors she wears in order to look healthy and radiant. Ideally, no woman should ever wear a color that looks pale or dull or washed out on her, nor should she wear a color that's too bright or overpowering. When you're wearing the right shades of color in the right clarity and intensity for you, both the colors and you will glow. The colors and you will look like you belong together.

Here is our rule of thumb: If a color looks dull or dusty on you, then you need to wear a clearer clarity, but not necessarily a *bright* or intense clarity. On the other hand, if a color looks so bright next to your skin that you look drab, then you should be wearing a color that is slightly more toned-down but not necessarily *subdued*.

Remember our motto: Every woman can wear all colors in the spectrum. *It's the shade and clarity of the colors she wears that matter.*

Our third key color concept is *value*, that is, a color's darkness or lightness. The lightest values of a color are often called pastels. The deepest values are termed dark colors. Those in between are, of course, medium-value colors. We have reproduced an example of a coral red in its different values in Plate 24. Also, Plate 47 shows all of Jennifer Ho's colors in their light and dark values. You will learn the rules for combining light and dark values in the section to follow on levels of contrast and in the chapter in Part II for your specific color type.

Striking the Right Balance Through Contrast Levels

No one can take all of their best colors and wear them just any old which-way. Even though you may know your best shades and clarities, you must know which colors can be worn in an all-one-color look, for example, which need to be accented, and which cannot be combined at all.

Knowing what level of contrast (which dark, light, and medium values of your best shades) you should wear is important because it tells you the best way to combine all those beautiful colors on your color chart. Any woman who wants to look her best must have a firm grasp of this concept. In fact, she must understand it so thoroughly that it's second nature to her.

In the Color 1 concept, we deal with three levels of contrast: strong, medium, and soft—the latter being a more blended look. Plate 25 illustrates these three levels.

What is a strong contrast? Just what the words imply—the two colors being combined are diametrically opposed to each other in terms of their relative lightness and darkness—the lightest value combined with the darkest value. The colors black and white create the strongest contrast imaginable, do they not? How about navy and off-white? Or dark brown and white? These combinations are all strong contrasts. And they are the *only* strong contrast combinations in our color concept. (See Plate 25.)

What is a soft contrast or blended look? The exact opposite of a strong contrast. The most obvious example of a soft contrast (or blended look) is white combined with a light beige—two light values combined. In terms of their relative lightness and position in the color spectrum, these two colors are close. You would also get a soft contrast effect if you juxtaposed pastels because the combination of any two light colors creates a blended look. (As in Photos 6.6 and 7.1.)

Colors of medium value (in the middle on the light–dark scale) can also be worn together in certain ways to generate a soft contrast look. To illustrate this for yourself, place next to one another two medium-value colors that are close on the color spectrum, for example, a medium blue-green with a medium green; or a medium-value rust with a medium brown. Together, they create a soft contrast effect.

The same is true of dark colors that are close to each other on the color spectrum. For instance, a dark red combined with a dark purple or a dark blue worn with a dark purple will give you a soft contrast or blended look.

A soft contrast look is also generated when a pastel is worn with a medium-value color from the same color family—when you mix light blue with a medium blue, let's say. Do the same with a dark blue and a medium blue. Again, you've got a blended look.

Finally, combine a medium-value color from one color family with a light color from a color family that's near it on the color spectrum. A classic case is the combination of pale lavender and a medium grape purple. Do the same with a medium-value color and a dark color that are close on the color spectrum, like a medium-value coral with a rust. That, too, gives you a soft contrast look.

What is a medium contrast? *All* the levels of contrast that are not extremely strong or very soft fall into this category—the combination of light values with medium values, of dark values with medium values, of two medium values, and a light value with a dark value other than black/white, navy/white, or dark brown/white. A light yellow combined with a medium gray is an example of this look. A pastel (the yellow) has been combined with a medium value of a color (the gray) that's far away from it on the color spectrum.

The combination of a pastel with the darkest value of that same color—for example, light lavender placed next to deep lavender—is also a medium contrast look.

Other medium contrast looks include: a pastel combined with any dark color, including black (see Plate 13); a pale blue worn with a dark brown; a pale pink worn with a dark blue; or two unrelated medium values together, say, a medium blue-green with a medium coral. (See Plate 28.) Another medium contrast combination is a medium value of one color worn with the dark value of a totally different color (as in Plate 37)—a medium-value red combined with a dark blue-green, for instance. Combining two dark colors from widely disparate color families, say a wine with a forest green, creates a medium contrast effect.

Finally, there's white or off-white combined with any dark tone of any color *except* black, navy, or dark brown. An example is very dark red worn with your best white. While such a dark–light combination may appear to have a great deal of contrast, it is not too strong a contrast for any color type. Such dark–light combinations are certainly less strongly contrasting than black, navy, or dark brown combined with white or off-white. That's why we call them medium contrast combinations.

All the combinations mentioned above create a medium contrast look—a look all women, no matter what their color type, can wear. But strong contrast and soft contrast looks are a different matter. In Part II you will learn which contrast levels are most enhancing on you, depending on your color type.

Universally Enhancing Colors— There Are a Few

It's a good thing there are some. Otherwise how would airlines choose uniform colors that look attractive on all their flight attendants? How would prospective brides select bridesmaids' gowns in all one color?

In the one case, a well-known airline has put its attendants in khaki. Khaki is an unbelievably bad choice because it isn't truly enhancing to anyone's complexion. Certain color types can wear it better than others, but right next to any skin tone, it is indifferent at best. True, khaki can be combined with other brighter colors to make it more acceptable, but this airline hasn't even done that. In another case, an airline chose a blackish navy suit worn with a stark white shirt. This contrast level does rate high on the authority scale, but it is too strong a dark–light combination for more than one-half of its flight attendants.

Two very attractive colors on most people are the medium values of blue-green—that is, turquoise—and pink-toned corals. They appear on almost every chart in the specific shade and clarity best for the individual (see Plates 39 and 41).

As we've pointed out repeatedly, for a woman to look her most enhanced, each color she wears must be in the best shade and clarity for her and her alone, because no two individuals are exactly alike. However, when a compromise is necessary as in the case of corporate uniforms, there is a medium level of clarity that works on all women, no matter what their coloring.

Let's take the example of navy blue. It is difficult to describe shades of navy blue because most people think that navy blue is simply navy blue. Not so. Color 1 Associates works with eighteen different navies. To pinpoint a shade and clarity of navy blue that is most universally enhancing, we would say to stay away from a *royal* navy blue, with its slight purple cast, and select a more typical medium dark nautical navy, one that has a little more yellow in it.

Of course, with a deep color like navy blue, there is one more consideration: contrast level. To look good on the most number of people, this navy blue must be incorporated in a medium contrast rather than a strong contrast outfit. In other words, to work for every Muted and Gentle color type, navy must be combined with a light beige or a pastel instead of white. Contrast and Light-Bright color types can effectively wear their navy shade with their white, and many Contrast and Light-Bright color types can also wear a pure white with their navy.

The most universally enhancing green is what people call "emerald green," but an emerald green that is neither too intense nor too dusty-looking (as illustrated in Plate 12). This emerald green has just enough blue in it to work on the vast majority of people. This cannot be said for kelly greens, lime greens, moss greens, and all the other green shades. Diligently avoid the yellow-greens that have a lime tone to them. They are anything but universally enhancing.

The best purple for the greatest number of people has the effect of equal parts of red and blue in it and is a medium-value color. (Note the blouses on our models in Plates 10 and 37.)

The whites we recommend are the off-whites and creamy whites—those with very little yellow, brown, or gray in them (like the blouse in Plate 14). Pure white is not universally enhancing because it looks too bright and overwhelming on many people, particularly those with Muted coloring.

Burgundy is another color to eschew in your search for a color that looks good across the board. And burgundy isn't the only one that is off limits. Many shades of beige, brown, and gray are equally difficult for a broad range of people to wear. Why? Because the shades aren't the exact ones that relate to an individual's coloring. The wrong shades of these colors, for example, will sallow or muddy the complexion and bring out lines under the eyes. In short, they can make a woman look drab, tired, ill, or older.

The most universally enhancing beige is neither a pink-beige nor a golden-beige—it falls somewhere in between. It must be "clear," meaning that it cannot have a grayed, brownish, or yellowish cast to it. Brownish beiges are often called "tan" and grayed beiges referred to as "taupe." Both of these shades are seldom enhancing to any skin color. Beiges with a yellowish cast are sometimes called "ecru," but garments described as ecru in color should be considered individually—some are not truly yellowish beiges, and may be flattering to some individuals.

Color Camouflage: Dealing with "Figure Faults"

We disagree with much of the conventional thinking on the subject of camouflaging so-called figure faults.

While we do believe you can use color and design to *improve* your total look, we do not believe you should try to hide a fuller figure behind small patterns, dark colors, and dresses styled like tents. Women—tall or short, heavy or thin—ought to accept and work with the things they cannot change, or are not willing to change, about their bodies. And if they can and want to change the things they dislike—lose weight, for example—they should do that instead of resorting to clothing camouflage.

The truth of the matter is this: No amount of color or styling trickery is going to transform a Shelley Winters body type into a Mia Farrow. It's just not meant to be. So if looking svelte happens to be one of your goals, go on a diet, lose that extra poundage, and exercise to redistribute your weight. It takes time and will power, but if you want a certain look, it's worth it.

The advice offered here is merely intended to help those women with a few specific figure problems achieve certain optical illusions. We believe that color—that is, the knowing use of light and dark values of a woman's best shades—is the ideal way to create what art directors and designers refer to as "a balanced look." And a balanced look is the greatest way anyone can deflect attention away from a figure problem. Our advice concerns the placement of your best colors on your body to minimize, but not eliminate, various types of perplexing "figure faults."

Advice for Women Who Think They're Too Heavy

You remember the shibboleth: Dark clothes are slenderizing; light or bright colors call attention to those extra pounds. If you believe this, please answer these questions:

Would a woman dressed in dark colors look larger or smaller standing in front of a light background?

Are most of our background colors (i.e., walls, upholstered furniture, woodwork, etc.) light or dark?

We'll wager you answered the first question "larger" and the second "light."

Most other books overlook the fact that the majority of office and home interiors are done in light colors—off-white and pastels. So if you really want to go into the subject of color camouflage in depth, you must take into consideration the effect your clothing's color values will have against lighter backgrounds.

When a heavier woman wears dark clothing to "hide" her weight, she's not hiding anything when she is viewed against a lighter background. In fact, her dark clothing emphasizes her size because her figure is clearly outlined for all to see. However, when this woman wears darker clothing and is viewed against a dark background—if she can find one—the configuration of her body would be hard to detect.

Our advice to women who want to appear thinner is to follow the Color 1 Associates dictates for women with their coloring and forget the mythology. We feel that an individual of whatever shape or size is most enhanced by wearing color shades and clarities, levels of contrast, and pattern sizes specific to her color type. By following the rules for her color type, a full-figured woman is going to look more fabulous than she could possibly look by attempting some form of color camouflage.

In other words, *whether you are overweight or underweight, tall or short, your color type is the key to dressing right and looking wonderful.* The rules that apply to your color type are the main factors to keep in the forefront of your mind at all times. Recite them to yourself when you are standing in front of a rack of clothes in a store deciding what to buy or when you are standing in front of your own closet back home deciding how to mix and match the items you already own.

Having said that, we can make a few concrete suggestions:

Any woman who wants to create the longest, tallest look possible can dress in one color from head to toe. Just be aware that certain styles can sabotage even an all-one-color look. (Any elongating monotone look, incidentally, includes your stockings and your shoes. But please, no opaque stockings unless your outfit is extremely casual or it's a high fashion look that calls for them.)

If you are wearing a solid-colored suit, a blouse in a contrasting color won't disturb the basic vertical line of your monotone outfit. Nor will a neck accessory—a scarf or necklace—in an appropriate color (see Photo 8.4).

You can also wear a skirt or slacks with a matching top and a contrasting jacket *provided* you leave the jacket open so people who look at you can see the vertical all-one-color look toward the center of your body (as in Plate 34).

If you have Gentle coloring, choose any of the shades on your color chart for your all-one-color look. A woman with Muted or Contrast coloring, on the other hand, is better off if she creates her monotone look in a medium value of one of her best colors. A Light-Bright color type with light hair can use either the lighter or medium values on her chart, while those with Light-Bright coloring and darker hair should stay with the medium values of their best colors.

A vertically striped dress also creates a long line. Just make sure the stripe is in the right scale, colors, and level of contrast for your color type.

Appropriate pattern size is the source of some controversy where full-figured women are concerned.

The conventional wisdom states that full-figured women shouldn't wear big, bold prints. Since Contrast color types are the only women who can wear large, bold patterns anyway, let's use a full-figured woman with Contrast coloring as an example of what to do and not to do:

Small patterns on a woman with Contrast coloring, no matter how large or overweight she might be, will not do her justice. A small print (unless it has strong contrast and is accented with a bright color) isn't going to play down her size. It's going to play down her natural coloring and make her look drab, washed-out, insignificant, and dull. At the other extreme, a large expanse of a jumbo-sized print might not be flattering to a very heavy woman— but for a different reason: There just may be too much of it. The overall effect can be overpowering.

Having said that, we can recall instances when we've dressed full-figured women with Contrast coloring in floor-length gowns that had large, high contrast patterns in their best colors. These women all got rave reviews. But it's important to emphasize that besides the details we've mentioned, the gowns had something else in common— styling. The overall lines of the gowns helped to balance the full figure and create an illusion of length, which the women needed.

In dealing with separates, where on her body a heavier Contrast color type chooses to wear a large pattern is crucial.

Let's say a full-figured woman with Contrast coloring wants to purchase a pair of plaid slacks. She loves plaid. But if the bottom half of her body is big, a large plaid could call attention to this fact. Consequently, a medium-sized plaid would be better. She could even wear a pair of slacks with a small plaid *provided* the plaid is a highly contrasting one.

And the rest of her outfit? On the top half of her body, she would wear a solid-colored top that picks up one of the colors in her plaid pants.

This same woman might find it more flattering to her body to reverse the solid and plaid on her body. She might wear a solid-colored base—a skirt and a matching top—and over it a loose, unconstructed jacket or a shirt with a large plaid. Medium-sized patterns, of course, can be worn by everyone. And full-figured Contrast color types can always wear large patterns in blouses and scarves. Again, the blouse's styling is important.

Traditionalists believe that a woman with a fuller bustline, no matter what her coloring, should always wear dark colors on the top half of her body and lighter colors on the bottom half. And that a woman with big hips and a smaller bustline, should do the reverse.

We couldn't disagree more. We say it's not a question of where you place the dark and light colors on your body, but *how you balance out the dark and light colors in the outfit on your body*.

In short, no matter what your perceived figure fault, your outfit must be balanced and harmonious. Balance is the key. If a woman with a full bustline wants to wear a light- or bright-colored blouse, fine—*provided*, of course, she sticks with her best colors and clarity. All this woman has to do to look great is to make sure that she brings a touch of her bottom color—her skirt or pants color—up to the top part of her outfit. She does this by repeating the bottom color in an accessory, a scarf, or beads, or an eye-catching pair of earrings.

Chapter 4

Makeup and Hair Coloring Magic

Universal Makeup Principles

Every once in a while one of the women's magazines runs an article about how to wear colors you've never been able to wear before, especially different shades of makeup base, with the idea that this will effectively extend the range of colors that look good on you.

If you've found a base that matches your skin tone exactly, don't change it no matter what advice pours out of the fashion columns. Should a beauty editor or cosmetics sales clerk exhort you to wear a different color foundation in the evening, don't do that either. A base that duplicates your skin tone is always the most enhancing any time of day or night and under all conceivable lighting conditions, even in television studios. Granted, candlelight may make your wrong foundation "mask" less obvious, but if your escort should happen to see you wearing that off-color base in normal light, be forewarned. He'll probably be alarmed.

One of our associates has a client, a woman in her fifties, who had spent her whole life wearing a dark foundation in a valiant attempt to mask her freckles. This woman was so determined to make her too-dark base look natural that she carried it down her throat and behind her ears. Unfortunately, her efforts were in vain. The base did not look natural and never would because it did not match her skin tone.

Our associate finally convinced her client to accept her freckles and wear foundation that matched her light skin tone. The idea came as a revelation to this attractive woman. Today, she looks like Mother Nature intended her to look instead of like a heavily made-up mannequin.

Please accept this as gospel: *Your base must match the skin tone on your neck exactly.* Foundation does not add color to your face. The purpose of foundation is to provide the look of a smooth, even complexion. It should be a sheer covering for your face that gives your face and body that all-one-color look. It is literally the foundation upon which you apply color to your face. That color comes in the form of eye shadow, blush, and lipstick.

Choosing the Right Base for Your Complexion

Your foundation should be the same color as your skin. Review the color chips in Plate 5 and take notes on Your Color 1 Color Chart. When you go to the store, take the lid off the bottle and look directly at the makeup base. If the product looks too pink, put the lid right back on and return the product to the sales clerk. It's not the right base for you. However, if it looks close to your skin-tone shade, by all means give it a try.

To test a foundation's color in a store, put a dot on the inside of your arm (just under or below your thumb) in the back of the wrist area. Why here? Because in other places on your forearm, inner arm, and hand your skin tends to be its palest or darkest. But in the area below your thumb you should find the closest match to the exact tone of your neck. To make sure, hold your arm up to your neck and look in the mirror in natural daylight. If the skin tone of your neck and that part of your arm don't happen to match, you'll have to test foundation directly on your neck.

No matter where you place the dot of base, don't rub it in. Just let it sit there on your skin while you evaluate how closely it matches the tone of your skin. You should perform this test in natural daylight. If the dot of makeup and your skin tones on your inner wrist match, then try another dot of foundation on your jawline and on your neck. The base shade will match your skin so well that you could dab it on a blemish and that blemish would appear to vanish.

Here are a few more tips for choosing among the available commercial foundation products:

Many bases sporting names with the word "beige" actually have a lot of pink in them. In contrast, bases labeled "ivory" usually have the least amount of pink. In choosing a base, let your eye, not a high-pressure sales clerk or the product's name, be your guide as to what matches your skin tone exactly.

The hardest foundations to find are light ivory shades that have a touch of brown-beige or golden-beige. If after a thorough search you can't find what you want in one bottle, mix the contents of two together. Do whatever it takes to get it right.

For example, if you have pink tones in your skin but are extremely fair and all bases seem too dark, try mixing the lightest beige you can find with a light ivory and keep testing your concoction on your skin until you get it right.

When we developed our own makeup line, we created foundation colors in the full range of skin tones from the lightest ivory to deep golden camels. Our Color 1 makeup line has fourteen different shades, including many that are difficult or impossible to find elsewhere. Even though we have this spectacular range, some of our clients still have to mix two shades to get their perfect color.

Exceptions to the Rule: If You Have to "Correct" Your Complexion

Women who have very angry-looking red blemished skin may want to use a "toner" to help ease the redness. In other cases, the skin on the face is a little pinker than the neck because it is sensitive. In such instances, a woman should still match her foundation to the skin tone on her neck, which, when applied to the face, will help tone down the sensitive pinkness or redness.

There are special greenish and purplish toners on the market designed especially to cancel out adverse skin conditions. (These are often called mint and lavender toners.) To cancel out that angry red you would apply—under your foundation—a mint toner on any blotches. Someone else might need to apply the lavender toner to cancel out very golden or brownish patches on their skin.

The catch with toners is that they must be applied very lightly or you may have to adjust your makeup base to a shade darker than your natural skin color in order to cover the toner color completely. As a consequence, you are liable to look very heavily made-up, resulting in the mask effect, which is not attractive. Thus, if you feel you must use a toner, apply it very lightly for the sheerest possible coverage. Then apply your makeup base, in the shade that matches the skin on your neck, over your entire face. Again, the watchwords are "light," "even," and "sheer."

What Difference Does a Tan Make?

Very little.

A lot of women don't understand the fact that when they tan their skin just becomes a darker version of its normal shade. For instance, if you have a golden-ivory complexion, with a tan you will look a golden-camel color. If you have pink-beige skin, a tan will give your skin more of a pink-camel tone or a red-tone brown.

For this reason, the clothing colors and her best lip, eye, and blush colors a woman can wear when she's tanned stay exactly the same as when she isn't.

If you tan, you need only two foundations to achieve the perfect base color, whether you are in the process of building a tan or in the process of fading. One must match your skin at its fairest. The other should match it at its darkest. When your skin is at an inbetween color stage, you simply mix the two foundations until you achieve the right tone.

Incidentally, when you mix your darker tan base with your lighter base, don't do it by pouring the liquid from one bottle into another. Rather, mix the two in the palm of your hand every time you use it. Obviously, the proportions will change depending on how tan you are.

A final note: Some women tan very dark. In order to match their deep tan shade, they may need to move into a makeup base product line created especially for darker skin tones. Of course, many women when they're tan don't feel the need to wear any foundation at all. It's when their tan is fading that they do.

What *may* change because of a deep tan is the way you choose to combine your clothing colors.

Many women when tan prefer to dress in the darker or brighter colors on their chart, whereas without a tan they may gravitate toward their more medium tones. They feel the bright or dark tones accentuate their tan, making it look deeper. Conversely, some tanned women prefer to wear their palest colors for a more contrasting effect. They feel the lighter shades showcase their tan and make it look darker.

These are simply examples of how many of our clients choose to use their colors when they're tan. It's all a matter of personal opinion and preference. We want you to be as adventurous as they are. Just remember to follow the rules for your color type concerning appropriate levels of contrast.

Your Skin Tone and Aging

Many women mistakenly think that their skin tone changes color as they grow older and start to gray because of the altered juxtaposition between their changing hair color and complexion. Now when they look in the mirror, they're puzzled. The visual effect is different from the one they projected before they started to turn gray. As a consequence, they may think they look more washed-out or pale or sallow than they used to look, and they don't like it. For this reason they assume they can no longer wear the colors they associate with their younger days.

Quite the contrary. Your color type only changes under one condition: if your skin tone changes. Your skin tone might change for a few reasons, for example, because you have permanently sun-damaged skin or are undergoing chemotherapy. It might also change if you have a vitamin deficiency or, at the opposite extreme, if you are taking megadoses of vitamins or some medication imparting a skin-tone transformation. Such a transformation may not be permanent, though. When you stop the chemotherapy or go off the medication, your complexion should return to normal, so do not be too hasty about redoing your color chart.

One of our European associates would normally be a Light-Bright color type but ended up as a Gentle/Light-Bright because she suffers from eczema. Her condition causes her slightly golden-toned skin to be pinker than normal in the neck and face area. This is the area that we pay most attention to when we decide a person's color type. If, on the other hand, her eczema condition one day miraculously disappears, she will go right back to having Light-Bright coloring, as her face and neck will return to the more golden shade of her arms.

Overweight people can also tend to experience a skin color change in the neck and face, again to a ruddier or pinker shade. This, too, can alter one's color type.

Our Color 1 associates have charted a number of children. When it comes to children, we should point out that human coloring is not always set until people reach adulthood. As children approach their early teens, their skin tone may change slightly and hair color may darken. Their hair color may darken even further after puberty, but this generally will not affect their color chart because hair color usually darkens in the same color family.

All About Lip Color

One of the most enhancing red shades you can wear is the color your lips are naturally. This is your body's natural red color. It appears in various light and dark guises on your body. Look inside your lower lip, at the color of your fingertips when you gently squeeze them, in the mirror when you're flushed. (This color is explained more fully in Chapter 2 under "Your Body Colors," and illustrated in Plate 8.) But any of your reddish shades, including coral, can be matched in lipstick and nail polish.

How many lipsticks do you really need?

You will want to own at least three: one that matches the red color on your chart; one that matches your coral;

and one in your raspberry and/or plum shade. (In Plate 10 our Gentle color type is wearing her toned-down raspberry, and in Plate 41 her toned-down coral.) Some women like to use a lighter lipstick in the daytime and a darker version of the shade in the evening. In that case, you need six lipsticks. Remember that these best shades are to be worn in your best clarity. You can see that in Plate 40 our model's lipstick is too bright.

For those women who want to own as few lipsticks as possible, choose a medium or medium-dark red color from your chart that will work both in daytime and evening. Supplement that with either a coral, plum, or raspberry, also in a medium to dark value. It is not an absolute necessity to own both a plum and raspberry lipstick. However, they do give different effects, and many clients enjoy using both.

Some women complain that even though they choose lipsticks that match their best red shades, it does them little good since the colors tend to change once they apply them to their lips.

It is true there are some women whose body acidity level makes the color of any product applied to their face change—and not only lipstick. It's just more noticeable with lipstick.

If you are one of these women, you need to test any makeup product you buy very carefully by letting it sit on your skin for some length of time. You might apply it at the makeup counter of your local department store and leave it on while you shop for a while in another part of the store. If the product changes color in the interim, you know you'll have to try something else. Depending on how your body has altered the color of the product, choose a shade that is a little bluer or more coral.

For example, if lipsticks always change to look more orangey, select one that is a shade bluer than you want to end up with. Thus, if you want a coral shade for your lips, we suggest you choose a lipstick color closer to the red color on your chart. On the other hand, if a red shade is what you're after and you know the opposite tends to occur—your lip color gets bluer—try a lipstick with a more coral orange tone in it.

Here's how you test lipstick: Take one of your lipsticks that you know changes on you and put some on the back of your hand or the inside of your wrist and let it sit there for a while. If it also changes on the back of your hand or wrist, you know you can do the same at a makeup counter and get an accurate reading. If you find out lipstick only changes on your lips, ask the saleswoman to use a cotton swab to take a little bit from the base of the lipstick. Then smudge it directly on your lips. Take that walk around the store again before you come back and make a final decision.

A footnote on lip-lining pencils: If you use one, make sure the shade of the pencil matches your lipstick color as closely as possible. Often, women use lip-lining pencils in shades that are very toned-down or brownish-looking. Then when they apply a clearer lipstick, they appear to have a dark line running around the edge of their lips. Covering the line completely with their lipstick color helps solve the problem but the difference in color is often still detectable. This also defeats the purpose of the lip-lining pencil, which is to keep your lipstick from "bleeding" and to define the exact lip area.

Adding Color to Your Cheeks

Blush—or rouge as it used to be called—is intended to give you a healthy efflorescence. The wrong shade of blush, to the contrary, can sallow your complexion and make you looked tired or ill. The best basic color of blush for you is always your red color. (Notice how in Plate 42 our model's blush makes her look tired. Not only is she wearing too much blush, but the color is too brownish—too toned-down for her Light-Bright coloring. See how much fresher she looks in Plate 43 wearing a lighter and *clearer* blush.)

Your best shade of coral can be used as a lipstick or polish color *but never for a blush*. After all, you don't blush coral or orange, do you? No. You blush your red color.

If you are wearing coral lipstick, you can experiment by combining your red blush color with a touch of a more coral blush. On most of you, your healthy glow will disappear! A coral or orange cast to your blush will negate that alive-and-well look of radiance you seek.

Glasses and Makeup

Women often ask us whether they should alter their makeup, especially their eye makeup, to compensate for glasses. Our answer is no. We recommend the same type of makeup, applied in the same way, that we recommend for anyone else.

We would, though, underscore the importance of eye makeup. Shadow colors and appropriate eye liner and mascara—all discussed in your color type chapter in Part II—are critical in projecting and enhancing the eye through the eyeglass frames. On the other hand, you should never apply so much eye makeup that it becomes a distraction, the main thing people notice when they look at your face.

Universal Hair Coloring Principles

If you are seized with the urge to color your hair, think long and hard about it before you proceed. And before you do, make sure you've had sufficient time to get used to how you look wearing clothing and makeup in your correct colors. You may find that your natural hair shade suits you just fine.

Helene Mills, our Santa Monica associate, recalls a client who was concerned about her hair color, which she dubbed "mousey brown." Her hair did look mousey, but that was because she was wearing all the wrong colors. She wisely decided to wear her right colors for a while before she rushed out to color her hair.

A few months later, the woman remarked:

"I just bought the most expensive blouse I've ever owned. I would never have looked at it if the color hadn't been on my chart. When I put it on, I *loved* it—and me in it!"

The color? The exact same brown shade as her own hair color, which no longer appeared to be a "mousey brown."

Choosing the most enhancing shade to color your hair is a tricky business. We recommend that if you want to lighten or darken your natural hair color, you do it in a shade that is highly complimentary to your skin tone.

Let's take the example of a woman who is a Contrast color type. She has natural black-brown hair and has been having her hair permanented regularly. In the process, she discovers that the chemicals in the permanent wave solution are turning her hair color progressively lighter, more golden bronze, rust, or reddish brown. This gradual lightening will happen whenever hair is subjected to permanents or the sun on a regular basis.

As this woman's hair changes color, superficially she begins to look more and more like a Muted color type—but not really because her skin tone has not changed at all. Her problem is her new hair color, transformed inadvertently. It's saying, "I make you look like you need more toned-down colors," but her skin tone is saying, "*I need clear colors.*" Unfortunately, her hair color and skin tone are increasingly out of sync. Despite what her altered hair color is saying, in order to glow, this woman must stick with the clear colors flattering to a Contrast color type and continue to avoid the toned-down shades needed by Muted coloring.

One remedy for the problem is for this woman to "reverse frost" her hair—in other words, have her hair pulled through a cap, especially the hair around her face, and darkened to approximate her natural darker hair color.

Do Blonds Have More Fun?

Many darker-haired women are curious. But do they dare risk it?

Most Caucasian women can look attractive as blonds *provided* the shade of blond is right with their skin tone. Although it can be done effectively, we do not encourage very dark-haired women with Contrast coloring to try it, however. With blond hair, they lose the dark–light contrasting effect that is characteristic of their natural coloring.

The natural-looking blonds are women who have made the effort to choose a shade that compliments their complexion. In general, the shades of champagne blond, beige-blond, wheat blond, and honey blond are the most enhancing on the widest number of women. The shades that are not universally effective are ash blond and very golden and bronze-toned blond—the blond colors we refer to as harsh or "brassy."

Why aren't these shades of blond universally enhancing? The ash blond shades look drab next to most women's complexions with the one exception of women with pink-beige skin tones. The very golden and bronze-toned blond shades are usually harsh, sallowing, and artificial-looking. The exception would be a very golden skin tone that was complimented by a very golden or bronze blond. (Study Plate 3 and imagine Brenda in ash blond hair. She would look drab by comparison—her honey-blond hair is wonderful with her clear golden skin.)

Should you, by accident, end up with one of these unattractive blond shades, there are remedies. For example, to make a very golden blond shade more palatable, we recommend toning with an ash-tone shade. But you don't want your hair to look ashy either. So use that shade to *cut* the brassy look so that your hair appears to be a more honey or wheat blond. On the other hand, if your hair has too much ash tone in it, making you look drab, you should reverse the process. Put more golden tones back in. The end result will be a warm-looking champagne or wheat blond color.

A woman can find her most flattering shades of blond by aiming for a color that incorporates the beige colors that are right for her with the camel shades in her hair or skin tone.

Here are some guidelines for selecting a blond shade complimentary to your complexion:

If you have an ivory skin tone (like Helene in Plate 12), strive for either a beige blond, champagne blond, or wheat blond shade, making sure that there is not too much ash tone in the latter.

If you have golden tones in your skin (like Jeanne in Plate 11), then you should move in the direction of a *slightly* golden-toned blond shade, like a honey blond.

If you have pink tones in your skin (like Patti in Plate 2), strive for a beige blond, a champagne blond, or a slightly ash blond.

Will I Change Color Types When I Color My Hair?

No, you cannot change your color type by changing the color of your hair. Why? Because it is your skin tone—not your natural hair color—that takes precedence in deciding what shades and clarity of color and contrast levels look best on you.

To prove it, we've taken clients and entirely covered their hair with a neutral piece of fabric. Without any reference to their hair color, we can still determine their best levels of contrast. And contrast levels are a most important factor for deciding in which color type to place a person.

Should I Color My Gray Hair?

This is a personal decision. During her whole life, a woman may feel she looks her most drab while she is in the process of graying, in the stage just beyond salt-and-pepper, when her whole head of hair is losing its pigment but has not turned uniformly gray or white yet. On the other hand, many of our women clients love their graying hair in all its various stages. And because of their "up" attitude about it, they look gorgeous throughout. Often these are lighter-haired women whose hair doesn't look startlingly different when it starts to whiten. Conversely, we also counsel women who simply feel old as they watch their hair turning gray. These women are candidates for hair coloring.

For graying clients with darker hair, there is an alternative to coloring your entire head of hair. It's called "reverse frosting." This is a process whereby your hair is pulled through a cap so that some, rather than all, of your hair is colored. The hair that is colored can be returned to your natural shade or any becoming shade you like. In this manner, some of your gray hair still shows. Highlighting or frosting can be used with the same natural-looking results by women with light to medium hair tones.

This halfway measure should be considered because coloring a full head of hair can tend to make a woman look harsh or like she definitely "dyes" her hair. Why? Because during the coloring process, all of the natural highlights end up being colored as well as the gray hair. A head of hair without highlights, no matter what the color, can look dull. However, a good colorist using a good product can color your hair entirely and you will look great *provided* the shade is right for your skin.

Part II

Coloramics for Your Color Type

Chapter 5

Wardrobe Advice for Muted Coloring

We suspect that more of our readers turn to this chapter than any of the chapters for the other three color types.

Why?

Because more than one-fourth of all American women have some variation of Muted coloring. Included among them are Nancy Reagan, Sally Field, Barbra Streisand, Ann-Margret, Carol Burnett, Raquel Welch, Shirley MacLaine, Lucille Ball, and Jane Fonda.

Think of Muted coloring as mid-range coloring. By that we mean coloring that is not quiet and gentle-looking at the one extreme or bright or contrast-looking at the other.

A woman who has Muted coloring needs to re-create the look of her natural coloring in her clothing and makeup color choices. In general, any woman with Muted coloring will look great wearing lots of different textures in fabrics (see Photo 5.2), leathers, and metals. You could say that texture and Muted coloring go hand in hand.

Maybe you have excellent color sense in interior design or when you help your husband mix and match his business wardrobe. But don't let this mislead you. It does

5.1

Our Castro Valley, California, consultant Betty Soblin has Muted coloring that is certainly not enhanced by the black and white dotted jacket she models in the photo above (Photo 5.1). This strong contrast effect gives the illusion of the jacket wearing the person rather than vice versa. Moreover, Betty's eye, lip, and cheek makeup is too pale for her lovely coloring.

Below (Photo 5.2), Betty is dressed in a textured, camel and beige striped jacket. It looks just right, creating a soft contrast look that compliments her Muted coloring. Betty's makeup is just right too, neither too pale nor too heavy.

5.2

not necessarily follow that you exercise the same level of judgment when you select your own clothes.

Jan Larkey, for instance, when she trained as a Color 1 associate, had a background as an art instructor teaching, among other things, color theory. She was also an experienced interior decorator, and she'd been selling her popular custom-designed jewelry for years. Nevertheless, through Color 1, Jan made a startling discovery about herself: She was wearing all the wrong colors to suit her Muted coloring! Not only that, she hadn't updated her look since college.

"I still wore long straight hair and no makeup combined with vibrant colors. My closet was filled with fire engine red, wipeout white, and enormous prints in high contrast black and white. I had been buying the colors and patterns I responded to psychologically, totally ignoring the visual impact they created with my more blended, muted body colors. It's no wonder I looked forty, fat, faded, and frumpy," she says in retrospect.

No longer. Today, Jan is always smartly dressed in the shades and clarities of colors most enhancing on her. Her hairstyle is contemporary. And she wears makeup in the colors that appear on her color chart.

Your Best Color Clarities

Toned-down colors look striking on women with Muted coloring. Bright and intense clarities can look harsh or garish.

Muted color types should never ever wear *pure* white because there is nothing even remotely muted-looking about that color (see Plate 27). Pure white is a bright color, just the opposite of the toned-down clarity that looks the most attractive on a Muted color type. Women with Muted coloring should substitute their best white, really an off-white, for pure white. Surprising as it may seem, on them their best white will appear whiter than it really is because of their bodies' natural color scheme.

The second-best clarity level for a Muted color type is subdued. (Study Plates 21–23 to review toned-down and subdued clarities. Then consider how enhanced our models in Plates 1, 9, 13, 17, 28, and 39 are by wearing toned-down and subdued colors.)

Best Clarity of Colors for Muted Color Types

Color Type	Best Clarity Level(s)	Second-Best Clarity Level(s)
MUTED	Toned-Down	Subdued
MUTED/CONTRAST	Bright	Slightly toned-Down Intense, provided the skin tone can handle them
MUTED/GENTLE	Toned-Down	Subdued

Your Best Level of Contrast

Women with Muted coloring must take care never to wear the strongest contrast of black or navy with white, as illustrated in Photos 5.1 and 5.3. And only dark-haired Muted color types should attempt the strong contrast of dark brown and their best white. (Plate 27 shows that the contrast level is too high—and the white too white—for JoAnn's Muted coloring.)

A medium level of contrast and a soft contrast (shown in Plate 28) are the appropriate looks for a Muted color type. (For more on strong and medium contrasts, go back to Chapter 3.) A Muted color type with *medium* or *dark hair*, though, should never combine two light colors unless a medium or dark accent color is added or the light colors are used in large blocks or in medium-sized to large patterns. (This is illustrated in Plate 38. Our model, Betty, appears washed-out—not only because of her overly pale makeup, but because she is wearing a small pattern combination of light colors.)

Here are some other medium and soft contrast effects that women with Muted coloring will find enhancing:

- *Light color with a medium color,* e.g., pale coral and medium blue, medium blue-green and light yellow.
- *Dark color with a medium color,* e.g., dark red-purple and medium blue, medium green and dark blue.
- *Two light colors—but never in a small pattern,* e.g., light coral and light green, pale yellow and light blue. Some Muted and Muted/Contrast color types may need to add a contrasting accent color.

- **Two dark colors,** e.g., dark raspberry and dark blue, dark green and dark plum.
- **Two medium colors,** e.g., medium red and medium blue, medium blue-green and medium purple.
- **Any neutral with any color,** e.g., light gray and red, navy and purple. Remember, do *not* combine light colors in small patterns without adding a contrasting accent.
- **Two neutrals that create a soft or medium contrast,** e.g., camel and rust, beige and navy.

Put another way, you can combine everything *except* black and white, navy and white, and light colors in small patterns. Unless you're a Muted color type with dark hair, stay away from the combination of dark brown and white, too.

Adding an Accent Color

What about the addition of an accent color to an outfit? Here are two rules for Muted color types:

1. When wearing all one color in a light or dark value— the monotone look—wear a soft contrasting accent near your face or at the waist. That accent could be a solid color or a pattern in the form of a scarf, ribbon, belt, or piece of jewelry. A blouse becomes the accent when it's worn with a solid-colored suit.

2. Medium-value colors can be worn with or without an accent. For example, in Plate 39 Betty would look great wearing this medium value of her blue-green head to toe, even without the accent of the scarf. But medium neutral colors—medium brown, camel, dark beige, and medium gray—may require the addition of a second accent color.

Your Best Neutrals

For women with Muted coloring, the neutrals you'll find most useful for pulling together a well-coordinated wardrobe are your best shades of off-white, cream, beige, camel, brown, and rust. They can be combined with all of your other best neutrals (discussed in detail below) and other colors to create effective medium and soft levels of contrast. These neutral shades can also be worn year-round in any region or climate the world over.

Here are a few examples:

Beiges and camels can be worn in the warmer months with all of your pastels and other light neutrals. A beige dress worn with turquoise and ivory beads, sheer beige hose, and shoes in either turquoise or beige would look elegant in any warm climate in the world. In the cooler months, a Muted color type can create the look of fall or winter by combining beige and camel with the medium and darker tones on her color chart.

Off-white can be worn in both the warmer and cooler seasons, too, depending on the shades you couple it with. For instance, you might create the look of autumn by wearing an ensemble consisting of off-white slacks, a rust top, a camel, off-white, and rust belt, and rust shoes. For a winter effect, you might wear off-white slacks with a sweater of deep purple, a camel, purple, and off-white tweed jacket accessorized with an ivory necklace, and shoes of purple or camel.

But in addition to the neutrals we just mentioned, there are others you'll want to consider to round out your wardrobe. Here is a rundown of all the neutrals, from the very darkest to the lightest, with tips about how to incorporate them in your wardrobe:

Black. Many, but not all women with Muted coloring can wear black. To decide whether you can, ask yourself: "Does a black item of clothing look as good on me as the same garment in a color that matches my hair color?" In short, black has to look *that good* on you if you are going to add it to your wardrobe and wear it regularly.

Even if you look enhanced in black, by now we hope you know *you can never wear black with white, although you can wear it with beige.* Also, try combining black with all of the light, medium, and dark values of your best colors.

Lighter-haired women with Muted coloring may need to have a lighter accent color near their face when they're wearing black or black combined with another dark color. On the other hand, there are many medium- and darker-haired Muted color types who can wear black alone, or with other deeper shades, never add a light accent, and still look lovely.

Black shoes are not a basic go-with-everything color for you. They are to be used only when black is incorporated somewhere in the outfit. What follows are typical outfits incorporating black that many Muted women find enhancing:

- A black dress accessorized with a copper and gold textured belt. At the neck, wear either a copper necklace or several gold chains. Shoes and purse could be black or metallic copper. If black, use sheer black hose; if metallic, use sheer skin-tone hose.
- Black slacks worn with a black, camel, and gray tweed jacket and a gray blouse. Complete the ensemble with a string of textured silver or black beads, sheer black hose, and black shoes and purse.
- A deep teal suit coordinated with a black, teal, and brick print blouse. This outfit's accessories include a small black leather belt, black leather shoes and purse, and sheer teal-tinted hosiery.
- A black skirt worn with a light coral blouse and a coral and black print scarf. Shoes and purse are black, and hose are sheer black or skin tone.

Camel. Camel, in a shade harmonious to the skin and hair tones, is one of the most useful neutrals for Muted color types.

Why? Because it's an extremely versatile neutral. Camel-colored clothing coordinates well with all colors, whether they're dark, medium, or light.

Some women with Muted coloring have distinct camel or caramel highlights in their hair. On these women, camel—that matches the highlight shade exactly—will look even more stunning because it focuses attention on one of their natural body colors. These women will want to own both dressy and casual shoes in their camel color.

Imagine these ensembles on a woman with Muted coloring:

- A camel suit worn with a medium-light plum blouse, an ivory necklace, ivory shoes, and sheer ivory hose.
- A camel skirt topped off with a coral blouse. The outfit is pulled together further by a necklace of camel-colored

wooden beads intertwined with a strand of coral beads. Shoes and purse are camel, and hose are sheer skin tone.

- A camel jacket over medium gray slacks, a cream-white shirt, and at the neck a gray or silver necklace. Shoes and purse are either gray or camel; hose can be skin tone or sheer gray.
- A camel dress worn with a patterned plum, green, and camel scarf at the neck, camel shoes and purse, and skin-tone or pale camel-colored stockings.
- A camel skirt combined with a pale gray blouse, a jacket, belt, shoes and purse in navy, and a textured gold necklace. Hose are skin tone or a sheer camel tone.

If you are a Muted color type with a medium to lighter look—your complexion and hair color are on the medium to light side—camel is an excellent color for shoes, handbags, and belts. It is also a fine choice for any item of clothing, especially for a jacket, blazer, or coat.

Gray. Here is another useful neutral, particularly when you wear your most enhancing shade of gray in its medium and lighter values. Darker charcoal grays are not enhancing to all women with Muted coloring. And keep in mind that any value of your gray is often prettier on you when accented with one of your other best colors near your face.

Gray is a good color for purses, shoes, and belts. It's particularly enhancing if your hair is gray or white or in the process of graying.

Gray combines well with all the light, medium, and dark values of your best colors as well as with all the neutrals on your chart. Visualize how you might look in these ensembles:

- A medium gray skirt worn with a medium purple blouse, rust beads, belt, purse, and shoes, and sheer gray-tinted hosiery.
- A medium gray suit worn with a medium teal blue blouse, gray pearls, gray shoes and purse, and sheer gray hose.
- Pale gray slacks topped off with a medium green blouse. At the neck, the whole outfit is pulled together by a gray-green-cream striped scarf. Shoes and purse are gray, hose are sheer gray.

5.3

In Photo 5.3, the strong contrast of the white blouse and navy suit is all wrong on a woman with Betty Soblin's Muted coloring. Her makeup colors, on the other hand, are too light. Betty's clothing stands out, while her face recedes.

• A medium-dark gray business suit worn with a cream blouse, silver beads, and sheer gray hose, gray shoes, and purse.

Navy. Solid expanses of navy can be overly dark-looking on many women with Muted coloring.

Thus, for even your best shade of navy to look enhancing, you must often combine it with all the other colors on your chart—with one exception. As we've said several times before, navy and any version of white creates too strong a level of contrast for you. (Compare Photos 5.3 and 5.4.)

Medium to lighter-haired women with Muted coloring often need a lighter color accent near their face when they're wearing navy, especially if they're combining navy with another dark color. For example, navy slacks and a dark green sweater might need a beige collar peaking out of the top of the sweater. Or you might add a patterned scarf with navy and green combined with other light colors.

Navy shoes are to be worn only when navy is incorporated somewhere else in the outfit.

Experiment with some of these looks:

• A navy suit worn with a pastel yellow blouse. Complete the look with a navy lapis necklace, navy shoes and purse, and sheer navy hose.
• Navy slacks worn with a light gray blouse and the same navy lapis necklace. Shoes, purse, and hose are (sheer) navy or gray.
• A navy skirt worn with a medium red blouse and a camel blazer, a red-navy-camel scarf, sheer navy hosiery, and camel or navy shoes and purse.

We don't recommend navy as a basic color for shoes and purses. However, navy accessories are lovely if the outfit has any navy in it. Navy can also look great as the "total accessory look" for an all-one-color effect (such as navy belt, shoes, and purse with a yellow dress) or with a two-color effect (such as navy shoes, necklace, and purse worn with a red skirt and beige blouse). A "total accessory look" means that the *odd* color (not appearing in the outfit) must be repeated twice. Purses do *not* count unless they are going to be carried and show every minute you are wearing the outfit.

Browns. If you are a light to darker-haired brunette with Muted coloring, your hair color brown is one of your very best neutral colors. Select your clothing and accessories in shades that match exactly or compliment your natural hair color. You will want to own both dressy and casual shoes, as well as purses and belts, that match your hair color.

Lighter-haired women with Muted coloring should stay away from very dark browns as the color is often too heavy for their look. But these same women should revel in the light to medium-dark values of their best brown. These brown shades will look wonderful.

Browns can be combined with all the colors—light, medium, or dark in value—on your color chart and nearly all of your neutrals. Brown can be particularly exciting when mixed with blues, corals, greens, purples, turquoise, reds, and yellows. Try out some of these combinations:

Notice how much better Betty looks (Photo 5.4) wearing the same navy suit with a pale peach blouse and the correct makeup. The medium level of contrast in her outfit is correct for Muted color types. The toned-down makeup colors give her face an unmistakable vibrancy.

- A medium brown skirt worn with a creamy white blouse, a brown, rust, and cream tweed jacket, rust beads and a belt, and either rust or medium brown shoes and purse. Hose could be sheer brown or skin tone.
- A medium brown suit worn with a medium red blouse and matching red shoes and purse. At the neck, wear a brown-red-cream patterned scarf. Hose can be sheer brown or skin tone.
- A light brown skirt combined with a pale coral blouse and finished off with the addition of a camel or cream jacket and camel or cream-colored shoes, purse, and hose. A strand of light brown beads in the same color as the skirt lends a nice touch.

Rust. Rust, when coordinated with other darker, medium, or light values of colors, creates a great Muted look.

- Picture an auburn-haired woman with a beige complexion wearing a rust suit from her main hair color family with a teal blouse. At her neck, she dons a patterned scarf of teal, rust, and red. Her hosiery is skin tone or sheer rust, her purse is rust, and on her feet she wears rust pumps.

• Or picture this: A brown-haired woman with camel hair highlights wearing a rust skirt topped off with a medium-value, toned-down green blouse. She wears a camel belt and beads, sheer camel or rust-tinted hose, and rust or camel shoes and purse.

Typically, women with Muted coloring have hair shades ranging from caramel blond to dark brown, sometimes with distinct rust highlights. Many redheads with rust-colored hair are also Muted color types. But no matter what your hair color, you will look smashing in your best shade of rust. You will want rust shoes, a rust belt, and a rust purse in your wardrobe.

Beiges. Beiges represent a basic shoe, purse, and belt color for Muted color types. Beige clothing and accessories also coordinate well with *all* the glorious dark, medium, and light values of every color and neutral on your color chart.

Choosing the right beige can be tricky, however. Let your skin tone be your guide, and if you are a light-haired Muted color type, your hair color beige may also be used. Obviously, a Muted color type with pink-brown beige skin shouldn't wear clothing in a golden brown-beige shade unless it matches her hair and a color break is utilized. The reverse is also true. A woman with golden brown-beige skin should not wear any beiges with a pinkish cast.

Here are some suggestions of ways to work with your best beige:

• A beige dress worn with a necklace, belt, shoes, and purse in a matching toned-down shade of red. Hose are skin tone.
• Beige slacks topped off with a navy, beige, and green striped shirt, a navy jacket, and beige shoes and hose.
• A beige skirt worn with a bluish purple blouse, a beige wood necklace intertwined with a gold chain, pale cream hosiery, and beige shoes and purse.
• A beige pair of slacks and matching blouse coordinated with a creamy off-white jacket, pearls, and beige shoes, purse, and hose.

This last outfit on a darker-haired Muted color type may look a touch too subdued. She may need to add a medium to dark color—say, a turquoise necklace intertwined with her pearls—to this outfit to increase the level of contrast.

White. All Muted color types can wear their best white (really an off-white shade) head to toe or combined with their other best colors and neutrals. What they can never do is combine their white with their navy, black (if it is one of their dark neutrals), and dark brown (if it is one of their dark shades *and* if their hair color is medium to light), for this creates far too strong a level of contrast for their toned-down coloring.

Picture yourself looking great in . . .

- Your white in a suit with a medium red blouse, ivory necklace, off-white hose, and either off-white or red shoes and purse.
- Your white in slacks with a medium teal blouse, pearls, and off-white hose, shoes and purse.
- Your white in a skirt with a plum blouse, ivory beads twisted with camel-colored wooden beads, sheer off-white or skin tone hose, and camel shoes and purse.
- Your white in a dress set off by a dark blue-green jacket and matching blue-green necklace, off-white hose, and either off-white or blue-green shoes and purse.

Wine and Burgundy. These "neutrals" find their way into many women's wardrobes because, by definition, they are a subdued clarity.

Be forewarned, though, that the exact shade of wine or burgundy you select is crucial since most women with Muted coloring cannot wear the deepest, almost blackened, tones of these colors; nor can they wear the dullest, extremely toned-down versions of these shades. But the right shade and clarity of wine and burgundy can be enhancing on Muted color types.

Shoes in these tones are only to be worn when that same color is incorporated somewhere in the outfit.

Here are some suggestions:

- A red-wine suit worn with a pale pink blouse, sheer pink hose, and shoes and purse in the same color as your hair.
- Burgundy slacks combined with a teal blouse, garnet necklace, burgundy sheer hose, and shoes and purse that match the color of your hair.

If you are a lighter-haired Muted color type who combines the colors of wine or burgundy with a dark second color—a navy or dark green, for example—you may need to wear a third lighter accent color at the neck. Sometimes it works if you simply open your blouse at the neck, exposing the lighter shade of your skin.

Dark Greens. You'll find you can combine your best shade of dark green with most of your other best colors and neutrals in their light, medium, and dark values. There is one exception: A light-haired Muted color type may need to add a lighter accent to an ensemble that combines dark green with another dark color.

Visualize yourself wearing . . .

- A dark green skirt, a rust sweater, a dark green-rust-camel tweed jacket, and rust shoes and purse and sheer rust or camel hose.
- A dark green suit with a cream blouse, accessorized with a gold necklace, a camel belt, camel shoes and purse, and sheer camel hose.
- A dark green dress with deep plum piping at the neck, plum earrings, sheer plum hose, and shoes and purse in plum or the color of your hair.

Fabric Textures and Weights

Fabric texture refers to the woven arrangement of its yarns or fibers. At the one extreme, there are the tightly woven, smooth fabrics. Included in this category are some silks, rayon, and various synthetics such as nylon. At the other extreme are the more loosely woven textured fabrics, among them linen, herringbone, tweeds, and raw silks. Cotton can be smooth and fine or roughly textured.

Muted color types can wear the full range of fabric textures. They look particularly enhanced in fabrics in which the texture is pronounced. This is because their natural coloring has a subtle textured quality to it. Repeating this subliminal effect in your clothing creates a look that is nothing short of fantastic (see Photo 5.2).

Another excellent look for Muted color types is the combination of a textured fabric with a smooth fabric—a mohair sweater worn with a wool gabardine skirt, for instance. Or you might want to use an ethnic necklace made of beads and carved pieces of ivory to accent a lustrous and shiny silk shirtwaist dress, if the styling allows.

The other consideration is a fabric's weight. Silk fabrics, for example, can come in weights so light they're gauzy or in weights so heavy that they actually have a nubby texture. Your color type allows the use of all fabric weights, *but* your weight and body structure are important variables to take into account when you're choosing fabric weights. Clearly, a very full-figured woman does not want to add pounds to her frame by wearing an overly thick fabric.

Patterns, Prints, and Designs

Generally, Muted color types look best in small tomedium-scale prints and designs. Small patterns need to have medium contrast, tiny patterns need to be avoided, since the only women who look attractive in tiny patterns are those with Gentle coloring and a few with Light-Bright coloring. You can wear larger prints *provided*: (1) the print's contrast level is somewhat blended-looking (see photo 5.7); and (2) small and medium-scale designs exist within the larger overall pattern.

So enjoy those florals, checks, stripes, dots, plaids, geometrics, and paisleys (see Plate 26). But avoid the traditional black or navy and white polka dots since this design is too high in contrast for you (see Photo 5.1).

Jewelry

Handcrafted, ethnic, textured contemporary, and antique jewelry look particularly attractive on Muted color types. Why? Because texture is synonymous with Muted coloring and these pieces generally incorporate texture as a predominant element of the design. (For example, the necklace in Photo 7.7 made of amber and African trade beads is too large visually for those with Light-Bright coloring, but would work well for many women with Muted coloring.) They range from the colorful and earthy designs of the ethnic pieces handcrafted by artisans of different cultures around the world to the ornate and symmetrical designs of the antique pieces. The latter are usually made of metals that have been brushed, oxidized, antiqued, florentined, or etched.

5.5

Betty Soblin's Muted coloring is showcased best by medium-to large-scale jewelry. In Photo 5.5, you see her wearing a tiny gold chain and pendant—a necklace a bit too delicate for her coloring. As a consequence, Betty has an unfinished appearance, even though her suit is in an enhancing shade, a toned-down orange. Another problem: Betty's makeup is too pale.

Here are the rules of thumb to keep in mind when you are choosing jewelry:

Size. Medium-sized to larger pieces of jewelry are best for you. Tiny, extremely delicate-looking pieces don't provide a strong enough focal point for women with Muted coloring unless you are a Muted/Gentle color type who has light-colored hair and you are wearing a pale-colored outfit that doesn't need much of a jewelry accent to look finished. To increase the effectiveness of your smaller pieces, wear several together.

When a Muted color type wears several pieces of jewelry together, it can be very becoming with the right outfit. Obviously, it's not an appropriate look when you're wearing a classic business suit.

Medium to dark-haired Muted color types can wear larger pieces of jewelry effectively. Lighter-haired Muted color types may wear larger pieces only if the design of the jewelry creates the illusion that they are light in weight.

Metal Colors. Good metal colors for you are gold, slightly tarnished or textured silver, pewter, copper, bronze, and brass. Combining gold and silver will also work for you if, for example, the necklace you are wearing is a mix of the two metals. Thus, your earrings and a bracelet could pick up either the gold or silver in the necklace.

If you have a golden brown-beige skin, golden olive, or olive skin, gold is your number one choice, but all other metals listed above will still be beautifully effective on you.

Metal Finishes. Both smooth and textured metals are fine, but avoid pieces with large surface areas that are shiny. In general, avoid any pieces that showcase large amounts of bright, shiny metals. In Photo 8.8 the necklace illustrated is made of black onyx and silver. This amount of shiny metal could call too much attention to itself on a Muted color type; however, if the silver were allowed to tarnish a bit, the necklace would be more flattering to Muted color types who look super in black.

One client had this reaction when we told her to avoid large amounts of shiny metal jewelry: "I feel like you're a fortune-teller consulting a crystal ball. You're telling me things about myself you really couldn't have known before and, not only that, you are telling me why I'm the way I am."

In particular, this client with her Muted coloring was referring to the fact that she had for years been avoiding the beautiful and expensive large pieces of bright, shiny silver jewelry decorating her jewelry box. She'd always felt guilty about owning the pieces but never wearing them. We had finally presented her with a rational explanation for her instinctively wise behavior.

Gem Stones, Semi-Precious Stones, and Costume Jewelry. Never wear costume jewelry in colors that are extremely bright and clear. The shades and clarities of colors on Your Color 1 Color Chart will be the most enhancing on you.

What about lovely expensive jewelry you already own whose colors aren't particularly flattering on you?

Don't panic. Such pieces can still be worn with an otherwise color-perfect outfit *provided* you keep the piece away from your skin.

For example, suppose you own a jade green necklace and your best shade of green is closer to an emerald green. Wear that jade necklace *on top of* a blouse that is in one of your best colors. It will look stunning worn against a blouse of purple, brown, yellow, or coral.

We hope you realize by now that pure white is *verboten* even in jewelry.

5.6

Photo 5.6 demonstrates how important the size of jewelry can be. This necklace of medium scale completes Betty's outfit. Betty's makeup is also stronger in this photo, giving her features just the right enhancement.

Handbags and Attaché Cases

In this age of free fashion expression, a purse need no longer match your shoes exactly. However, both your handbag and shoes must go with your outfit. If they both relate well visually to your outfit, they'll both go well with each other.

What materials should you seek out in purses? Natural materials are your first choice. A good-quality leather purse is a staple in every woman's wardrobe, and if you take care of it, it will last for years.

For late spring, summer, and early fall wear, straw and wicker purses are particularly effective. They add that dimension of texture so flattering to women with Muted coloring. For every season of the year, consider a suede or reptile-skin purse.

Patent leather is the one material you must avoid in

large amounts. Its shiny finish is not for you except in small amounts mixed with leather, suede, canvas, or straw.

Your best year-round color choices in handbags are your hair colors and your skin tones. Your second best choices are the other neutrals on Your Color 1 Color Chart.

Your best camel shade is one of your most versatile purse colors on your chart because it works for all seasons. It goes with medium or light-toned clothing as well as dark-toned clothing.

In terms of size, if you are five feet six inches or taller, you can carry any size purse you wish. Note that larger purses may look like "totes", though, even on tall women. Women under five feet six inches need to stay with small to medium-sized purses (eleven by eight inches or less). Because small purses in smooth leathers and skins can be used with both dressy and casual clothing, we recommend they be first purchases, no matter what your height.

You can't go wrong if you own a handbag or an attaché case in a color that matches your hair color exactly. No matter what color outfit you are wearing, this item will always look coordinated because it repeats a predominant theme in your body's natural color scheme.

Of course, if you are a light blond or a flaming redhead, it's more difficult for you to find an attaché case that duplicates your hair color. So for blonds, we suggest you match your camel color—in other words, your hair color taken darker. Redheads should look for briefcases in the rust and brown on their charts.

Shoes

Much of the material and color information about handbags and attaché cases applies equally to shoes.

Your basic shoe wardrobe should contain both dressy and casual shoes in colors that match your hair exactly and in a beige shade that matches your skin exactly. No patent leather, please, except in strap sandals. Supplement these hair- and skin-toned shoes with shoes in your other best neutral shades such as camel, brown, beige, rust, navy, and gray.

If pure black does not exist on your color chart, there is no need for you ever to own a pair of black shoes.

Shoes in such colors as your best red, blue, and green are fabulous to own but a definite luxury unless you wear that color a lot. Concentrate on building a shoe wardrobe in your best neutral tones first. Then add shoes in your favorite colors, colors that you wear the most frequently.

Eyeglass Frames

No Muted color type can go wrong if she selects her eyeglass frames from her best beige color (skin tone) or her main hair color. She might also repeat a hair highlight color in her frames *provided* it is a predominant highlight color that is apparent under all lighting conditions, not just in direct sunlight.

A tortoiseshell might be a good choice. Just make sure the colors running through it are good ones for you. The drawback here is that tortoiseshell is too casual-looking a frame to wear for dressy and formal occasions. So, if you can only have one pair, select a flattering solid tone.

Frameless glasses can give a nice effect and show off your eyes very well.

If you lean toward metal frames, we recommend a soft-toned or textured gold. Gray-haired women with Muted coloring look lovely in silver frames that pick up on their hair tone. Slightly toned-down and textured metallic finishes are your best bet.

Naturally, any neutral-colored frame is less limiting than a colored frame. But for those of you who crave color and can afford more than one pair of eyeglasses, go ahead. Choose frames in any of the colors that appear on Your Color 1 Color Chart.

Evening Wear

Night lighting conditions are very tricky, partly because they're hard to predict. Of course, if you're going to a discotheque, you know you might be subjected to the bright flashing spotlight effect of strobe lighting as well as very dim, dark lighting. Elegant restaurants usually feature soft flickering candlelight. Other than that, artificial night lighting conditions are anybody's guess.

For after-five wear, a woman with Muted coloring should wear the strongest clarity she can possibly sustain.

Generally, that means medium shades of a toned-down clarity. Medium values afford the brightest look on women with Muted coloring. In terms of texture, smooth shiny fabrics are a good choice. They add luster to any color. For example, a shimmering lamé—a fabric with metallic threads—is fine for you *provided* it is in one of your best shades and it is not overly bright. Sequins and beads are fine as well if they have a slightly toned-down look to them.

Dark and pale colors are not good choices because they fade to a noncolor look under most night-lighting conditions.

A Muted color type will find that toned-down golden and bronze metallic finish shoes and bags are striking in the evening, or she might select any other toned-down metallic finish or dressy leather or fabric shoe that repeats her most prominent hair colors or skin tones. Gray-haired women will look smashing in silver or pewter metallic shoes. You can also match a prominent color in your outfit.

Furs

Select furs in your best shades of off-white, beige, camel, brown, rust, or gray—and, of course, black if it is on your color chart.

Solid-colored furs are more versatile as they can be worn with dressy as well as more casual outfits. In addition, they can be worn over patterned as well as solid-colored clothing.

Multicolored furs such as lynx and raccoon are sensational. But we warn you, they are sportier in look and, therefore, are more limiting for women with multifaceted life-styles.

Makeup and Hair Coloring Advice

When a Muted color type errs in her choice of makeup, it is often because she selects colors that are too bright.

Keiko Couch, our Fort Worth associate, will never

forget her color charting session with one client in particular. The woman, in her early seventies, is a wealthy rancher's widow. Despite her pronounced Muted coloring, this woman walked into Keiko's studio wearing a brightly colored outfit with the makeup to match: far too pink a foundation; orange-brown cheek color; and a brilliant red lip color that was bleeding out to her wrinkles. Not only was the makeup too bright, the colors didn't even go well with each other.

The client explained her garish image in this way: "My mother always dressed me in bright colors so I got in the habit, I guess. I make my face up to match my wardrobe."

Because the makeup shades were wrong, Keiko had her client remove it completely so she could work with her natural skin tones. By holding up patterned fabric swatches in Muted colors and medium contrast levels, Keiko showed her the right look, the one she'd been missing out on all these years. The woman was speechless. Today she dresses like the Muted color type she is and loves her look!

Makeup Colors

How and where to apply makeup on your face is not the province of this book. Our mandate is color. We are going to discuss what makeup colors to wear to dramatically enhance your natural beige-on-brown, brown-on-brown, or red-on-brown rich Muted coloring.

Foundation. Your foundation, or makeup base, *must match your skin tone exactly*. Don't let a saleswoman talk you into anything different, say, a base with too much pink in it, "to give you that all-American, peaches and cream look." Stay away from foundation that is too pink on the one extreme and too orange on the other. The skin tones of many Muted color types are brown-beige or a golden brown-beige. When you shop for foundation, study all the bottles lined up in a row, and first try those that appear to have the least amount of pink in them.

Blush. Blush is intended to give you a healthy glow. All your best red, plum, raspberry, and red-purple shades are excellent choices for blush colors. Your best shade of coral can be used as a lipstick or polish color but never for a blush except perhaps as a light touch *underneath* your red blush.

5.7

Betty Soblin, a Muted color type, should be able to wear this softly contrasting top with its stripes of pale gray, coral, yellow, peach, and camel (Photo 5.7). The problem is her makeup. It's too pale. Women with Muted coloring must make sure their makeup colors have enough strength to compliment their medium to strong coloring, but not so strong that they overpower them.

Lipstick. You can combine all of your best lipstick colors with impunity to create new shades. And don't be afraid to match your lipstick shades in nail polish. One of your best colors for lipstick is your best shade of red—the color you turn when you blush or flush. Other possibilities are your best shades of coral, plum, raspberry, red-purple, and possibly wine—each in the best clarity to enhance your Muted coloring.

Eye shadow. Your eye shadow colors should be in the same toned-down colors you wear in clothing to emphasize and enhance your natural Muted coloring. The one exception are women with Muted/Contrast coloring, who can wear makeup colors that are brighter and clearer.

All of your best colors can be used for eye shadow, keeping in mind that different colors create different effects. How many basic eye shadow colors should you own? We recommend brown, gray, a highlighter in your pale skin-tone shade or a creamy white, blue, green, blue-green, and at least one shade of bluish purple. Purple, incidentally, goes with everything. Certain eye shapes will need both light and medium-to-dark values of each shade.

For a conservative-looking eye during the day, your best neutrals and/or your eye colors translated into shadows, subtly applied, are your best bet (refer back to Chapter 2). This look is appropriate for conservative business attire or any ensemble requiring a more understated look in eye makeup.

For a less conservative effect, wear eye makeup that repeats the colors in your clothing. Study Plates 38 and 39. The first shows a woman with Muted coloring made-up incorrectly; the second, the same woman looking fantastic. Or you might mix and match eye makeup colors, combining eye shadows in your clothing colors with a shadow or eyeliner in one of your neutral colors or a shadow or eyeliner in one of your eye colors.

For example, a green-eyed woman with Muted coloring who is wearing a purple dress might wear a soft purple shadow and duplicate the green in her eyes with a soft green eyeliner.

Eyeliner and Mascara. Many Muted color types look better in brown mascara than they do in black. Black may be used *provided* it does not give you a harsh or unnatural look. Navy and other dark colors may be used for special fashion effects. Use eyeliners in any of your charted colors. Just be certain to diffuse the line—smudge it—particularly if the color is dark in value.

Darker vs. Lighter Color Values. In deciding whether to wear a dark, medium, or light value of your best makeup colors, take your outfit, the occasion, the time of day, your eye shape, and your hair color into account.

For example, a dark-haired Muted color type can wear makeup that is darker and applied a little more heavily than Muted color types who have lighter hair and slightly gentler coloring. Or if it is daytime and you are casually dressed, you'll probably feel that less makeup is more appropriate. You could achieve this less made-up effect either by applying your usual makeup with a lighter hand or by wearing more medium or lighter values of your best colors instead of your darker makeup tones. Be careful not to go so light and pale that you look washed-out like our model in Plate 38. Though Betty is wearing full makeup (foundation, blush, lipstick, eyeshadow, eyeliner, and mascara), there's just not enough of it to enhance her Muted coloring. See how much more radiant she looks in Plate 39.

Medium makeup tones are always appropriate for conservative business dress as well as for daytime and evening casual looks. Lighter tones of lipstick give more of a nonmakeup look that is strictly casual. Lighter eye shadows are most often used as highlighters and placed in different places on the eye depending on the shape of the eye and the effect you are seeking.

Wear your darker tones of lipstick and eye makeup for dressier daytime and evening occasions or anytime you wish to create a particular high fashion look. However, if you're a Muted/Gentle color type, don't overdo it or you'll get that overly made-up look.

Blushes can be purchased in medium or dark values. Apply them lightly or more strongly depending on the effect you want.

5.8

A medium contrast look is ideal for women with Muted coloring. In Photo 5.8, Betty's sweater has stripes of toned-down blue-green and rust. The correct makeup tones on her eyes, cheeks, and lips give Betty a balanced, radiant glow.

Coordinating Your Makeup and Clothing Colors

To give you an idea how best to mix and match your makeup and clothing colors, we're going to describe several outfits with some suggestions about the makeup you might wear to accompany them.

- You are wearing a medium brown pair of slacks—a color that matches your hair—with a cream blouse, a rust belt and necklace, brown hoisery and shoes, and a rust or brown handbag.

  Here are two of your makeup options:
  One way to keep your eye look neutral would be to wear a cream-color highlighter, gray eye shadow tones, a brown eyeliner, and brown mascara. Complete the look with a medium to medium-dark coral lip and polish color. On your cheeks, your best medium red tone mixed with just a hint of your coral lip color if you wish.
  A more colorful and contrasting effect could be achieved with eye shadows of purple or blue-green with the same cream-tone highlighter. The other colors remain as described above.

- Your outfit consists of a medium red dress with a necklace made by twisting a gold chain and a strand of turquoise beads together. Your earrings are textured gold hoops. You are wearing skin-tone stockings and medium brown shoes. Your purse is either brown or red.

  And your makeup?
  For a stronger eye effect, good eye shadow colors would be shades of medium brown and turquoise with a cream or skin tone highlighter, turquoise eye liner, and brown mascara. A more conservative option is to drop the turquoise and stay with the cream highlighter and medium brown shadows exclusively. Your eyeliner and mascara would be brown. Your lip, cheek, and nail color need to match the red shade of your dress.

- Suppose you have on a pair of medium purple slacks and a deep green sweater. The outfit is pulled together further by a green, purple, and cream print scarf, sheer purple hose, purple shoes, and a purse in your hair color.

With this ensemble, your best eye shadow colors repeat the purple and/or green tones of your clothing. Again, wear a cream or skin tone highlighter. Your eyeliner could be purple and/or blue-green. For mascara, either use brown or a fashion shade of dark purple. In this case, your best lip, cheek, and nail colors are any of your plum, coral, or red tones.

- You're dressed conservatively for business: a brown suit and a beige blouse accessorized with a gold necklace, skin-tone hose, and brown shoes and purse.

To compliment this outfit, one suggestion would be eye shadows of medium brown and gray, with a gray or brown eyeliner, and brown mascara. Brush your cheeks and lips with your best medium red shade. Either match that red shade for nail color or use a clear nail polish. If your eyes are greenish, bluish, or blue-green, you could wear a very subtle touch of your eye color with the brown or gray shadow as a subtle eye liner.

Hair Coloring

When a woman with Muted coloring colors her hair, she should avoid the two most common mistakes: (1) making the hair color too brassy; and (2) giving the hair too much ash tone.

Our associate Caryl Krannich remembers the time she had two clients within the space of a week, both making the first mistake. Both women were Muted color types with pink-brown beige skin, yet they had added brassy gold tones to their hair.

"In each case, I demonstrated in a kind of show-and-tell session that there was a dissonance between the client's pink-toned skin and golden-toned hair," Caryl explains. "I did this by matching each woman's skin and hair colors to color chips, then placing them next to each other. They didn't look good. Once my client could see the conflict, I had her look in a hand mirror, noting that same conflict in her body colors."

Since both her clients wished to keep their lightened hair color rather than darken it, Caryl suggested that they change the blond shade to a champagne or beige blond—that was more complimentary to their skin tone.

Many of our associates deal with just the opposite problem: people with Muted coloring who have lightened their hair to blond shades that were too ash in tone. It then becomes our associates' problem to help these women find a satisfactory way to fix their hair color mistakes.

One client wanted to return to her natural hair color and add highlights to brighten it. We advised her to use the camel shade on her chart as a guide. Another client, who was lightening her gray hair, wanted to return to a brown shade but not a color as dark as her original hair color. We advised her to color her hair to match the medium brown shade on her chart, a shade that looks lovely with her skin tone. It was the right recommendation, for this client now looks lively and vibrant instead of drab and washed-out.

A Muted color type who wants to change her hair color has three choices. She can choose to be a blond, a redhead, or a brunette *provided she selects the right shade of those colors*. Here are some guidelines:

Red Hair. You will look the most natural as a redhead if your original hair color has an apparent reddish highlight and you match it exactly. (Reread "Determining Your Main Hair Color and Highlights" in Chapter 1.) Otherwise, we suggest you color your hair to your best rust, rust-brown, or copper shade—in short, a shade that keeps your skin looking clear and radiant. Let your color chart and skin tone be your guide.

Blond. An appropriate blond shade can be chosen by repeating the beige tone of your skin in your hair color. If your hair has natural camel highlights, then you may lighten your hair to that camel shade. Caramel highlights can be matched to create a caramel or strawberry blond effect. (Note the camel and caramel highlights in Plates 39 and 1, respectively.) Definitely avoid ash blond shades and brassy golden blonds. Honey or golden blond shades are fine *provided* you have golden tones in your skin.

Brunette. Great care must be taken to choose a shade that is enhancing to your skin tone. Only then will your new hair color look natural. Choose a brown that is a darker verson of your beige skin color—the camels, medium browns, and darker browns on your chart.

Your Muted coloring is truly unique, and you now know how to use colors in their best shades, clarities, and levels of contrast to help you look terrific in your clothing and makeup. You are ready to begin Part III, where you can apply all of your new knowledge and learn to cast your own special and fabulous color spell!

Chapter 6

Wardrobe Advice for Gentle Coloring

The colors you wear have a potent effect on other people. You probably don't even realize it, but Peter A. Willms, our Color 1 associate in Camp Hill, Pennsylvania, does. He relates an anecdote demonstrating that when you don the wrong colors for your color type, you can actually induce unwanted negative behavior in those around you.

Peter's wife Mary is a schoolteacher. Until Peter did her color chart, she had a habit of wearing colors that did battle with her natural Gentle coloring. They were much too clear, and she often combined colors in ways that created too strong a level of contrast.

When her colors were toned down, she remained dubious until her friends started showering her with compliments. Then she began to notice something else. The atmosphere in her classroom had changed. Her students' behavior improved markedly, and she was able to maintain better discipline. Improved visual image gave her more visual power, confidence, and positive energy, which affected how her students responded to her teaching.

Mary's case isn't unique. Women with Gentle coloring often err in the direction of too much contrast, at the same time wearing colors that are too bright and clear.

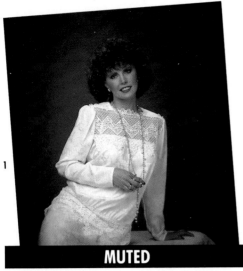

MUTED

Muted Color Type. Our associate Lin Marie of Portland, Oregon, is an exquisite Muted color type. Here she is shown dressed in a cream-colored silk and lace dress. She chooses a muted red shade for blush and lipstick.

GENTLE

Gentle Color Type. Patti Sparks, our Newport Beach, California, associate, models a lace dress in pale dusty rose and cream colors—wonderful shades to showcase her Gentle coloring. Her lip and cheek color is also a light rose.

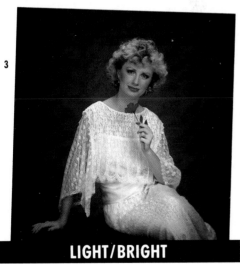

LIGHT/BRIGHT

Light-Bright Color Type. Brenda Perham, a professional singer, makeup artist, and photographer's stylist from California, has Light-Bright coloring that is framed to best advantage by the pure white lace dress she is wearing. But her look would not be complete without the bright accent of clear red blush and lipstick. Her coloring requires that extra splash of a bright clarity.

CONTRAST

Contrast Color Type. Color 1 associate Dolly Boyd of Los Angeles has the striking dark–light coloring typical of her color type. This dress of black velvet with the pure white lace collar is just the kind of high-contrast outfit that looks radiant on women with Contrast coloring. Her makeup is equally dynamic—strong clear red cheek and lip color.

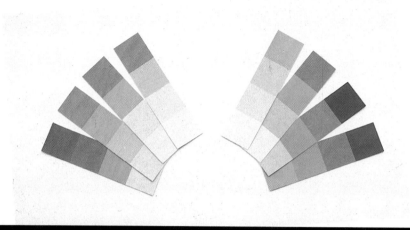

SKIN TONES

When you are analyzing your skin tone, there are three considerations: the shade; the undertones (are they pink or golden?); and your complexion's lightness or darkness. The four skin-tone strips on the left side of this photo are examples of shades where pink tones predominate.

Those on the right are examples of shades where golden tones predominate. Note that the four gradations on each strip of color go from light to dark examples of the same shade. Some women develop deep tans that approximate these darker color values.

These nine strips of color depict specific skin tones, moving from the pinker tones on the left to the golden tones on the right. From left to right, they are: (1) the very lightest pink porcelain to the deeper shade of pink ivory; (2) a pale pink-brown beige to a darker version of the same; (3) a porcelain to a darker porcelain, usually called ivory; (4) a light golden-brown beige to a darker version of the same; (5) a light golden porcelain to a golden ivory; (6) a light golden-brown beige to a darker version of the same; (7) a golden porcelain to a light clear golden; (8) a light olive to a medium-dark olive; and (9) a light clear golden to a clear golden olive.

CAUCASIAN SKIN TONES

These seven color strips represent black women's skin tones. Again the shades with pink tones are shown on the left and the more golden tones on the right. Moving from the left side of the fan to the right, the actual shades on the color strips are: (1) from dark pink-brown to pink-brown camel; (2) light pink-brown beige to medium ivory beige; (3) black-brown to light brown-beige; (4) medium-dark clear brown to medium-toned ivory; (5) clear golden camel to clear golden ivory; (6) clear golden brown to clear golden beige; and (7) light golden-brown beige to medium ivory beige.

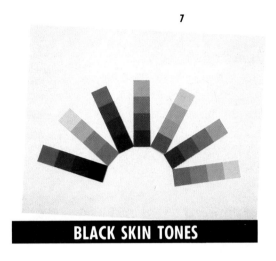

BLACK SKIN TONES

The top fan of color strips shows clear red shades ranging from coral tones on the left to blue-red tones on the right.
The lower fan shows toned-down reds, again the coral tones on the left and blue-red tones on the right.

LIP COLORS

SKIN COLOR

MAIN HAIR COLOR

Lin Marie, our Color 1 associate in Portland, Oregon, is a lovely example of Muted coloring. Here she is shown wearing clothing and makeup colors that enhance her natural coloring: her toned-down blue and purple eye shadows and muted red lip and cheek color pick up the dusty blue, red, and purple tones of her scarf and medium blue dress. Altogether, it's a fabulous Muted look.

9

MUTED

SECOND HAIR COLOR

MAIN EYE COLOR

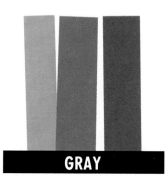

SECOND EYE COLOR

WHITE

RED

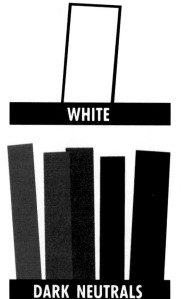

DARK NEUTRALS

GRAY

GREEN

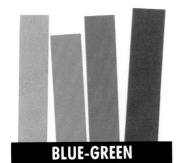

BLUE-GREEN

GREEN-BLUE

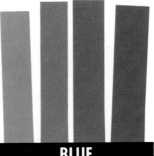

BLUE

BLUE-PURPLE

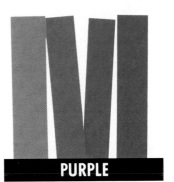

PURPLE

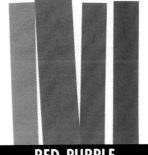

RED-PURPLE

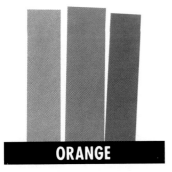

ORANGE

RASPBERRY

CORAL

SKIN COLOR

MAIN HAIR COLOR

Myrt Arthur, our associate in San Mateo, California, is a beautiful Gentle color type. She is dressed in two of her ideal colors: a slightly toned-down pink jacket with a purple blouse, accented with a string of pearls. Her eye shadow colors are various shades of purple, and her cheek and lip color is a toned-down raspberry.

10

GENTLE

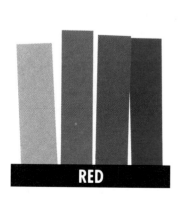

SECOND HAIR COLOR

MAIN EYE COLOR

SECOND EYE COLOR

RED

WHITE

DARK NEUTRALS

GRAY

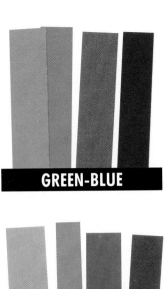

GREEN-BLUE

BLUE-GREEN

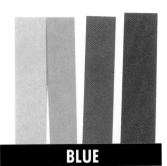

BLUE

TEAL

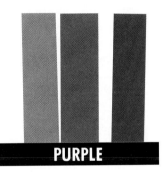

PURPLE

PLUM

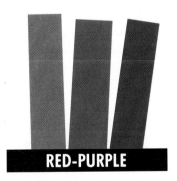

RED-PURPLE

RASPBERRY

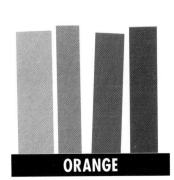

BLUE-PURPLE

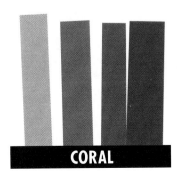

CORAL

ORANGE

SKIN COLOR

MAIN HAIR COLOR

An exciting example of Light-Bright coloring is Jeanne Schoenfeld, our associate in the Del Mar/La Jolla area of Southern California. Jeanne models a dotted blouse, which showcases the colors of clear red and pure white. Her earrings are also pure white. The shadow on her eyes is in clear bluish tones, and her lipstick and blush are a clear red, bright but at the same time light-looking.

11

LIGHT/BRIGHT

SECOND HAIR COLOR

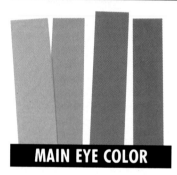

MAIN EYE COLOR

SECOND EYE COLOR

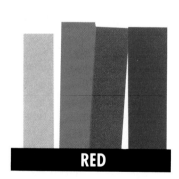

RED

WHITE

GRAY

DARK NEUTRALS

GREEN

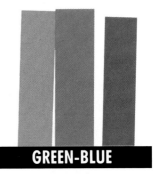

GREEN-BLUE

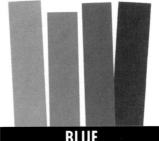

BLUE

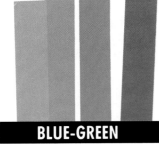

BLUE-GREEN

BLUER-GREEN

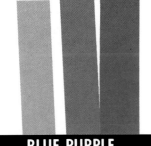

BLUE-PURPLE

PURPLE

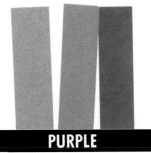

RED-PURPLE

CORAL

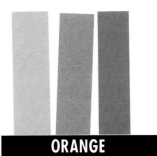

RASPBERRY

ORANGE

SKIN COLOR

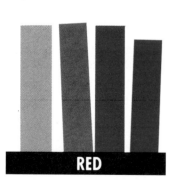

MAIN HAIR COLOR

Helene Mills, one of our associates in Los Angeles, exemplifies the drama of Contrast coloring. She is dressed in a clear, bright purple blouse worn as a jacket over a bright green man-tailored shirt, accessorized with a black onyx necklace. Her eye shadow is a combination of clear purple and clear green. The final makeup touches are a clear medium red blush and a lip color of clear medium-dark red.

12

CONTRAST

SECOND HAIR COLOR

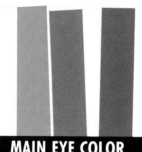

MAIN EYE COLOR

SECOND EYE COLOR

WHITE

RED

DARK NEUTRALS

GRAY

GREEN

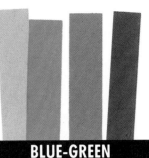

BLUE-GREEN

BLUE-PURPLE

BLUE

ROYAL BLUE

RED-PURPLE

PURPLE

PLUM/FUCHSIA

RASPBERRY

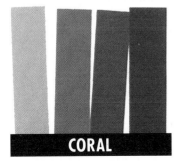

CORAL

ORANGE

Emmaline Jansing, from Lake San Marcos, California, is an example of a gray-haired woman with Muted coloring. Here she models a toned-down, dark purple jacket and a soft yellow blouse. Her earrings and pin repeat the two colors of her outfit. For eye shadow, Emmaline chose various toned-down shades of purple. Her lip and cheek color is a medium toned-down red.

Marguerite Melton, from San Bernardino, California, is a Gentle color type. The colors of this outfit are ideal for her: a toned-down coral jacket combined with an off-white blouse. Her eye shadow colors are understated yet enhancing. Her blush is a toned-down pink color, and her lipstick is a deeper value of toned-down pink-coral.

MUTED

GENTLE

13

14

15

16

LIGHT/BRIGHT

CONTRAST

Evelyn Ford, a Color 1 Associates' client and coauthor Judy Lewis-Crum's mother, is an excellent example of a Light-Bright color type whose hair is now gray. The bright red of her jacket is repeated in her earrings. Her pale gray blouse, in turn, matches the gray tones of her hair. Her eye shadow colors are clear grays, and she wears a clear red shade on her lips and cheeks.

Sally Wilder, an associate in Fort Worth, Texas, is an example of a salt-and-pepper gray-haired woman with Contrast coloring. The clear bright red blouse combined with the large-pattern red, white, and black scarf creates the strong contrast effect that looks so handsome on women with Sally's coloring. For eye shadow she chooses clear tones, and for cheek and lip color she wears a clear bright red.

Marilyn Overton of Riverside, California, is wearing colors in the right clarities and level of contrast to enhance her Muted coloring. Her toned-down purple suit jacket creates a medium level of contrast next to her cream-colored blouse. Her makeup underscores the look: She wears pale purple and gray eye shadows, a medium toned-down red lip color, and a lighter version of the same red on her cheeks.

Grace Washington proves that black women, too, have Gentle coloring. She is dressed in a medium dusty blue blouse set off by a scarf with stripes of blue, pink, yellow, and white. Pink cheek and lip tones beautifully complement her Gentle pink-brown skin.

MUTED

17

GENTLE

18

19

20

LIGHT/BRIGHT

Bennetta Butler is a black woman with Light-Bright coloring. She wears a white shirt and multistriped nautical scarf showcasing the clear bright shades of white, blue, green, yellow, red, and navy. The clear medium tones of her eye shadow pick up on several of the scarf colors. Her lipstick and blush are clear red shades.

CONTRAST

Reeta Bess-Barnes, a professional model from Los Angeles, is wearing a large-pattern black and white blouse with bold earrings to match. Clear deep lipstick and blush complement her Contrast coloring.

Clarities of Green. The word "green" is a catchall term referring to various shades and clarities. In this photo you see different clarities of green in similar shades. The fabric on the left is subdued; the middle one is a bright clarity; and the right one is toned down.

Clarities of Red. Here are examples of three different clarities of red in similar shades. The fabric on the left represents a subdued red. The red in the middle is clear and bright. The red on the right is just slightly toned down.

Clarities of Blue. The clarities depicted go from a subdued blue on the left to a clear, bright blue in the center to a toned-down blue on the right.

21

22

23

CLARITIES

These blouses are all the same shade of coral red, but they range in value from light (left) to dark (center) to medium (right).

VALUES

Contrast Levels and Print Sizes. These four fabrics depict two levels of contrast. The black and white swatches on the left are examples of the strongest level of contrast. The black and beige swatches on the right represent a medium level of contrast.

The second variable shown here is print size. Contrast color types look best in strong and medium levels of contrast. But, ideally, that contrast should be contained in a large- to medium-bold print. Hence, women with Contrast coloring would look enhanced in the fabric on the upper left. Contrast color types can only wear the small black and white pattern on the lower left if they add a bright solid-colored accent.

Light-Bright color types can also wear strong and medium contrast levels, but they cannot wear them in large-scale prints. Thus, the fabric on the lower left would be suitable for them.

The black and beige fabric swatches on the right are small to medium in scale and represent a medium level of contrast. Muted and Gentle color types can wear

these, although really tiny patterns only look good on women with Gentle coloring. Contrast and Light–Bright color types can also wear black and beige because it creates a medium level of contrast. But on a Contrast color type, the black and beige pattern should be medium to large in scale. On a Light–Bright color type, it should be medium to small.

CONTRASTS

26

Fabrics for Muted Coloring. All of the fabrics pictured have an overall "muted" look about them. The clarities are toned down, the contrast levels range from medium to soft or blended, and the prints range from medium-large to small in scale. Note that there is no pure white in any of the fabrics.

MUTED

27

28

MUTED WARDROBE

JoAnn Grose, our Color 1 associate in Mill Valley, California, (Plate 27) is wearing an outfit that is all wrong for her dramatic Muted coloring. The color scheme of her top—clear bright purple, black, and pure white—is too strong a contrast. People will notice JoAnn's blouse before they look at her face. JoAnn's makeup is also incorrect. Her eye makeup is too pale and her lips too bright, creating an all-mouth, washed-out-eyes look.

What a difference the right colors make! In the photo on the right (Plate 28), JoAnn is wearing an outfit in toned-down versions of red and teal blue. Her red blouse proves that redheads can wear red *provided* it's the right shade and clarity of red. Her eye shadows pick up the teal tones of her skirt, while her blush and lipstick repeat the toned-down red of her blouse.

Fabrics for Gentle Coloring. All the fabrics shown are excellent choices for women with Gentle coloring. Why? The clarities are toned-down to subdued. The levels of contrast range from soft to medium. And the designs are tiny to medium in scale.

29

GENTLE

WRONG

30

RIGHT

31

GENTLE WARDROBE

Myrt Arthur's Gentle coloring is overwhelmed by the dark–bright color combination in Plate 30. (Myrt is our San Mateo, California, associate.) The bright yellow-gold blouse is too intense in color, as well as the wrong shade for her. Also, the medium and dark tones on her eyes, cheeks, and lips create an overly made-up look.

How much more alive and exciting Myrt looks in Plate 31. The reason: She's wearing the shades, clarities, and levels of contrast designed to enhance her coloring. The toned-down yellow suit with the gray collar trim and bow create a medium level of contrast. To bring out her eyes, she is wearing medium to light shades of gray eye shadow. Her cheek and lip color is a toned-down red.

32

LIGHT/BRIGHT

Fabrics for Light-Bright Coloring. These are typical fabrics that a Light-Bright color type might wear. Wouldn't you agree that they have a "light and bright" look about them? This is because the colors are all clear and bright as well as being medium to light in value. None of the colors are toned-down or overly intense-looking. The sizes of the various prints range from medium to small, while the levels of contrast within the prints range from medium to strong.

33

WRONG

RIGHT

34

LIGHT/BRIGHT WARDROBE

To look their most enhanced, Light-Bright color types need to wear bright clarities. Jeanne Schoenfeld, our Color 1 associate in Del Mar, California, is wearing just the opposite in Plate 33. The bronze-colored dress is a bad shade and does nothing for Jeanne's Light-Bright coloring. Another problem illustrated here: Jeanne is wearing makeup that is too dark in tone and too heavily applied.

The correct look is demonstrated in Plate 34. Jeanne has, in effect, duplicated her natural light and bright color scheme in her outfit. She wears a pure white skirt and camisole combined with a bright blue jacket and accessorized with a bright gold neckband and bracelet. On her eyes, she wears medium-toned blue shadows and a clear but light-looking red on her cheeks and lips.

Fabrics for Contrast Coloring. This eye-popping collection of fabric swatches only a woman with Contrast coloring could wear. The bright colors and large, bold scale of many of the designs would overpower women with any other type of coloring. But women with Contrast coloring need such patterns in strong levels of contrast and bright or intense colors to look their most enhanced.

35

CONTRAST

36

37

CONTRAST WARDROBE

Jennifer Ho's dramatic Contrast coloring is not showcased to best advantage in the pale blue and white floral dress she models in Plate 36. (Jennifer is one of our associates in the San Francisco area.) In fact, the dress combined with the matching pale blue eye shadow and soft dusty rose cheek and lip color make Jennifer look downright insignificant. Dainty little prints are not the province of the woman with

Contrast coloring. Neither are two light colors worn together.

Can you believe Jennifer is the same woman when you look at her in Plate 37? The black jumper, clear deep purple blouse, and purple, red, and blue scarf bring Jennifer's natural coloring to life. This dark–bright combination is fabulous for Contrast color types. Jennifer has repeated her outfit's colors in her makeup.

With her Muted coloring, Betty Soblin—our Castro Valley, California, associate—looks washed out in makeup colors that are too pale. In the photo on the left (Plate 38), this is Betty's problem. The "faded look" is further exacerbated by a blouse whose colors are too blended-looking for her. Muted color types need gutsier color combinations.

The oomph lacking in the first photo is present in the one on the right (Plate 39). Here Betty is wearing the right clothing and makeup to enhance her Muted coloring: a slightly toned-down blue-green blouse set off by a scarf, also blue-green with accent colors of yellow-gold and rust. Her toned-down eye shadow colors pick up on the blouse and scarf colors. Her medium coral-red lipstick and blush give Betty a radiant glow.

RIGHT

WRONG

39

38

MUTED MAKEUP

Because of her Gentle coloring, Myrt Arthur, our San Mateo, California, associate, runs the risk of looking too heavily made up if she wears dark tones of makeup. That's one of her problems in Plate 40. Here you see her wearing a blend of dark blue, gray, and purple eye shadow, a clear pink-red blush, and a bright but deep shade of lipstick. The bright colors and strong contrasts of her outfit are equally disturbing. There is nothing Gentle about this look!

The difference between night and day is the way we'd characterize the difference between Photos 40 and 41.

In the latter photo, Myrt has created an exciting complement to her natural coloring: Her eye shadows consist of toned-down medium shades of light blue, purple, and peach. Her blush is a toned-down medium pink. Her lipstick shade is a pink-coral. She's dressed in a toned-down coral blouse with a coral and creamy white scarf.

RIGHT

41

WRONG

40

GENTLE MAKEUP

In Plate 42, Jeanne Schoenfeld's makeup is too dark and applied too heavily for a woman with her Light-Bright coloring. (Jeanne is our Del Mar, California, associate.) Not only is the blue eye shadow too dark, but her blush and lipstick shades are similarly strong in tone. Her outfit doesn't help matters either. The combination of the blue blouse—clear and bright—with the black jacket and bow scarf creates a bright–dark look that is visually very heavy and dark-looking.

See what a difference the right shades of makeup and a lighter and brighter clothing look can make! (See Plate 43.) Jeanne's eye shadows are clear medium tones of blue. On her cheeks and lips, she wears a clear but light-looking bright red. In essence, Jeanne has repeated the light and bright effect of her natural coloring in the colors she's applied to her face. The light (her jacket) and bright (her blouse) effect of her clothing completes the look.

WRONG

RIGHT

43

42

LIGHT/BRIGHT MAKEUP

At first glance you may wonder why we label this look "Wrong." Our model does look attractive, but not smashing! Not only is Helene Mills's eye shadow too pale for her Contrast coloring (Plate 44), but it's also too toned-down a color for her. She is far more enhanced by using clear colors. Her cheek and lip colors are wrong for the same reasons. Her blouse, too, is just a little too pale.

In Plate 45 we see Helene, one of our Los Angeles area associates, with clear blue and plum eye shadow tones and a clear plum red color on her lips and cheeks. Her outfit repeats her makeup colors and consists of a bright-on-bright combination in a medium level of contrast. We'd call this a spectacular Contrast look!

RIGHT

WRONG

CONTRAST MAKEUP

This array of clear, bright color clarities—28 in all—comprises the color chart of Jennifer Ho (Plate 46). When you have your color chart done by a Color 1 associate, a Personal Color Harmony folder displaying your colors as well as an accordion-fold pocket shopping guide will be created just for you. Both are depicted in Plate 47.

46

47

JENNIFER HO'S COLOR CHART

Another client, with ivory skin and red hair, dressed as if she had Contrast coloring until she realized the subtle power of Gentle color combinations. Where her color choices were once overwhelming and jarring, now they're subtly vibrant and glowing. Since she is president of a hair styling studio, she finds her new image, capped off by her marvelously coiffured hair, an excellent advertisement for her business.

Famous women who have Gentle coloring include Candice Bergen, Meryl Streep, Faye Dunaway, Jane Pauley, and Linda Evans.

Your Best Color Clarities

The most enhancing clarity for a Gentle color type to wear is toned-down. The next best clarity is subdued. Only those rare women with Gentle/Light-Bright coloring can wear bright clarities. On them, that clarity looks beautiful.

To see how out of place bright colors look on the typical Gentle color type, look at the right and wrong photographs, Plates 30 and 31, and 40 and 41.

A Gentle color type can wear pure white, but only in small amounts in a print or as a trim. When you are wearing a solid expanse of white—a plain white blouse or skirt, let's say—we caution you to stick with *your* best white, which will be slightly off-white.

To review color clarities, study Plates 21–23.

Your Best Level of Contrast

A decade ago, when the notion of the "power look" for businesswomen—the dark navy suit worn with the stark white blouse—was promulgated, a large cross-section of women were misled. Among them were women with Gentle coloring, who are overpowered by this strong contrast combination.

Best Clarity of Colors for Gentle Color Types

Color Type	Best Clarity Level(s)	Second-Best Clarity Level(s)
GENTLE	Toned-Down	Subdued
GENTLE/LIGHT-BRIGHT	Bright	Slightly Toned-Down
GENTLE/MUTED	Toned-Down	Subdued

6.1

Women with Gentle coloring do not look attractive wearing overly large patterns, particularly when those patterns create a strong contrast. The dress Myrt Arthur models in Photo 6.1 is a perfect example. You see the dress long before it occurs to you to notice Myrt. Myrt's makeup is also too dark and too strong for her coloring.

But don't let this worry you too much because women with your Gentle coloring can wear a navy tailored suit, all right, but only under the following conditions: It must be in an enhancing shade of navy and be accompanied by a blouse in a color that creates a soft or medium level of contrast—light beige, light gray, or any of your best pastels, for example (see Photos 6.3 and 6.4).

Here are some further suggestions about how to combine the colors on Your Color 1 Color Chart:

- *A light color with a medium color* (as in Plate 41), e.g., light yellow and medium coral, light blue-green and medium red.
- *A dark color with a medium color,* e.g., dark purple and medium blue, dark raspberry and medium raspberry.
- *Two light colors,* e.g., light green and light coral, light blue and light pink.
- *Two medium colors* (see Plate 31), e.g., medium red and medium blue, medium red-purple and medium blue.
- *Two dark colors,* e.g., dark green and plum, dark gray and rust. This combination—without any accent—may be worn by darker-haired women with Gentle coloring. Light-haired women may need to lighten such an outfit by adding a third medium or light accent color.
- *Any neutral with any color,* e.g., light gray and light blue, camel and coral.
- *Any two neutrals that create a soft or medium level of contrast,* e.g., medium gray and camel, off-white and beige, navy and light gray.

Put another way, we are saying you can wear every combination except black and white and navy and white. You cannot wear dark brown and white either unless your hair is a dark ash brown.

Adding an Accent Color

What about accent colors?

A Gentle color type can wear all one color—the mono-tone look—with or without the addition of an accent. For example, our model in Plate 18 would look wonderful in her blue from head to toe, even without the addition of the scarf.

Your Best Neutrals

Some women wear a lot of neutral colors—black, gray, navy, brown, rust, camel, beige, white, burgundy, or dark green—because it makes them feel safe. After all, camel is camel, isn't it?

No it isn't. Neutrals, such as camel, come in various shades and clarities and values just as other colors do. You have to wear neutrals in the right shade, clarity, and dark or light value to emphasize your rich yet Gentle natural coloring. In addition, you must always create the right level of contrast for your color type when you combine neutrals with other colors in the outfits you wear.

If you have Gentle coloring, you won't want to be without your creamy whites, beiges, camels, and light to medium grays for clothing as well as accessories. These light and medium neutrals coordinate well with all the other dark, medium, and light colors on your color chart—with three glaring exceptions. As we mentioned earlier, *most women with Gentle coloring cannot wear white in any form with the dark neutrals of black, navy, or dark brown.* (Compare Photos 6.3 and 6.4.) The level of contrast these combinations create is far too strong for a Gentle color type's delicate coloring.

Using her lighter and medium neutrals, a Gentle color type can assemble sophisticated outfits that will look stunning any month of the year no matter where she lives or what the climate.

Let's say you want to create an autumn or winter look. How about these combinations?

Wear off-white slacks with a rust sweater and a plaid jacket of off-white, rust, and camel. Complete the ensemble with an ivory necklace, sheer off-white hose, and matching rust shoes and purse.

6.2

Myrt displays the correct look for a Gentle color type in Photo 6.2. This time, you notice Myrt's face, not just her dress. The colors of the dress are aqua blue and raspberry pink. This medium level of contrast and small-sized print are extremely effective with Myrt's coloring. Also effective are the medium tones of eye shadows, lipstick, and blush she is wearing here.

Don the same pair of off-white slacks and sheer off-white hose, but this time coordinate them with a medium gray blouse and medium red jacket. At the neck, wear a strand of pearls, or the same ivory necklace, and choose matching red shoes and purse for accessories.

In the spring and summer, picture yourself in a light gray linen skirt and a light blue blouse. Your necklace and belt are in coral, and your shoes, purse, and hosiery are gray or your skin-tone beige.

For another spring and summer effect, you might coordinate a camel linen suit with a pale pink blouse, pale camel or beige shoes, hose, and purse, and camel-colored wooden beads at the neck.

But light and medium neutrals are not your only choices. We'd like to introduce you to all the available neutrals—dark, medium, and light—and discuss how you can incorporate them all into your wardrobe.

Black. Not all women with Gentle coloring can wear black effectively.

If you can wear black, you must be careful *how* you wear it. A solid expanse of black is almost guaranteed to look too heavy on you unless you add the leavening effect of a medium to light toned-down color. But, as we've said, that light color cannot be any form of white, as this creates far too strong a level of contrast. Also, the medium value color cannot be too bright or intense (as in Plate 30).

So how do you deal with black?

Keep in mind that your objective is to make black—or other dark neutrals like navy or dark brown—appear as delicate as possible.

One sure-fire way to take some of the wallop out of black is to wear very little of it—a little bit of black in a print scarf or blouse, for instance. Another way is to always wear a light or medium accent color near your face. Pearls won't do because they are white, although rose quartz beads might do the trick. Some of you may need a more pronounced item—a blouse or scarf, for example—to tone down the powerful effect of black.

A third way is to expose a lot of skin in the neck and chest area. If you are wearing a black blouse, leave a few buttons open at the neck. For evening a sheer and/or lacy blouse that enables your skin tone to show through has a very delicate look. For most Gentle color types, a black turtleneck will be too dark and heavy-looking with your soft and gentle coloring.

Even if you can wear black, we do not recommend accessorizing outfits with black shoes, hosiery, or purses unless your outfit incorporates black somewhere in it. You cannot use black shoes, for example, as a basic go-with-everything shoe color.

We once had a blond Gentle/Light-Bright client who insisted that all blonds look terrific in black. Only she didn't. Black made her look ghostlike. Not even makeup in the right colors and correctly applied could counteract black's negative effect on her. Unfortunately, her wardrobe was awash with black—everything from black T-shirts to evening dresses. Naturally, this woman was quite upset when she was told black did not look good on her.

However, being a good sport, she agreed to stop wearing black and give the colors on her chart a try. After three months, she reported how happy she was now that people were complimenting her regularly on her newfound sense of color. She no longer looks old, pale, and worn-out before her time.

If black does compliment your Gentle coloring, try . . .

- A black skirt, a pink sweater, and a scarf in a delicate pattern of pink, black, and gray. Finish off the look with sheer gray hose and black shoes and purse.
- A beige suit, black blouse that you leave open at the neck, a turquoise necklace twisted around an ivory necklace, turquoise earrings, skin-toned hose, and black shoes and a black purse.

Camel. This is an extremely useful neutral for women with Gentle coloring, particularly if the woman's hair has an obvious camel tone or highlights. If it does, those are the shades of camel to match. If it doesn't, your best shade of camel will be a darker version of your skin tone.

The beauty of camel is that it coordinates with all the dark, medium, and lighter values of your best colors as well as with your best neutrals. You will want to own both dressy and casual shoes in your camel.

Picture yourself in one of these ensembles:

- A camel suit worn with a pastel blouse in either pale coral, blue, or plum. Complete the outfit with camel shoes, a camel handbag and skin-tone hosiery, and a gold chain at the neck.

6.3

The dark navy and white "executive look" (photo 6.3) is a good one for women whose coloring can sustain such a strong contrast. Myrt Arthur's Gentle coloring cannot. And that's not all that is wrong here. Her makeup tones are also too dark and strong.

- Or how about the same camel suit worn with a medium-value blouse in red, green, or yellow? You could adorn the outfit with the same accessories and actually look quite different because of the blouse substitution.
- Finally, try a camel skirt or slacks with a turquoise blouse, gold jewelry at the neck, a camel belt with a moderate-sized gold buckle, skin-tone hose, and camel shoes and purse.

Gray. Gray in its medium to lighter incarnations is another neutral rivaling camel in its usefulness. It too coordinates exquisitely with all the other light to dark colors on your color chart. In addition, it can be worn with all of your other best neutrals. It's a super shoe, purse, and belt color and will be an absolute necessity when your hair has gray or white in it.

Visualize yourself in these combinations:

- Light gray slacks combined with a medium blue blouse, silver earrings and necklace, sheer gray hose, a purse and shoes that are gray or the color of your hair.
- A medium gray suit worn with an off-white top—a sweater or blouse. Accessorize the outfit with your best toned-down red in jewelry, a belt, and shoes. Your handbag and hosiery are gray.

Navy. Much that we said about black applies with equal force to navy.

If you are going to wear navy, make it appear as soft and delicate-looking as possible using the *trompe l'oeil* effects we outlined earlier. Navy shoes are not to be worn unless navy is incorporated somewhere in the outfit.

Navy can be combined with other darker neutrals such as rust, deep raspberry, and wine as well as with the medium and lighter colors on your color chart—with the exception of white. If you are combining navy with any other dark color, you will probably need to lighten the look by adding a medium to light accent near your face.

You may want to try one of the following outfits:

- A navy skirt and matching sweater vest, a coral blouse, a coral-and-navy print scarf, and sheer navy or skin-tone hose, and navy shoes and purse.

- Navy slacks, a beige blouse, your toned-down red in a blazer, navy lapis beads, sheer navy hose, and navy shoes and purse.

Browns. While medium-dark to lighter browns in your best shades look smashing on all Gentle color types, dark brown is often a problem, as we've said repeatedly. Like black and navy, it may be too dark and heavy-looking when worn in large expanses.

If dark brown looks good on you, we still must add a cautionary note: Be careful when combining it with other dark colors or dark neutrals such as rust. Such a dark–dark combination creates a heavy visual effect overall, which is diametrically opposed to your delicate coloring. Most dark–dark combinations need to be lightened and softened by the addition of a lighter or medium accent.

Your best browns will match your hair color or be a darker version of your hair color if your hair is light-colored. This shade of brown is an excellent choice for accessories: shoes, purses, attaché cases, and belts.

Here are our suggestions for some gentle-looking yet lovely outfits built around the color brown:

- A medium-value brown suit with a light blue blouse, a camel-brown light blue scarf, a camel belt, shoes, and purse, and skin-tone or sheer camel hosiery.
- Light gray slacks and a matching sweater, a medium brown jacket, brown shoes and purse, and light gray hose.

Rust. Like brown, rust is a darker neutral that can be worn effectively with all your best neutrals and complimentary colors. However, we suggest you only combine rust with neutrals and complimentary colors in their medium to lighter values. Otherwise, you will encounter the dark–dark effect we just described to you.

Rust is not a basic shoe, belt, or purse color for you unless you have distinct rust tones in your hair. If you are a blond or brown-haired Gentle color type, only wear rust shoes when you've incorporated rust elsewhere in your outfit.

Here are some wonderful ways to utilize rust:

- A rust purse and shoes would look handsome when coordinated with a subtle tweed jacket of rust, cream,

Next we see Myrt (Photo 6.4) in the same "executive look" suit and blouse, only this time she is wearing a medium level of contrast because the blouse color is a pale, toned-down coral. In addition, her makeup is more attractive in this photo because she's now wearing the right medium to light tones to suit her coloring.

and camel worn over a cream skirt and a rust blouse with a strand of pearls. Your hose would be your skin tone or a sheer camel shade.

- Rust slacks, a blue-purple blouse, and a beige jacket with rust beads, rust hose, and rust or hair-colored shoes.

Beiges. It sometimes happens that beige appears on a Gentle color type's color chart in two different shades. This is because the woman has a skin tone of one shade of beige and a hair color in a different shade of beige. For example: skin with a pinkish cast and blond hair color with a golden cast.

Should this describe your coloring, be forewarned: You cannot combine those two different beiges in the same ensemble. You cannot wear golden beige slacks with a pink-beige blouse, for example. Moreover, clothing worn in your hair color beige—that golden beige—will always need a "color break" near your face. Otherwise, that golden beige worn by itself will not enhance the pink-beige of your complexion.

What's a "color break"?

It's one of your other best colors worn in the form of a scarf, blouse, or necklace. On a golden beige dress, a color break might be an off-white collar at the neck and cuffs at the sleeves. (The concept of the "color break" is described at greater length in Chapter 11.)

Beiges are basic shoe, belt, and purse colors for women with Gentle coloring. Why? Because it is your skin tone and thus is already part of every color scheme you create. Beige coordinates superbly with all your best dark, medium, and light colors and neutrals as well. (See how lovely Myrt Arthur looks in her beige and white blouse in Photo 6.8.)

There are hundreds of ways for you to look smashing in beige. Here are two:

- Beige slacks with an off-white blouse, a jacket, belt, and earrings in blue-green, skin-tone hose, and beige shoes and purse.
- Light gray slacks and a medium purple blouse over which you wear a beige vest. Complete the outfit with a silver necklace and earrings and gray hose, shoes, and purse.

White. We are really referring to a slight off-white here since Gentle color types cannot wear pure white except in very small doses—as trim or in a small amount in prints, for example.

We've said it before, but we cannot emphasize it enough: You can never wear white, even off-white, with the dark neutrals of black, navy, or dark brown. These combinations would overpower you with your soft coloring.

You can, however, wear your best creamy white with *all* of the other colors and neutrals on your chart, even with your dark red, rust, and dark blue (but *not* navy). One of a Gentle color type's best looks combines the subtle, toned-down shades of white, beige, camel, and/or light gray.

We guarantee you'll look wonderful in any of the following:

- An outfit that envelops you head to toe in your best white. You don't even have to add a second-color accent.
- Your white in slacks worn with a medium-dark plum blouse, an ivory necklace, ivory shoes and purse, and ivory hose.
- Your white in a dress topped off with a pastel blue jacket, a pastel blue, coral, and white scarf, bone hose, and your white or bone shoes and purse.

Wine and Burgundy. It's very possible these colors won't be flattering to you. What will be lovely are colors that give *the look* of wine and burgundy on you.

These dark reddish shades—often darker values of your best red, raspberry, and plum—should be worn with medium or light-colored garments to avoid that overall dark-on-dark look that can be oppressive to women with Gentle coloring. Shoes in these shades are to be worn only if the color is incorporated somewhere else in the outfit.

- For example, you might want to wear a pearl necklace or add a scarf in a lighter value (rapsberry pink) to a solid dark raspberry dress. It would also help if you accessorized the outfit with bone or sheer pink hose and shoes and purse either in bone, your skin tone, or your hair color.

6.5

Everything about the scarf Myrt Arthur wears in Photo 6.5 conflicts with her Gentle coloring. The black and white stripe is too visibly overpowering, too strong a level of contrast for her. And the pattern is too bold. Moreover, her makeup is heavy-looking.

- Slacks in a dark plum might be coordinated with a light gray blouse and pulled together at the neck with plum-toned beads. Shoes and purse could be your hair color; hose could be sheer plum, gray, or your skin tone.

Dark Greens. Your best shade of a forest green can be an exciting dark neutral for your Gentle coloring. This dark green works in combination with nearly all the other medium or lighter colors on your chart.

However, should a Gentle color type attempt to combine her best dark green with another dark neutral—a plum-burgundy, let's say—she'll usually need to add a light or medium accent to the outfit.

Two great dark green looks are . . .

- Coral slacks and a matching sweater, a dark green jacket, skin-tone hosiery, and shoes, belt, and purse in a color that matches your hair.
- Dark green slacks and a plum blouse, a jacket, shoes, hose, and purse in light gray, and silver jewelry.

Fabric Textures and Weights

Texture refers to the weave or the arrangement of the fibers in a piece of cloth.

In general, smooth and slightly textured fabrics are the best choice for Gentle color types. Finely woven cotton, some silk, and synthetics such as nylon are examples of tightly woven, smooth fabrics. A nubby raw silk fabric, seersucker, or a lamb's wool sweater are examples of the slightly textured look. In Plate 2 you can see that the wide lace adds texture to our model's silk dress. Because the lace is soft and lightweight-looking, it is a wonderful use of texture for a Gentle color type.

Highly textured fabrics you should avoid include wide-wale corduroy, coarse, rough, burlaplike weaves, and heavy rough tweeds. The tweeds you can wear are those that are finer and light to medium in weight. But stay away from all stiff, rough, or very coarse fabrics.

The same fiber—cotton or wool, for example—comes in different weights. Your delicate coloring requires that you remain a loyal supporter of light and medium-weight fabrics.

If you like to effect the "layered look"—a blouse worn under a pullover sweater, for example—just make sure the end result doesn't look too heavy or thick.

Patterns, Prints, and Designs

A Gentle color type looks her most attractive in prints ranging from tiny to medium in scale.

Actually, tiny prints are unique to women with Gentle coloring. On a Gentle color type, miniature prints look stunning. On everyone else, they look unexciting.

Regardless of your height, you may wear a large print if it is *very blended-looking* and incorporates medium and smaller-scale designs within the overall large pattern. For example, you may find that a large floral or paisley made up of light beige, light blue, light blue-green, and light coral looks extremely handsome on you because of the design's delicacy and the lightness of the colors.

Experiment with all types of patterns and prints—florals, checks, dots, geometrics, stripes, and plaids. Just make sure they adhere to the size parameters and levels of contrast we discussed earlier (see Plate 29).

Should you fail to heed our advice, Photos 6.1 and 6.5 demonstrate how unwise a decision that would be. In Photos 6.2 and 6.6 you see the same woman doing everything right.

6.6

In Photo 6.6, Myrt has on the same creamy white shirt, but she's substituted a multicolored scarf featuring all pastel tones. Such soft contrasts are made for Gentle color types. Myrt has also changed her makeup. In this photo, she's wearing light to medium shades of her best colors.

Jewelry

No matter how large your build, you simply do not have strong enough coloring to carry a massive, heavy-looking piece of jewelry. Be wary of the blandishments of jewelry sales clerks who say, "You're lucky. You're tall so you can wear large pieces of jewelry well."

Should you go ahead and purchase that large necklace to accessorize your new knit dress, you might be sorry. Back home in front of your own mirror, you may be wailing, "This necklace doesn't look right. It's too prominent. Where did I go wrong?"

If you went wrong, it's because you thought your height was the only consideration in choosing the size of a piece of jewelry. You failed to take your Gentle color type into account.

6.7

It's plain to see that the necklace Myrt Arthur wears in Photo 6.7 is too large and prominent for a woman with Myrt's Gentle coloring. Her eye shadow, cheek, and lip color is also too heavy-looking to be attractive.

Here are some rules that will keep you from wasting money at the jewelry counter:

Size. Small and medium-sized pieces of jewelry—or larger pieces that look light in weight—are your best bet. Your goal is to avoid the appearance of being weighted down. The rule of thumb is this: Never wear too many pieces or pieces that are overly large and heavy. In general, the larger the piece of jewelry, the more airy and lightweight it should look (see Photos 6.7 and 6.8).

Metal Colors. On you, the most enhancing metals are soft-toned gold, white gold, rose gold, copper, slightly tarnished silver, and pewter. Stay away from brighter yellow golds, brass, and bronze unless they are prominent hair colors.

You may mix metals on your body if you are wearing one piece of jewelry that combines the metals. For example, if you have on a belt that is studded with gold and silver, you might wear a silver bracelet and gold earrings. If your necklace is a mix of white and soft-toned yellow gold, you might wear silver or white gold earrings and a soft-toned yellow gold bracelet, or vice versa.

Metal Finishes. Toned-down metals are the most enhancing on you. Both smooth and textured metals are also fine as long as the piece has no large surface areas that are extremely shiny. Large amounts of smooth, shiny jewelry is proscribed, definitely off limits to you.

Gems, Semi-Precious Stones, and Costume Jewelry. Remain faithful to the colors on your color chart in selecting jewelry in these categories.

If you already own a piece of jewelry in a less than enhancing shade, take heart. You can still wear it *provided*: (1) you coordinate it with an otherwise color-perfect outfit; and (2) you wear it *on top of* a garment, not against your skin.

Suppose you own a strand of amber beads you love. Unfortunately, the beads are a more golden amber than is ideal for you. But fortunately, you also own blue, green, and purple blouses in shades that are ideal for you and coordinate well with those amber beads. We suggest you wear that amber necklace on top of those color-perfect blouses. You'll be surprised how good your amber beads suddenly look on you.

Handbags and Attaché Cases

Your color type can determine much about the handbags you carry. You don't need to have a lot of purses. But you do need to know the colors and sizes that are right for you with your Gentle coloring.

It's a smart move to buy a purse or attaché case that exactly matches the color of your hair. You'll always look coordinated carrying it since it repeats a color you always wear on the top of your head—your hair. For a second basic purse, try to match the shade of your skin exactly. You will also want to find a straw purse in this color for the warmer months.

Your next best color choices are your dark, medium, and light neutrals. Your dark neutrals are navy, black (if it enhances you), rust, medium-dark browns, dark green, plum or burgundy, and medium to dark grays. Your light and medium neutrals are off-whites, beiges, light to medium gray, and camels. Indeed, camel is one of the most flexible shades on your color chart. It's a color for all seasons that coordinates well with all your best light, medium, and dark clothing colors.

In Photo 6.8, Myrt wears the same beige and off-white ruffled blouse, but this time her necklace is in the correct medium scale. She has also toned down her makeup, using medium shades of her best colors. The overall effect is extremely pleasing.

There is one restriction on purse materials. You should avoid any solid expanse of patent leather. It falls in the same negative category as overly bright, shiny jewelry. However, patent leather mixed with other leathers, suede, straw, and canvas is fine.

A purse for everyday use should be small to medium-sized—measure eleven by eight inches or less—if you are a shorter Gentle color type. For women who are five feet six inches and taller, a larger purse might be in order provided it's lightweight-looking. However, keep in mind that the larger the purse, the more casual it is. The dressier the occasion, the smaller your purse should be. Having said this, it should be obvious to you that small and medium-sized handbags are far more versatile.

Most of the above advice about purse size applies to women of all color types. For those with Gentle coloring, no matter what their height and body structure, purses that look light in weight are best. Avoid stiff, structured shapes and all overly thick-looking leathers and other materials.

For late spring and summer, a straw purse is a nice addition. For any time of the year, an excellent-quality leather bag is your wisest investment. If you take good care of it, a good leather handbag will serve you well for years.

Shoes

Much of what we've said about purse materials and colors applies equally to shoes.

Your basic shoe wardrobe should contain both dressy and casual shoes in colors that match your hair and skin tones. Supplement these with your other best neutral shades such as camel, beige, brown, rust, navy, and gray.

Shoes in such colors as your red, blue, yellow, etc., are wonderful to work with but are more of a luxury. That's why we recommend you build a shoe wardrobe of neutrals first and then gradually add pairs in your other favorite, most used colors.

If you have light-colored hair, shoes in your hair shade will work well with all your colors, even your medium and darker outfits. Picture a beige-blond woman wearing a navy skirt and powder blue blouse that she accessorizes with light beige hose and shoes and a purse that match her hair color. Guaranteed, she'll look terrific.

If you own a dress in your best white, you are not limited to white as a shoe color since you look enhanced in soft contrast or blended combinations. You might substitute a beige shoe, one that matches your skin tone. Skin-tone shoes will relate even better to a white dress if you also pick up that beige color in some other accessory—a scarf, necklace, or belt, for instance.

As we said before, the only material you need to avoid is solid patent leather. But even you can wear patent leather if the shoe is a small strap sandal, not a pump.

Eyeglass Frames

By now, you've probably picked up on the fact that all your accessories, including your eyeglass frames, should be light, never heavy-looking. Your Gentle coloring mandates it.

No Gentle color type can go wrong if she selects her glasses frames from her beige color (skin tone) or main hair color. She might also consider the highlight color in her hair *provided* that color is prominent enough so that it is apparent in all lighting conditions, not just in direct sunlight. Take the case of a woman with pink-beige skin and medium brown hair with slight golden highlights. It would be a mistake for her to try to duplicate her hair's faint golden highlight in a frame.

If a metal frame is your preference, we suggest toned-down silver, pewter, or a soft-toned gold. Make sure the gold's finish isn't too bright, shiny, brassy, or yellow.

Don't overlook frameless glasses. They allow more of your eyes to show and create a nice effect.

Evening Wear

Everyone can wear their own best pastels in the daytime, but they are not necessarily effective in night lighting. Night lighting conditions have a tendency to make light colors fade to obscurity. If any color loses its power, it also loses its ability to make you glow! To wear an effective "pastel" look in the evening, choose clearer and darker pastels—more toward a medium-light value.

Very dark colors can also be ineffective at night. Under low light conditions, they usually get darker, or as we term it, they "black out." At night, a purple might look like a purple-toned black instead of its true shade, for example. Each individual has her own level at which dark colors start to black out. Avoid these dark colors at night.

When trying on evening clothes in a store, seek out a mirror in dim light. If the color fades out or blacks out, it will never make you look radiant. At home, try lighting a candle in the bathroom; if the problem occurs and you cannot return the garment, intensify your makeup (especially your blush) and see if there is a way to add a color accent near your face.

Since black is the absence of color, you can wear it in the evening if it appears on your color chart and you make it look delicate so that it won't overpower you visually. To help you achieve a more delicate effect, experiment with jewelry, silk or chiffon scarves, or ribbons of satin or velvet. If you are wearing a low-cut dress, your exposed skin may provide you with enough relief from the black to make it look less weighty on you.

In general, choose evening clothes in medium dark to medium light color values in the strongest clarity of color you can possibly sustain and still look radiant and in control of the outfit. Remember, never let a clarity of color become so clear and bright that it seems to be wearing you.

Lamé—that shimmering fabric with the metallic threads—is one possibility for you *provided* it's in your best shades and the overall effect is not overly bright. Sequins and beaded garments in a toned-down clarity are also good choices.

For shoes and bags, you might try metallic shades of pewter, soft-toned silver, or soft-toned gold. You can also match your outfit or wear dressy shoes that match your skin or your most prominent hair colors.

Furs

Stay with short- and medium-haired furs. If you are tall, you may be able to wear longer-haired furs. Just make sure they look very delicate, airy, and light in weight. Because you have Gentle coloring, you must at all times avoid heavy looks, bulk, and extreme thickness, even in furs. "Delicate" is your watchword.

Select a fur color in your best white, beige, camel, brown, gray, or black, if the latter is on your chart.

Keep in mind that solid-colored furs are more versatile. They can be worn over casual clothes as well as with formal evening wear. And they coordinate with both patterned and solid-colored outfits.

We think multicolored furs, such as raccoon or lynx, are terrific, but they are definitely more limiting. These furs look grand on sportier occasions, but if elegant evenings on the town are an important part of your life, a solid-colored fur would be a wiser choice.

Makeup and Hair Coloring Advice

If you've been wearing the wrong makeup and wardrobe colors and you suddenly switch to the right ones, the change is guaranteed to elicit favorable comments. But don't be surprised if people's remarks focus on the wonderful change in some part of your anatomy other than your facial features or clothes. Why? Because a change in the colors you wear will have a profoundly positive, but subliminal, effect on your total image.

This happened to one of our clients, a black woman with Gentle coloring who ill-advisedly wore very brownish colors, particularly in her makeup. After we introduced her to the lovely reds, raspberries, plums, and corals on her color chart, she charged off on a two-week shopping spree in New York. When this woman went back to work wearing her new makeup and clothing colors, the reaction was immediate. She still laughs to herself about it:

"Everybody told me I looked terrific. But not one person figured out why. Most people wanted to know what I'd done to my hair. It looked fantastic, they said. I hadn't done anything to my hair, of course. But I'd done plenty to the rest of my body."

Another client wore makeup in the wrong colors, too dark in value and often too strong in intensity for her Gentle coloring. In addition, she was coloring her hair the wrong shade, a mistake we'll discuss later in this chapter.

When we finished the makeover, our client was using the same number of makeup colors, but the shades and intensity of the colors had changed. The client adopted a softer look in her makeup. Specifically, her foundation is no longer too pink or too dark, but matches her ivory-beige skin tone exactly. The new base is lighter and slightly more golden in tone. She discarded her overly dark eye shadows and now wears eye shadows that are medium to light in color value. Her lipstick colors are medium to medium-dark toned-down shades, a far cry from the deep, intense colors she used to wear on her lips.

If you have Gentle coloring, this softer look should be your goal, too. Keep the word "gentle" in the forefront of your mind at all times when you are purchasing makeup as well as when you are applying it. With your delicate coloring, a little makeup goes a long way. You can, however, create as much drama in your makeup look as any color type. It's just that with Gentle coloring you can achieve this drama with less intense, toned-down, light to medium values of colors.

Study the makeup on Myrt Arthur in Plates 40 and 41. In the first photo, Myrt is wearing overly dark makeup that overpowers her Gentle coloring. In the second photo, she has adopted an enhancing "gentle" look to bring out the understated drama of her Gentle coloring.

Makeup Colors

The art of makeup application is something about which we hope you already know. If not, there are a number of good books on the subject. What we want to enlighten you about here is color: which makeup shades you should wear to enhance your natural coloring.

Foundation. Many Gentle color types have a touch of pinkness to their skin, which some feel they need to tone down. The correct shade of base will automatically do this unless you have extreme ruddiness or blotchy red spots. In these two instances, you might consider using a toner under your foundation, but be careful. Follow the advice in Chapter 4 about "correcting" problem complexions.

It's common for women with Gentle coloring who have been wearing a base too dark or too pink to feel that they look pale once they start matching their skin tone exactly. Their eye hasn't yet adjusted to their true Gentle look. Also, they haven't yet accepted the notion that *color is added to the face with eye shadow, blush, and lipstick—not with base!* Inevitably, these women come to relish their new, softer look. In retrospect, they comment, "How could I ever have worn that mask on my face?"

Blush. Your best reds, raspberry, and plum colors are ideal rouge shades. But as we've said elsewhere, your best shade of coral can be used as a lipstick or polish color but *never for a blush.* However, if you are wearing coral lipstick, you can experiment by adding a hint of coral to your cheeks and then blending it with blush in your red color (as in Plate 41, where our model is wearing a coral lip color with her red color blush).

Lipstick. Your lipstick—and any matching nail polish—must have that softened or toned-down quality essential for bringing out the best in your Gentle coloring. There is one exception. Gentle/Light-Bright color types have clearer colors on their charts, and their lipstick, polish, and blush should reflect this fact.

Good choices for lipstick are your best red, raspberry, plum, and coral colors. And feel free to combine your best lipstick colors on your lips with impunity to create new shades.

Eye Shadow. "Soft" and "subtle" are the watchwords when you're making up your eyes.

Stick with light to medium eye shadow shades in your best toned-down clarity. A basic collection of shadows for you would include gray, brown, blue, blue-green, green, at least one shade of purple, and beige or creamy white for a highlighter.

Eye shadows that repeat colors in your eyes (reread "Your Body Colors" in Chapter 2) and your best neutrals are good ones to accompany a conservative business outfit or to use any time you want to have a less obvious eye makeup effect. You will find that your more bluish-purple shadows, too, are very basic because they work well with all of your most enhancing colors and compliment every conceivable eye color.

Another possibility is to duplicate the colors of your clothing in your eye shadows. To create the right blended and medium contrast effects, mix your medium eye shadow tones with your light tones and, if you are a Gentle/Muted color type, with an occasional medium-dark tone.

A cautionary note: Gentle color types must be on guard to apply their eye shadow—indeed, all their makeup—rather lightly. It doesn't take much for a woman with Gentle coloring to look overly made-up. (See Plates 30 and 40, which illustrate this problem.)

Eyeliner and Mascara. Brown mascara is generally more enhancing for many Gentle color types than black. However, if your hair is quite dark, you may find black an effective color for nighttime occasions and for any daytime occasion when you are very dressed up. If it looks at all harsh on you, please use brown instead. Navy and other enhancing dark tones are also possible mascara choices.

Use eyeliners that match any of your charted colors. Just be certain to diffuse the line—smudge it—of any medium to darker eyeliner shade to eliminate any chance of it appearing too harsh.

Lighter vs. Darker Color Values. Light-haired Gentle color types should keep their eye shadow, lipstick, blush, and polish in the medium to light range of color values, while dark-haired Gentle color types can wear somewhat darker color values.

The rule of thumb for eye, lip, cheek, and nail color is this: Medium color tones are always appropriate for daytime business looks as well as for day and evening casual attire no matter what the color of your hair. Slightly stronger or darker tones may be called for if you are wearing outfits in stronger mixes of your best colors or you are simulating a certain high-fashion effect. For lighter-haired women with Gentle coloring, this would mean moving to medium-dark values, or simply applying your medium-value shades with a slightly stronger hand.

Makeup for evening always needs to be deepened enough to give you the effect you want, but not so much that you look overly made-up. Let your outfit, the occasion, and your good judgment dictate how dark and how much makeup to apply when you're attending afterdark events.

To achieve a strictly casual "nonmakeup" look, wear your lighter lipstick colors. The lightest shades of your best eye shadow colors are usually used as highlighters to achieve specific effects depending on your eye shape.

Purchase blushes in medium to medium-dark values. Then simply apply them lightly or with a heavier hand, keeping the guidelines outlined above in mind.

Coordinating Your Makeup and Clothing Colors

How do you decide which eye, lip, cheek, and polish colors to wear with an outfit?

To educate you on this score, we'd like to describe several outfits and then give you a few makeup suggestions:

• Pretend you are wearing a conservative business suit in a medium gray with a creamy white blouse. You've encircled your neck with a sophisticated gray and creamy white patterned scarf. For accessories, you've chosen textured silver earrings, skin-tone stockings, and a gray purse and shoes.

Now for your makeup: We suggest eye shadow colors in medium and light tones of gray and cream. Use a gray eyeliner. Use brown mascara—or black if it doesn't look harsh on you. For lip and cheek colors, use your medium red, raspberry, or plum. Either match that shade in your nail color or select a clear or neutral nail polish.

- This time you're wearing off-white slacks with a yellow blouse and a strand of pearls twisted around a gold chain. Your gold earrings are small to medium in scale. Your shoes, purse, and hose are all off-white.

With your eye shadows, you've got several choices: On the one extreme, you could go for a more neutral look and wear soft shades of gray or medium brown and cream. At the other extreme, you might want to wear the stronger tones of medium and lighter purples, blues, blue-greens, or greens and cream. The neutral eye look requires gray or brown eyeliner. The more accentuated eye demands that color in a liner. The best mascara color in both cases is brown.

Select medium coral or red lipstick and a matching nail polish color. Brush your best shade of red blush on your cheeks.

- This next ensemble consists of a medium blue dress topped by a camel jacket and a scarf at the neck of blue, camel, purple, and white. Add camel shoes, a camel purse, and skin-tone hosiery.

The blue of the dress affords you the perfect opportunity to repeat it in your eye shadows. You could either restrict your eye shadows to that medium blue shade augmented with a pale camel-beige highlighter. Or you could add a purple shadow to the blues for a broader-spectrum effect. Wear brown mascara and an eyeliner of blue and/or purple. On your lips, cheeks, and nails, we recommend plum, raspberry, or your best red.

- Finally, imagine yourself dressed to the nines in a coral suit with a cream blouse and a necklace with delicate coral, turquoise, and ivory beads. You complete the ensemble with tiny ivory earrings, skin-tone hose, and shoes and a purse in your hair color.

How would you decorate your face?
To draw attention to your eyes, blend together coral and blue-green eye shadows accented with a cream

highlighter and a blue-green eyeliner. For a more subtle eye effect, you could wear a camel-toned eye shadow with a brown or gray liner and cream highlighter. Stay with brown mascara. Your lip and nail color will be your coral with your medium red on your cheeks, possibly blended with just a touch of your coral lip color.

Hair Coloring

Remember that client who wore the wrong makeup colors in shades far too dark and strong for her Gentle look? Well, she also had a problem with her hair color. Her favorite hairdresser was coloring her hair too brassy. The brassy-looking hair made her complexion look more florid than it really was. Using the Color 1 concept, she solved the problem by substituting a beige tone for the bright golden tone her hairdresser was using.

The mistake this woman was making—coloring her hair too brassy—is a common one among women with Gentle coloring. When Gentle color types, whether they're blonds, brunettes, or redheads, wish to lighten their hair color, as a rule they should lighten or highlight their hair with beige-blond and champagne-blond shades. These happen to be colors that are flattering to ivory and pink-beige skin tones, which many women with Gentle coloring have.

When you lighten or color your hair, your objective is to look like you were born with hair in your new shade. (We suggest you reread the sections on skin and hair color in Chapter 1.) No matter what new hair color you choose, always make sure it compliments rather than clashes with your complexion. The average Gentle color type, as we've mentioned, has an ivory complexion or skin with a pinkish cast and therefore must avoid hair too golden in tone.

One way to select a new lighter shade is by using a lighter version of your main hair color, by matching a prominent highlight color in your hair, or by repeating your skin-tone beige.

If you are a blond with Gentle coloring, it is likely your hair has an ash, beige, champagne, camel, caramel, or strawberry look to it. If you have Gentle/Light-Bright coloring, it will probably have a golden highlight. If you wanted to darken your hair, use a deeper value of your natural hair color or a deeper value of your skin tone (e.g., if skin has a golden tone, hair should be a golden camel or a golden brown).

The shades we just listed are also common highlights for Gentle color types with light to medium brown hair. Thus, if a brunette wanted to lighten her hair, she might select lighter versions of her highlight colors.

If your hair is white or gray and you want it to be blond, brown, or red, you must choose a shade that looks fabulous with your skin. Match the beiges, camels, browns, and rusts on your chart.

Your Gentle coloring is truly unique. You now know how to use colors in their best shades, clarities, and levels of contrast to help you look marvelous in your clothing and makeup. You are now ready to begin Part III, where you can apply your new color knowledge and learn how to cast your most special and exciting color spell!

Chapter 7

Wardrobe Advice for Light-Bright Coloring

There's a common mistake many women with Light-Bright coloring make. They think because their coloring is on the light side, they should wear only soft, light-looking colors. As a consequence, they tend to wear colors that are so pale and often so toned-down they wash out their skin coloring and end up fading into the surroundings.

What should women with Light-Bright coloring wear? They should wear clear, bright clarities to emphasize the light and bright radiance of their natural coloring. Besides giving them a striking new image, the correct colors will also greatly improve their self-confidence.

In the United States, at least, women with Light-Bright coloring are fewer in number than women of the other color types. Even our experience in color charting over forty thousand women last year worldwide indicates there are fewer of them in the global population than Muted, Gentle, or Contrast color types.

However, we can name a number of American movie stars who have Light-Bright coloring: Marilyn Monroe, Ginger Rogers, Shirley Jones, Dolly Parton, Farrah Fawcett, Suzanne Somers, Cheryl Ladd. The French actress Catherine Deneuve is another.

Your Best Color Clarities

People with Light-Bright coloring need to re-create their body's natural look in their clothing colors and color combinations. This means wearing colors in a clear, bright clarity. But it also means combining light colors with bright colors, as the phrase "Light-Bright" implies (see Plate 34). It does *not* mean combining dark colors with bright colors. That particular color combination does *not* reproduce the look of your natural coloring, as there's nothing light and bright about it.

Your skin tone is your guide to how clear, bright, softened, muted, dark, or light you wear your best shades of colors. A color is too bright for you if it appears to jump off your skin and causes people to look at the color instead of you. At the opposite extreme, a color is too muted if it looks muddy or dead next to your skin.

The second best clarity for a Light-Bright color type to wear is very slightly toned-down. Let us emphasize the adverb "slightly." (To review color clarities, study Plates 21–23.)

Pure white is one color all Light-Bright color types can wear. White gives Light-Bright coloring a fresh, crisp look that's extremely appealing. (See Plate 3.) White is particularly effective on them when it's combined with other bright colors. To see what we mean, study the way the Light-Bright color type model has combined white with other colors in Plate 34 and Photos 7.2, 7.4, and 7.6.

Best Clarity of Colors for Light-Bright Color Types

Color Type	Best Clarity Level(s)	Second-Best Clarity Level(s)
LIGHT-BRIGHT	Bright	Slightly Toned-Down
LIGHT-BRIGHT/CONTRAST	Bright Intense—provided they are accented with light accessories.	Slightly Toned-Down
LIGHT-BRIGHT/GENTLE	Slightly Toned-Down	Bright—provided the skin tone can handle them.

7.1

The combination of two light colors can be lovely on a light-haired Light-Bright color type if the tones are clear. The blouse and slacks Jeanne Schoenfeld models in Photo 7.1 is an example. The culprit here is Jeanne's makeup, not her clothing. Jeanne's makeup shades are too dark, and her eye shadow, blush, and lip color have been applied with a heavy hand, creating a painted look.

As they mature, some women with Light–Bright coloring come to the erroneous conclusion that they should forsake the bright colors of their youth and move into toned-down, dustier shades. This is not so.

Joan Stone, our Dousman, Wisconsin, associate, remembers her encounter with two clients with Light–Bright coloring. Both were handsome women in their sixties. One had gray hair, the other had colored her gray hair blond.

As young women, both had worn clear, bright colors, but now they felt more subdued colors were "appropriate" for them. Their advancing age and their social status dictated it, they argued. Their husbands were presidents of large, important companies, and these women felt bright colors might cheapen their appearance and make them look garish, an image that would be out of place at corporate social functions.

Joan countered their objections. Clear, bright colors would not look excessive and tawdry on them. Because of their bodies' natural color scheme, such colors on them look eye-catching, to be sure, but also lovely, classy, and correct. To prove it, she draped them in their best colors, followed by the toned-down shades they were defending, and made them study themselves carefully in the mirror.

In fairly short order, they came around. Joan was right. They looked older, pale, and drained in the toned-down colors. They looked younger, more vital, and more rested in the lighter, brighter colors. The moral of the story: Once a Light–Bright color type, always a Light–Bright color type.

For an illustration of a gray-haired Light–Bright color type wearing her best colors, see Plate 15.

Your Best Level of Contrast

Strong and medium levels of contrast are the most enhancing on women with Light–Bright coloring. Light–Bright color types with light hair can wear a blended look if the clarity of the colors is clear.

Here are some specific pointers about how to mix and match the shades on Your Color 1 Color Chart:

- **A bright color with a light color** (see Plates 11, 15, and 19), e.g., bright red and pure white, light gray and bright yellow.
- **A dark color with a clear light color,** e.g., navy and a light clear coral, dark clear blue-green and a light clear yellow.
- **Two bright colors, provided both are light-looking,** e.g., a light, bright yellow and a light, bright red, a light, bright purple and a light, bright blue.
- **A bright color with a light- or medium-toned neutral,** e.g., bright green and light gray, bright blue and camel.
- **Two neutrals that create a medium to strong level of contrast,** e.g., white and dark gray, beige and navy. A light-haired Light-Bright color type may combine two light neutrals such as white and light gray without adding a third contrasting accent color. But medium- and darker-haired Light-Bright color types need a bright or dark accent to bring such a combination to life (e.g., beige and light gray with a bright blue accent).

7.2

How much more attractive Jeanne looks in Photo 7.2! The small-striped, clear red and pure white blouse is an ideal look for women with Light-Bright coloring. Jeanne has amplified the positive effect of her clothing by choosing her best clear medium to light makeup colors.

Adding an Accent Color

There are several color combinations Light-Bright color types can *never* wear unless they add the grace note of a conciliatory third accent color near the face:

Do not wear a dark color with a bright color unless you add a light accent near your face because a dark with bright combination is overall too strong-looking. A navy suit worn with a bright red blouse, for instance, requires a white or other lighter color accent to make the entire ensemble palatable with your coloring. A small- to medium-sized print scarf in navy and red with a large amount of pure white background is one way to bring the needed lightness to this outfit. (See Photo 7.3 and Plate 42 for an example of what *not* to do.)

Do not wear two light colors together unless your hair is light or unless you add a dark or bright accent near your face. For example, a clear pastel blue-and-white outfit usually needs a bright or dark accent to increase the level of contrast. A light-haired Light-Bright color type can wear this light-on-light combination without adding the accent *provided* the pastel is a clear clarity. (See Photo 7.1.)

In Photo 7.3, you see Jeanne Schoenfeld in a bright red and black lumberjack plaid jacket worn over a solid black blouse. Any bright–dark combination is too visually overpowering for a woman with Jeanne's Light-Bright coloring. Her makeup matches the outfit. It's too strong and dark in tone.

Do not wear two dark colors together unless you add a light accent near your face. A dark clear royal blue and clear dark green combination needs the addition of a good deal of light accents to make the outfit relate to Light-Bright coloring. (In Plate 42 you can see how the dark-bright color combination is visually too heavy-looking for this model's Light-Bright coloring. Her makeup is obviously too strong as well.)

What about monotone looks?

You may wear an all-one-color look in your best medium-toned bright colors. Our model in Plate 43 would look great wearing the color of her blue blouse from head to toe, without the accent of pearls or the white jacket. Light-haired women with Light-Bright coloring can even wear all-one-color looks in their clear vibrant pastels. But darker-haired women with Light-Bright coloring cannot. These darker-haired women must accent any all-one-color looks in their light shades with a bright or dark color.

There is one monotone look no woman with Light-Bright coloring can wear. That's an outfit consisting of one dark color, even if it's one of a Light-Bright color type's most enhancing dark shades. Always accent your darker values of color with light values.

Your Best Neutrals

If you wear a lot of neutrals—black, camel, gray, navy, brown, rust, beige, white, and burgundy—did you ever ask yourself why? It's probably because neutrals seem to mix and match so well with other colors. Moreover, they make you feel safe. After all, how can you go wrong wearing gray?

You can go wrong if it's the *wrong shade* of gray, or brown, or any other neutral. Neutrals, just like your complimentary colors, come in different shades and clarities. Thus it's crucial that you choose the right shade and clarity to enhance your natural Light-Bright coloring.

As a woman with Light-Bright coloring, you'll find the light and medium neutrals of beige, white, off-white, camel, and light-to-medium grays are mainstays in your wardrobe. Light-Bright color types—no matter how light or dark their hair, no matter what the season of the year—will want to own several items of clothing and accessories in these lighter and medium neutral colors. Those items might range from suits and blazers to sweaters, blouses, shoes, and purses.

For example, for summer use you might want to own several major white cotton, linen, or silk clothing items. In the winter, wool wardrobe staples in white, off-white, your skin tones, camel, and gray will see you through the season. In fact, any month of the year, most of your light and medium neutrals make equally fine choices for accessory items—scarves, necklaces, earrings, belts, shoes, and purses.

Don't misunderstand, though. We are not precluding the notion of including the darker neutrals in your wardrobe, too. It's just that you must take more care in how you mix and match separates in darker neutral shades. Keep in mind that a woman with Light-Bright coloring always needs a fair degree of lightness in any outfit to make it relate to her natural light and bright body coloring. Too many dark colors in an ensemble can easily overwhelm her.

What follows is an overview of all the light as well as dark neutrals you may want to utilize in your wardrobe:

Black. Whether you can wear black effectively is an individual matter. However, if you can, you still have to be careful *how* you wear it. Too much of a good thing can be a bad thing with your delicate coloring.

A Light-Bright color type who can wear black can combine it with pure white, creating the highest possible level of contrast (see Photo 7.4). She can also mix it with all the other light neutrals and colors in their lighter values on her chart. What she must *not* do is combine black with any of her best bright colors in their medium or darker values or any dark color on her chart. The effect, visually, would be too heavy for her.

One other word of advice:

When you're putting together an ensemble with black in it, many of you will need to use one of your clear light colors or light neutrals to frame your face. Sometimes baring your skin at the neck and chest area creates enough relief. So with a black blouse, for instance, leave a few buttons open. Most of you need to avoid wearing a black turtleneck or other high-necked black item. Remember your goal: to lighten the look of black to create a light and bright effect.

7.4

Photo 7.4 depicts Jeanne wearing a light–dark contrast combination that enhances her coloring. Her blouse is the same solid black one as in Photo 7.3, but her jacket is a pure white. Her makeup in medium clear tones is equally enhancing.

Here are some outfits you may want to duplicate:

- Black, white, and camel can be a dynamite combination for you. Wear a pure white blouse with black slacks, topped with a camel blazer. Add a black strand of beads, or a necklace that combines black and white, black and camel, or all three colors. For a terrific look, twist a gold chain around your black beads. Hose could be sheer black; shoes and purse black.
- Wear a black pleated skirt with a pure white blouse, perhaps one with some black trim on it. Complete the ensemble with black patent leather shoes and purse, a very sheer black tint in hose, a dressy black snakeskin belt with a shiny gold buckle, and gold earrings. Or wear the same skirt with a satiny-looking, skin-tone blouse and the same accessories, only this time substitute shoes and purse that match your hair color exactly, and use skin-tone hose.
- To test just how much black you can sustain, assemble an outfit consisting of a light gray skirt, a black blouse (no high necks, please), shiny silver jewelry, black sheer stockings, and black shoes and purse. If there is too much black, use sheer gray hose; still too much black, add a white or off-white jacket.
- Instead of using black as a clothing color, try it for accessories only. Wear a light, yet clear and vibrant, purple skirt and matching blouse accessorized with a black belt, purse, and shoes and a black necklace and earrings. Hose can be skin tone, or a sheer tint of black or purple.

For Light-Bright color types black—even if it does appear on your color chart—is not a basic go-with-everything neutral for such staples as shoes and purses. Use black shoes and purse only when you are wearing an outfit that incorporates black, or for a more total black accessory look as in the outfit mentioned above. If black is not flattering to your coloring, there is no need to own any accessories or garments in black at all.

Camel. This is one light to medium neutral that looks fabulous on you, especially when you coordinate it with other light to medium-dark best neutrals and colors. It's an ideal choice as an accessory color, too. You will want to own both dressy and casual shoes in your camel.

If your hair is a camel color or has distinct camel highlights, a camel blazer in this shade is an absolute necessity for you. You'll be able to wear it over everything you own, and it will always look good because it repeats a shade in your natural body coloring. If your hair is light, your best camel shade will be a darker version of your hair color.

Camel and a medium or light gray is a lovely neutral color combination for you. Picture yourself in . . .

- A camel skirt worn with a medium gray blouse and adorned with either a silver or gold piece of jewelry, a pin or necklace. You could also twist one silver and one gold chain together for a handsome touch. Skin-tone hose, camel shoes and purse complete the look.
- A camel suit with a crisp, pure white blouse, skin-tone hose, and a red belt, purse, and shoes. Red or red, white, and gold earrings top off the combination.
- Camel slacks with a clear light blue blouse topped off with an off-white jacket. For accessories wear a gold necklace and earrings, skin-tone or bone hosiery, and camel or off-white shoes and purse.

Navy. Every woman with Light-Bright coloring has navy on her color chart in her best shade.

Navy should be treated like other dark neutrals—with care. Too great an expanse of it, especially near your face, could have a negative effect. Your goal: to create a light and bright look with navy.

If you want to wear suits, slacks, or shirts in navy, make sure you always wear them with light neutrals or *clear* pastel colors. Do *not* wear them with medium-toned bright colors, dark colors, or dark neutrals, for there is nothing at all light and bright about such combinations.

Many women with Light-Bright coloring discover, to their delight, that they already own several medium-toned blouses and tops in good shades and clarities for them. These tops are to be worn with light colors, light to medium neutrals, and, in some cases, other light-looking, medium-toned bright colors—but *never* with navy or any other dark color.

Try these navy looks:

- A navy suit worn with a pure white blouse, a scarf of navy, red, gray, and white, sheer gray hose, red shoes, and a navy purse. Accent with red or white earrings.
- Navy slacks, a clear, light yellow blouse, navy beads, sheer navy hose, navy shoes and purse.

Gray. Here is another very useful neutral that always appears on your color chart in your most enhancing shade.

The rules we've already enunciated for dark neutral color combinations apply to dark gray as well. Light and medium gray are another matter, for both fall into the light-to-medium neutral category. You will want to own both dressy and casual shoes in your medium to light gray because they will work well with almost your entire wardrobe. They become necessities if your hair is gray or white.

You would look great wearing . . .

- A clear light gray wool dress with a crisp white collar and cuffs and red accessories—a red belt, earrings, shoes, and purse and sheer gray hosiery.
- A medium gray suit with a light, yet bright, yellow blouse, a silver necklace, and gray hosiery, shoes, and purse.
- Slacks in a clear medium purple coupled with a clear light blue top and accented with gray beads (silver or gray pearl), a gray belt, hose, shoes, and purse.

Light and medium gray clothes adorned with silver jewelry are particularly striking on women with Light-Bright coloring whose hair is gray or in the process of turning. Indeed, for such women gray and silver are a joy to work with because, wearing them, they always look pulled together, "finished."

Gray-haired Light-Bright color types often make extensive use of gray as a basic accessory color—lining their closet and drawers with gray shoes, belts, handbags, and scarves.

Browns. Brown doesn't have to be too deep in value before it becomes a dark neutral in a Light-Bright color type's color lexicon. Even though your best "dark" brown is probably really a medium brown, you must treat it according to the rules for dark neutrals we've already enunciated. Again, your goal is to make your best dark brown look light and bright so it can enhance your coloring.

Your most enhanced browns are darker values of your hair, match your hair, or in the case of gray-haired Light-Brights, would be a darker value of your skin tone.

Camel is generally more versatile than dark brown for most of you as it can be combined with light, medium, and dark values of all your best colors and neutrals. With your best medium-dark and dark browns, you are limited to either clear light neutrals—light gray, off-white, white, and light beige—or your best vibrant-looking *pastels*. No bright color, regardless of its color value, can ever be coupled with medium-dark or dark brown.

If your hair is fairly dark, medium-dark and dark brown will serve you well as a basic shoe, belt, and purse color. If your hair is lighter, only wear brown shoes when you are incorporating brown elsewhere in the outfit.

Here are two light and bright-looking outfits with brown:

• Medium brown slacks, a clear light pink blouse, a turquoise belt and necklace, skin-tone hose, and shoes and purse in your hair color.
• An off-white skirt worn with a light gray blouse and a medium brown tweed blazer with gray and off-white flecks, an off-white necklace, bone or sheer gray stockings, and gray shoes and purse.

Rust. Every woman with Light-Bright coloring has some shade of rust on her color chart.

Even though rust appears on your chart, it is not a go-with-everything accessory color. Why? Because it is not a hair shade—either a main hair color or highlight color—for any Light-Bright color type.

Nonetheless, rust is a practical dark neutral to include in your wardrobe *provided* you follow the guidelines for mixing and matching dark neutrals with other colors—in short, create light and bright looks by using rust with light tones.

These outfits will look lovely on you:

• Camel slacks with a white blouse, a rust jacket and belt, skin-tone hose, camel shoes, and a rust or camel handbag. Add gold earrings for a special finish.

- A plaid skirt that is rust, light gray, and off-white worn with an off-white sweater, light gray hose and shoes, and a rust purse. Silver earrings finish the look.

Beiges. If you have light hair, you have two best beiges on your color chart. One is your skin tone and the other is your hair color.

Often, the skin tone and hair color match. But it's also possible that these are two different shades of beige. (Study Plates 34 and 43 to see how closely Jeanne's hair and skin tone match.) For example, you might have golden beige hair and ivory-beige skin. If we've just described you, by all means wear both shades of beige *but never at the same time*. Moreover, heed the following advice when you wear your hair-tone beige:

Clothing that matches a hair-tone that is more golden than your skin tone beige needs a "color break," that is, a splash of another good color for you that you wear near your face to take the onus off that hair-color beige. A color break could be in the form of a blouse, scarf, or jewelry *provided* the piece of jewelry is prominent enough. Here's a specific example:

- Under a hair-color beige blazer, wear a shirt in your best medium bright green or any other super shade for you. Leave the shirt unbuttoned at the neck and arrange the collar so that it is on top of the blazer's lapels. You can stand the collar up if you like.

Light-haired women with Light-Bright coloring use their beige with every other color on their chart. Darker-haired Light-Bright color types can too, but they may have to add a bright or dark accent when they combine beige with another light neutral or pastel.

Off-white, camel, and beige blazers are a necessity in every Light-Bright color type's wardrobe. Beige is also a necessary neutral for you to use as a purse, belt, and shoe color. We recommend that you purchase both casual and dressy shoes in your best beige.

Experiment with these beige looks:

- A beige suit and raspberry blouse accessorized with pearls, bone hosiery, and off-white shoes and purse.

- Turquoise slacks with a clear light yellow blouse, a beige jacket, turquoise beads, and shoes and purse in a color matching your hair; wear skin-tone hose.

White. Pure white as well as off-white love you, so we hope you love them. You would be wise to include lots of your best whites in both your clothing and accessory wardrobes.

We are not discouraging your use of your best off-white, certainly one of your most versatile and necessary neutrals. But we want you to realize that the sharp, clean look of pure white creates an especially fantastic image for a woman with your coloring (as it does for Brenda in Plate 3). This is particularly true when pure white is worn in contrast with clear, vibrant colors—white and bright red, white and clear vibrant blue, etc. Your creamy whites can also be combined with other colors to create medium and strong contrast effects.

Here are some lovely ways to wear white:

- A white dress, hose, shoes, and purse with a ribbon belt of hot pink and matching hot pink earrings.
- Medium vibrant blue slacks and a matching top. Over it wear a white jacket and add white accessories—belt, hose, and shoes. Earrings in white, silver, or gold complete the look.

Wine and Burgundy. Wines and burgundies, as you might normally think of them, do not appear on the charts of women with Light-Bright coloring. In their place, you may find various shades of deep red, medium-dark vibrant red-purples, bright medium-dark plums, and clear raspberries.

These deeper values of your best reds, plums, and raspberries must be treated as dark neutrals, and you must apply the same mix-and-match rules to them as you would to any other dark neutral. In other words, create light and bright looks with them.

You may be puzzled because your chart is devoid of more typical wines and burgundies. Let us explain:

Wines and burgundies may be "neutrals," but they're also toned-down neutrals. Visualize, if you will, a burgundy. Now summon up the mental image of a cranberry red. Don't you agree that the burgundy is muted-looking,

In Photo 7.5, Jeanne Schoen-feld's Light-Bright coloring is overpowered by the large scale and boldness of the clear blue dots on the pure white skirt. Moreover, her makeup is too heavy and dark.

whereas the cranberry red looks clear, even somewhat bright?

As we've said many times before, you need to wear *clear* colors at all times.

Try these outfits in clear versions of your dark reds, plums, and raspberries:

- Clear plum slacks, a light clear pink blouse, a light clear blue-purple jacket, plum beads, pink hosiery, and shoes and purse in your hair color.
- Light gray slacks combined with an off-white blouse, raspberry sweater vest, silver necklace and earrings, and gray hose, shoes, and purse.

Dark Green. Dark greens seldom appear on a Light-Bright color chart. Instead, you will find a vibrant medium-dark green—the darkest version of your best shade of green—because it's so much more flattering to you.

Fabric Textures and Weights

"Texture" refers to the weave of a piece of fabric. Take a piece of nylon cloth. Its synthetic fibers are tightly knit, creating a smooth, shiny fabric. Silk and cotton, on the other hand, are both natural fibers. They are sometimes woven tightly, giving the resulting fabric a smooth finish, and sometimes woven more loosely, affording a nubby texture—raw silk fabrics and handknit cotton sweaters, for example.

Light-Bright color types look great in smooth and slightly textured fabrics. Thus, they can wear twills, her-ringbones, basket-weave woolens, and tweeds *provided* they have a fairly fine texture and the cloth is neither heavy in actual weight nor simply heavy-looking. They can also wear loosely woven knits and weaves *provided* they are open weaves and give an airy, light appearance. (In Plate 3, our model's lace dress has lots of texture, but since the lace is soft and lightweight-looking, it is lovely with the delicate coloring of a Light-Bright color type.)

Your coloring is a bit at odds with any texture that is overly coarse, thick, rough, or burlap-looking. Nor will you look enhanced in material with substantial bulk or weight to it, such as very heavyweight woolens.

Patterns, Prints, and Designs

Regardless of your height or weight, you'll always look great in small and medium-scale prints (see Plate 32). Large, bold designs are not your forte, but you could wear a fairly large pattern if it is airy and light-looking. In Photo 7.5 you will see an example of what *not* to do when it comes to patterns. Photos 7.2 and 7.6 show you what to do.

In choosing prints—whether they're plaids, checks, geometrics, dots, stripes, or florals—it's important to adhere to the right levels of contrast. For you, these levels of contrast are, as we've noted, strong and medium. No soft contrast or blended looks unless you have light hair and the light colors in the prints are very clear and vibrant-looking.

Jewelry

In selecting jewelry, follow these guidelines:

Size. Light-Bright color types are most enhanced by small and medium-sized jewelry (see Photos 7.7 and 7.8). A tall woman will be able to wear one larger piece *provided* it looks light in weight. But the large necklace in Photo 7.7 looks just the opposite—massive.

Wear as much or as little jewelry as your outfit, your personality, and the occasion demand. On the other hand, never let yourself look overloaded or overpowered—a risk you always run in selecting accessories to grace your delicate coloring.

Metal Colors. Most Light-Bright color types prefer gold because it relates so well to their golden skin tones. Other good metals are shiny silver, brass, and bronze. White gold can be worn if your skin is light ivory in tone.

Metal Finishes. You may wear both smooth and textured metals, but even your textured jewelry must have a shine or at least a subtle glow. Toned-down or slightly tarnished metals, which look terrific on women with Muted and Gentle coloring, are most assuredly off limits. On you, they'll look dull and drab, as if you were just too lazy to polish them.

Gems, Semi-Precious Stones, and Costume Jewelry. When you're buying jewelry, match the colors on your color chart.

To prove that women with Light-Bright coloring can wear dots in the right scale of pattern, study Jeanne in the bright red and pure white dotted dress in Photo 7.6. Doesn't she look 100 percent better? Further underscoring the just-right look of the dress are the clear light to medium makeup colors she wears.

The necklace Jeanne Schoenfeld wears in Photo 7.7 doesn't bear any visual relationship to her Light-Bright coloring. It's too large and heavy-looking. And her makeup is too dark and too heavily applied.

Should you happen to have a favorite piece in a color that's less than perfect for you, don't worry. There's a way not only to salvage the piece but to make it look absolutely terrific on you.

The trick is to keep this less-than-ideal color away from your skin. If the item is a necklace—an amethyst that's too toned-down a purple for you, let's say—that's easy enough to do. Simply wear that amethyst necklace *on top* of a dress or blouse that is a perfect color for you. You might wear it with your best medium bright green or red, for example. Also make sure you create a medium to strong level of contrast between the necklace and the garment. In the case of the toned-down amethyst beads, you should never wear them against light colors.

Handbags and Attaché Cases

You can be perfectly dressed in all the right colors. Yet if you are carrying a handbag or attaché case in the wrong color or made of a cheap material—even if it is the right color—it can make your whole outfit look second-rate and uncoordinated.

The rules here are really very simple:

You need only own one briefcase provided it's a leather one of good quality and a good shade for you. Your best camel or your hair color is an outstanding choice. We feel it is also better to own fewer handbags that are perfect in color and size for you than a lot of purses of poorer workmanship. Select them from your best neutrals, particularly those neutrals that match your hair and skin tones. Purses in colors that you wear a lot are also very useful. The most useful neutrals are camel, beige, light gray, off-white, and black if it's on your chart.

If two purses are all your budget will accommodate, buy one in your hair color and the other in your skin color. You'll always look coordinated sporting handbags in these colors since you are repeating tones that appear in your body's natural color scheme.

In terms of size, we recommend you stay with purses that are medium-sized or on the small side. Large handbags tend to overwhelm women with Light-Bright coloring. Besides, small and medium-sized bags are more versatile since, in purses, largeness and dressiness are mutually exclusive.

Avoid stiff, structured, heavy-looking purses, even if they are medium to small in size.

You've heard it before but we'll say it again: Natural substances make the best handbag and briefcase materials. Calfskin, cowhide, patent leather, suede, straw, canvas, even wooden beaded bags, as long as they aren't heavy-looking, are all fine choices for women with your coloring. For spring and summer, a straw purse in your skin tone or hair color is a great go-with-everything accessory.

One final point: When you're considering the purchase of a purse or attaché case with metal ornamentation, hew to our guidelines about smooth, shiny metals and complimentary metal tones.

Shoes

Our advice about shoe colors and materials echos what we said previously about handbags and attaché cases.

The day has long passed when women's shoes and handbags must match. As long as your shoes and purse are in colors that go with your outfit, you'll look coordinated. Start your shoe wardrobe off with both dressy and casual shoes in your hair color and your skin tone. Add shoes that match any of your other most used neutrals, or most used colors. For example, light to medium camel (main hair color tones) is one of your most versatile neutrals, so you may use camel-colored shoes a lot; or if you wear red regularly, shoes in your red might be wise to own, too.

All good-quality shoe materials are fine choices, including patent leather. If you don't like white shoes, you may be able to coordinate shoes in your off-whites or light beiges with outfits containing a lot of white. However, when a white shoe is the perfect one for your outfit, we would prefer that you get rid of any old prejudices against white shoes and wear them. Try strap sandals with neutral heels so there is *less* white on your feet.

7.8

Now look at Jeanne (Photo 7.8) wearing a medium-sized necklace. It's just right. She's scaled down her makeup as well. The clear medium tones she wears on her eyes, cheeks, and lips balance out her Light-Bright look.

Eyeglass Frames

You can't be led astray if you select eyeglass frames that match your skin tone or hair color. Of course, the type of glasses that allow more of your eyes to show are frameless ones.

Whatever frame you choose, just make sure the frame appears light in look and weight. Heavy or dark-looking frames are a poor choice. Your Light-Bright coloring won't stand for it.

In selecting metal frames, follow the dictates about metallic colors and finishes we laid down under "Jewelry."

Evening Wear

When it comes to nighttime dress, you're fortunate, for bright, clear colors hold their own better than toned-down colors under artificial night lighting conditions. Your coloring can also accept the ultra-bright look of lamé, dazzling metallic fabrics, sequins, and beads in your best shades—all made especially for after-hours wear.

By and large, stay away from very light pastels and most dark colors after five, even with the requisite dark, light, or bright accent. Pastels usually wash out, and extremely dark colors usually "black out" under night lighting conditions. The end result: As they fade out or become blacker, you fade out with them. And you can never look vibrant wearing what appears to be the wrong colors for you!

You may be able to wear black without a light accent if it is a low-cut dress that leaves a lot of skin showing in the neck, chest, and shoulder region. If an accent is necessary, consider shiny gold jewelry, rhinestones, or pearls. These add lovely finishing touches to black evening ensembles for Light-Bright color types.

Furs

With your Light-Bright coloring, it's advisable to remain a devotee of short and medium-haired furs. If you're tall, you might try such lightweight-looking furs as fox and lynx even if the hairs are a mite long. Do not overwhelm your delicate coloring.

Since a good fur must serve you day and night for a range of occasions, we recommend your most *versatile* neutral colors. Your best shades of white, off-white, beige, camel, medium brown, gray, and black—if black is on your chart—are all possibilities. Your rust will be sportier-looking on you and therefore would not be a wise choice if you need a fur that will work over evening wear.

We must caution you that solid-colored furs are more versatile than their multicolored counterparts. They can be worn for both formal and casual occasions and over patterns as well as solids. Multicolored furs have a sportier look; therefore, they're more limiting for some lifestyles.

Makeup and Hair Coloring Advice

Change can be scary.

Mary Lawson, one of our Denver, Colorado, associates, has calmed the tremors of several clients whose color charts dictate a significant adjustment in their wardrobe and makeup.

In particular, Mary recalls one client with Light-Bright coloring who had been wearing toned-down clarities. Her reasons were psychological rather than visual. Toned-down clarities made her feel safe and unobtrusive. Faced with the prospect of switching to a clear, bright but light-looking clarity, especially in her makeup, this woman panicked. Wouldn't such colors call too much attention to her?

Mary's response: "You just looked at yourself in a hand mirror wearing the correct clear makeup colors for a woman with your Light-Bright coloring and you're amazed. Perhaps you're even a little shocked at how different you look. Of course, you look different. You look wonderful!

"But in your surprised state, I think you're overlooking something important. When people look at you, they see all of you from head to toe, not just your face. Once you begin wearing the correct clarity of colors and levels of contrast in your clothing, you'll need this clearer but delicate-looking makeup to balance out your image. Otherwise, you'll look incomplete, like you cared enough to choose the right clothes for yourself but were too lazy to finish the job by applying the right makeup."

Mary's client was afraid of makeup. The opposite is often true. Many women with Light-Bright coloring are too heavy-handed with makeup, applying too much of it in colors that are too dark, too strong, or too muted. That problem is depicted in Plate 42. The right shades and amount of makeup for a woman with Light-Bright coloring is shown in the accompanying Photo 43.

When a Light-Bright color type goes astray in her makeup color choices, the reason is usually simple. Her problem is that she hasn't captured the exciting "feel" of Light-Bright coloring. She somehow misses the point that her best makeup colors coincide with her natural coloring. They're light and bright. They're never dark, strong, or toned-down.

Makeup Colors

If you're insecure about makeup colors, the purchase of cosmetics is probably a chore for you, a project you dread. This needn't be the case.

The advice in this section has a twofold purpose: It's intended to remove any questions you, as a Light-Bright color type, have about makeup colors. And, having done that, it should surely make the process of buying and using makeup more fun for you, perhaps even highly enjoyable.

Foundation. One of the reasons you are classified as a Light-Bright color type is because you have clear golden or ivory tones in your skin. Thus, if you are wearing a base with pink in it, you are probably wearing the wrong shade. At the other extreme, if you are wearing a base with too much brown or peach in it, you're making an equally grievous mistake.

Selecting a base is relatively easy. All you have to do is duplicate your skin tone exactly. We outline the process of choosing the right makeup base for your complexion in Chapter 4.

Blush and Lipstick. One client of ours, a legal secretary, learned a lesson in the importance of clear vs. toned-down lip and cheek clarities.

This woman has striking Light-Bright coloring, but the brownish red makeup colors she'd been wearing were all wrong for her. A couple of days after her charting session, she called to thank us for the invaluable advice. She said so far she'd done nothing more than change her blush and lipstick to the clear colors on her Color 1 Color Chart and she'd received compliments all day long! (Plates 33 and 42 illustrate what too browned a lip and cheek color can do to a Light-Bright color type.)

Your best clear, bright red shade in medium to light tones is one of the ideal colors for you to wear as lip, cheek, and nail color. This is your red color, the color you turn when you blush or become flushed. (Consult Chapter 2.)

You've other options as well: Your best raspberry and clear light plum (red-purple) shades can be matched in lipstick, blush, and nail polish. Remember to wear these colors in their clear, vibrant, as well as light incarnations. Avoid dark, strong, intense, brownish, dusty, or muted-looking shades in any makeup you wear. A woman with Light-Bright/Gentle coloring, though, will need to wear a more toned-down clarity, but she still needs to avoid dark, brownish, dusty, and very toned-down clarities.

Your best shade of coral can be used as a lipstick or polish color but *never for a blush*. After all, you don't blush coral or orange, do you? No. You blush your red color.

Eye Shadow. There are several guidelines to keep in mind here:

First, stick with clear to very slightly toned-down eye shadow colors. (Again, Light-Bright/Gentle color types must limit themselves to more toned-down shadows.) By the same token, make sure your eye shadow colors are light to medium in value. In other words, *do not wear dark, intense eye shadow shades or dusty, brownish, muted shades.* They'll look either too overpowering for a woman with your delicate coloring on the one extreme or too drab and dull on the other.

What color eye shadow is best? Any color that appears on your color chart, bearing in mind that each renders a different effect. To create a range of looks, you will want eye shadows that match your medium brown, gray, light beige (for a highlighter), blue, blue-green, green, and at least one shade of purple.

For conservative business looks or any understated look, eye shadows that repeat the colors in your eyes and neutral shades are your best bet. Neutral colors and your eye color shades are always less obvious than interjecting a color that isn't already contained in your eye. You will find that your more bluish purple eye shadows are also very basic as they work well with all of your best shades in addition to complimenting every eye color.

For less conservative looks, it's nice to repeat the colors of your clothing in your eye shadow.

For example, whether you have blue, blue-green, brown, or green eyes, you can wear different combinations of green, blue, turquoise, and purple eye shadows depending on the color of your outfit that day.

Eyeliner and Mascara. Brown, black, and navy mascaras are fine for most Light-Bright color types. But some Light-Bright color types may have to forgo the black if it looks harsh on them.

Eyeliners can match all of your charted colors. Just make sure such colors—or the way you apply them—do not create a harsh or heavily made-up look. If your eyeliner color seems slightly too dark or pronounced, smudge the line to diffuse the darkness.

Darker vs. Lighter Color Values. Although it is Light-Bright and Contrast color types who have the clearer colors on their charts, it is Light-Bright and Gentle color types who have the more delicate coloring. On both of these delicate color types, less makeup goes further. On these types, dramatic looks can be achieved with relatively medium and light, less intense colors. Thus, both Light-Bright and Gentle color types should always endeavor to keep their makeup *light*-looking, but not washed-out or pale-looking.

On the other hand, nighttime lighting conditions pose certain challenges that can't be overlooked. After the sun sets, a woman with Light-Bright coloring should apply her makeup with a slightly stronger hand. Otherwise, she'll look pale. Her lipstick, blush, and eye shadows can all be stronger-looking, but she mustn't overdo it and create a heavy look, like that of a painted kewpie doll.

Here are some other general makeup guidelines:

Hewing to your lightest makeup tones, especially in lipstick, gives you more of a "nonmakeup" look that is strictly casual.

You can wear your medium-dark—but never deep—lipstick, shadow, and blush tones when you are very dressed up whether it's a daytime or evening event. Medium-dark makeup tones may also be called for with a particular high fashion look you are trying to achieve. Just make sure you don't overdo it with colors that are too strong or intense.

Your clear and vibrant blushes can be purchased in light, medium, or medium-dark values. Obviously, apply medium or medium-dark tones of blush more lightly. On the other hand, if your blush is very clear and light, you may have to wear more of it to achieve the desired effect. You will always be wearing less blush in the daytime to accompany conservative business attire than you will wear at night for festive occasions when lights are low.

Any time you wear ensembles comprised of stronger color combinations—wearing two of your lighter-looking, vibrant colors together, for example—you will need to increase the level of your makeup accordingly. However, under no circumstances must you ever wear very strong or dark, heavy-looking makeup. It looks harsh, hard, and out of keeping with your delicate coloring. If we really wanted to frighten you enough to keep you from doing it, we'd say it would make you look old! It will.

Coordinating Your Makeup and Clothing Colors

Maybe you're still puzzled about the best makeup colors to wear with specific outfits. We're about to give you several hypothetical examples to help you get a feel for how it's done for Light-Bright coloring.

• There you are, dressed in a red-white-and-turquoise sundress accessorized with a bright yet lightweight-looking necklace and bracelet of turquoise and silver. Your accessories are red patent leather shoes and belt. Your purse could be red, white, or turquoise. If you are wearing hose, they would be sheer white or skin tone.

So, you ask, what colors do I apply to my face?

This colorful outfit demands makeup colors to match. We recommend turquoise eye shadow and eyeliner with an eye shadow highlighter of clear silver gray, white, or light beige. For mascara, choose black or dark brown. Your lip, cheek, and nail color should match the red shade in your dress—a clear, bright, but *light-looking* tone.

• Now you have on a bright raspberry-pink blouse, a medium or light green skirt, an ivory jacket, and a green malachite pendant that matches the green of your skirt. Your hose, shoes, and handbag are ivory.

For an enhancing makeup look, match the green of your skirt and pendant in your eye shadow and eyeliner. Use a highlighter eye shadow of ivory or light beige or even pink, if you wish. Your mascara is black or dark brown. Repeat the raspberry shade of your blouse in your lipstick, blush, and nail polish.

• Suppose you're dressed for business in a golden camel suit. Your blouse is coral, your earrings and a simple neck chain are gold, your shoes and purse are camel or a medium golden brown, and your hose are skin tone.

Your goal is an understated makeup look so you would choose to create a neutral eye with camel to medium brown eye shadow and cream or beige highlighter. Select eyeliner in a medium golden brown, and finish off your eyes with dark brown or black mascara. Adorn your lips and nails with the coral shade of your blouse.

If you'll recall what we said earlier, you must never use a coral shade of blush on your cheeks. Substitute instead your best red shade. The only concession you might try is to place a tiny amount of your coral blush on your cheeks and apply your red blush over that to bring your blush shade a mite closer to your lip and nail color.

• Finally, you're dressed up in a white wool suit topped off with a navy and white printed blouse, navy and white spectator pumps on your feet, and a navy purse. Your hose are very sheer white, navy, or your skin tone.

This time your eye shadow should be blue with a very light beige or off-white highlighter. Your eyeliner is navy. Your mascara is either navy, black, or even dark brown.

For lipstick, blush, and nail polish, select from among your best light plum, raspberry, coral, or red. If you choose coral, remember not to wear it on your cheeks—or if you do, to mix it with your red blush.

Hair Coloring

In lightening their hair, the most common mistake Gentle color types make is to allow too much of a golden tone in it. Beige or champagne tones would be more flattering.

Conversely, women with Light-Bright coloring tend to err in the opposite direction: They allow too much ash, rather than golden tones, in their hair. This often happens because their hair loses color rapidly during the lightening process, often faster than the colorist anticipates. The result is hair that ends up too white or ash-looking because the hair has been completely stripped of its pigment. Fortunately, there are now products that lighten hair just to the perfect shade and then the lightening action stops.

What colors are possibilities for women with Light-Bright coloring wishing to lighten or color their hair?

You can't go wrong if you pick out one of your hair's natural highlight colors and lighten your hair to that shade. Or simply take your main hair color several shades lighter.

On women with Light-Bright coloring, the most prevalent hair highlight color is golden in tone but not brassy-looking. Thus, if it is your intention to darken your hair from a natural golden camel color to a medium brown, let's say, make sure that the medium brown you choose retains a strong golden highlight. Otherwise your new medium brown color will clash with the golden tones or clear ivory tones of your skin.

Should you decide to lighten or highlight your hair or want to hide your gray hair by coloring it, be careful. Don't overdo it by allowing too much of a golden tone to your hair. Your hair will end up looking brassy. Work for a honey blond, a wheat shade, or a champagne blond.

Your Light-Bright coloring is truly unique, and you now know how to use color to help you look gorgeous in your clothing and makeup. You are ready to begin Part III, where you can apply all of your new color knowledge and learn to cast your very special color spell!

Chapter 8

Wardrobe Advice for Contrast Coloring

You may think wearing the right colors is important. But did you ever consider *how* important? One of our St. Louis associates reports that switching to the right colors after wearing the wrong ones for years actually kept one of her clients from being fired.

The client was a professional woman who handled one of her firm's largest accounts. She was a Contrast color type but according to our associate you'd never have known it from the outfits she wore. Her closet was filled with muted, toned-down colors—lots of browns, khaki, and heathery tweeds. On her, a woman with high contrast coloring, they looked absolutely blah!

Our associate steered her client away from the colors that were making this highly competent professional woman appear so insignificant. She replaced those old, do-nothing colors with clear, bright, vibrant colors and strong contrast color combinations. The client loved her new look. And so did this woman's employer. Months later, her superior at work admitted that the executives at the firm had been on the verge of firing her simply for having the wrong image. It was her color and wardrobe transformation that helped to save her job.

Like this client, Elizabeth Taylor, Liza Minnelli, Audrey Hepburn, Kate Jackson, Jaclyn Smith, and Joan Collins need to follow the rules we are about to enunciate. For they, too, are Contrast color types.

Your Best Color Clarities

The primary mistake the client was making concerned clarity of colors. She was wearing toned-down and subdued clarities when she should have been wearing just the opposite—either intense clarities or bright clarities. (Look at the vast difference color can make in a Contrast color type's appearance by comparing Plates 36 and 37.)

This color crime is frequently committed by women with Contrast coloring. Our associate Alice Marie Livingston of Pendleton, Oregon—a Contrast color type in her own right—admits she too labored under similar color misconceptions.

"I used to wear toned-down colors because of a number of silly notions I had about color in general," Alice says. "One of them was that toned-down colors are more expensive-looking, more modest, and dignified. Needless to say, a whole new world has opened up to me now that my wardrobe is filled with the bright cavalcade of colors I should have been wearing all along."

Some Contrast color types in their late thirties and forties who are starting to have a middle-aged weight problem and graying hair are often the worst offenders in regard to clarity of color. Dressed in muted colors, they think people won't notice them as much.

But the opposite is actually true: In toned-down colors, such women appear ten to fifteen years older than they really are.

Best Clarity of Colors for Contrast Color Types

Color Type	Best Clarity Level(s)	Second-Best Clarity Level(s)
CONTRAST	Intense Bright	Slightly Toned-Down
CONTRAST/LIGHT-BRIGHT	Bright	Slightly Toned-Down Intense—provided the skin tone can handle them
CONTRAST/MUTED	Slightly Toned-Down	Bright—provided the skin tone can handle them

8.1

Contrast color types need to duplicate their natural coloring with medium to strong levels of contrast in the outfits they wear. Helene Mills, our Santa Monica, California, associate, has not done that with the taupe blouse and small gold-beaded necklace she models in Photo 8.1. Her makeup is too pale and gives the same toned-down effect, making Helene look undistinguished and ordinary.

The photographs (Plate 36 and Photos 8.1, 8.3, and 8.5) show how undistinguished and ordinary a woman with Contrast coloring looks in outfits that are too toned-down. (To review color clarities, study Plates 21–23.)

Your Best Level of Contrast

Contrast color types must always create contrast in their color combinations. This means mixing and matching colors in such a way as to create strong or medium levels of contrast.

There are only three strong contrast combinations: black and white, navy and white, and dark brown and white. Any other dark–light combinations—such as black and beige—are considered medium levels of contrast. Other examples of medium levels of contrast are dark red and white, dark purple and medium blue-green, black and light gray.

If you are a Contrast color type, these color combinations will work on you:

- **A dark color with a light color,** e.g., dark clear blue-green and clear light purple, navy and clear light yellow, clear dark green and clear light coral.
- **A dark color with a bright color,** e.g., black and bright red, as in Photo 8.6, dark clear purple and bright green, dark clear plum and bright blue-green.

- **A dark color with both a light and a bright color,** e.g., black, white, and bright blue, as in Photo 8.2, dark clear purple, white, and bright red.
- **A bright color with a light color,** e.g., bright blue and white, bright turquoise and clear light pink, bright purple and clear light green.
- **Two medium-toned bright colors** (as in Plate 45), e.g., bright purple and bright blue-green, bright blue and bright coral.
- **A bright color with a light, medium, or dark neutral** (see Plate 37), e.g., bright fuchsia and medium gray, camel and bright green.
- **Two neutrals that create medium to strong levels of contrast,** e.g., black and white; navy and light gray. Many neutral combinations look best when a third bright accent color is added to liven them up, e.g., dark gray and white with a bright red accent.

Adding an Accent Color

The above represent combinations you can wear forever, knowing you'll always look beautifully enhanced and well coordinated. On the other hand, there are two color combinations you can *never* wear unless you add a third accent color:

Do not wear two dark colors together unless you add a light and/or bright accent near your face. You might, for example, wear a navy and clear dark red outfit with a white accent. Or add white to the combination of black and brown. (See Plate 37 for an example of two darker colors worn together with a bright accent.)

Do not wear two light colors together unless you add a dark and/or bright accent near your face. (Plate 36 shows how washed-out our model looks in this light blue and white combination.) A clear light pink and light gray outfit could be accented with a dark gray or bright hot pink accent. A clear pastel blue and white dress would need a bright red belt and shoes, for instance. Photo 8.3 shows a Contrast model wearing two light colors together without an accent. Photo 8.4 shows the same model in the same suit, but this time she's added a bright accent. Isn't the difference remarkable?

If you want to wear all one color head to toe, we

8.2

"Undistinguished" and "ordinary" are certainly not adjectives you would use to describe Helene in Photo 8.2. Here she wears a bold-patterned dress. The stripes of white, black, and bright blue create a light–dark–bright combination that only a Contrast could carry off. Her makeup colors duplicate the strength of the outfit's colors.

recommend using your medium-toned bright colors. For example, our model in Plate 16 would look great in her red worn head to toe, even without the accent of the scarf. The monotone look is not as successful in light or dark colors with the possible exceptions of all white or all black. A solid dark brown dress, for example, would require a light or bright accent at the neck or waist—perhaps in both places—to create the needed contrast. A dark clear blue-green blouse and skirt might need a bright fuchsia belt, necklace, or scarf. A matching clear light blue slacks and sweater outfit could use rust accessories.

Your Best Neutrals

While it's true that neutrals—black, camel, gray, navy, browns, rust, beiges, and white—coordinate well with other colors, this does not mean that a neutral is a neutral is a neutral, so to speak. If you've seen one brown, you've seen them all. This couldn't be further from the truth.

Neutrals come in different shades and clarities and values just as other colors do. So when we discuss the various neutrals, bear in mind that the beige or navy or camel that looks good on you may not be the same shade of beige or navy or camel that looks good on your friend who also happens to be a Contrast color type. The subtle variations in your natural coloring require subtle shading variations in all the colors you wear, including neutrals.

There's no doubt that neutrals are handy colors to have in your wardrobe. You can build all kinds of looks—from summery to wintery, from conservative to high fashion, either by using your neutrals alone, your colors alone, or a mixture of your neutrals and other colors.

What follows is a rundown on the neutrals—both dark and light—you may want to include on your shopping list if they aren't already hanging in your closet:

Black. The majority of all Contrast color types can wear black. However, many Contrast color types need to accent black with light or bright colors for their most enhancing look.

Those bright or light colors can either be colors such as red, yellow, or purple, or other neutrals such as light gray, camel, beige, or white.

If you are a Contrast color type with black hair—or hair a deep brown shade that is very nearly black—you may be able to wear black in an all-one-color look. Your skin tone, bright lipstick color, blush, and eye makeup shades are providing the only color accents on your body.

On the other hand, you may be a brunette Contrast color type. Your hair is dark but unmistakably brown. Anytime you wear black, you probably need to use a light or bright color accent near your face—or, at the very least, at your waist. Large, shiny metal jewelry worn at the neckline is often all that is needed to provide that extra fillip near your face.

Women with Contrast coloring will find black an extremely practical neutral for shoes, belts, and purses. Even for Contrast color types whose hair is salt-and-pepper or has already turned gray or white, black accessories look wonderful.

Black shiny patent leather accessories are an option for women with Contrast coloring.

Here are some lovely ways to wear black:

- Wear a black suit with a vibrant turquoise blouse. Accessorize the outfit with a silver necklace, turquoise and silver earrings, sheer black hose, and black shoes and purse.
- Coordinate black slacks with a light gray blouse and a scarf of black, light gray, and red. Finish the look with sheer black hose and red shoes and purse.

Browns. For brunettes who are a Contrast color type, the brown shade of your hair is an excellent color for you, either in clothing items or accessories. You will want to own both dressy and casual shoes in this shade. A Contrast color type will want to coordinate her best brown with her best medium-value bright colors or the vibrant light pastels on her chart.

For example, imagine a Contrast color type with dark brown hair wearing this outfit:

- A dark brown suit with shoes, a belt, and a purse— the latter two accessories with shiny gold ornamentation—that match her hair color, a blouse in a medium-tone vivid red, and the finishing touch of a brown and gold beaded necklace with gold earrings. Hose can be sheer brown or skin tone.

- Or the same dark brown skirt worn with the same accessories; a vibrant medium-toned blue blouse, an off-white jacket, and the same handsome gold earrings and necklace of brown and gold beads.

If you're a Contrast color type with hair that is black-looking, even though it is really very dark brown hair, your brown will be a good shoe, belt, and purse color for you. But it still won't be as basic as black.

Camel. Camel is a good neutral for women with Contrast coloring *provided* they are careful to select it in the right shade and avoid too blended a look when they combine it with other colors. Your best shade of camel is in the same color family as your skin tone.

Camel and dark brown combined, for instance, create a soft contrast, which is *not* a look enhancing to any woman with Contrast coloring. Camel worn with black will work since these two neutrals combined create a medium contrast look.

It's always great to combine camel with your best medium-toned bright colors. For example, imagine yourself in these handsome casual outfits:

- Camel slacks, socks, and loafers, a bright green cashmere sweater, a scarf with a bold geometric design in camel, bright green, and beige, and gold earrings.
- Matching red slacks and blouse, camel-colored blazer, belt, shoes, and purse, camel hose, and earrings and necklace in gold.

Gray. On Contrast color types, medium gray worn with another neutral most often requires a third color to add the necessary contrast effect. You might wear:

- A medium gray suit with a pure white blouse and bright red belt, shoes, and handbag, for example. Use sheer gray or skin-tone hose.

Light or medium gray worn with a second color that's bright and vivid—now that's another story.

- A light gray suit coordinated with an intense blue or purple blouse will look stunning. It would be interesting to accessorize such an outfit with sheer black hose and black shoes and purse, but you could also use gray accessories, as well as add a shiny silver necklace and earrings.

- A medium gray and white vertical-striped skirt—fairly wide stripes, a crisp white blouse, white hose, fuchsia belt, shoes, and purse, and silver earrings and bracelet.

Charcoal gray is a dark neutral which, like black, should be coordinated with light or bright colors. Gray shoes, belts, and purses become an absolute necessity when your hair is salt-and-pepper, gray, or white. You will want to own both casual and dressy shoes in your best gray.

Here is a smashing way to wear dark gray:

- Dark gray pin-striped slacks, worn with a print blouse of cream, black, and gray, black shoes, purse, and hose, and silver earrings.

Navy. This is another dark neutral that always needs a light or bright color to create needed contrast. Among the many possibilities are a clear, vibrant, light-looking shade such as a vivid pink or yellow, a medium-toned bright color such as a medium bright coral or blue-green, or a light neutral such as stark white or light gray.

When you wear navy or any of your other neutrals or colors on the bottom half of your body as skirts or slacks, don't forget to balance your ensemble by bringing a touch of the bottom color up to the top half of your body in the form of a scarf or necklace or, at the extreme, a matching jacket. It is especially crucial to add this finishing touch if you are putting together a three-color look.

One suggestion: If you wear a lot of navy, you might consider buying a lapis lazuli necklace, as this is a natural semi-precious stone in a deep rich blue color that works well as a navy accent.

Experiment with these smart-looking navy outfits:

- A navy skirt, vibrant fuchsia blouse, white jacket, navy lapis beads, sheer bone stockings, navy and white spectators, and a navy purse.
- A navy suit with a light gray blouse, a gray-navy-red scarf, sheer gray or sheer navy hose, navy shoes and purse, and silver earrings.

8.3

The pale-on-pale outfit Helene Mills models in Photo 8.3 might be salvaged with the addition of a clear bright or dark accent. Still, soft contrast effects such as this should never be the first or even second choice of women with Helene's Contrast coloring. Her similarly pale makeup doesn't help matters either.

White. What about pure white on women with Contrast coloring? *Pure* white is a light color that acts like a *bright* color.

Here are some guidelines:

Pure white is always fine in a print or as a trim.

Pure white is fine from the waist down.

You may wear pure white above the waist with a bright or dark color accent (e.g., a scarf, necklace, earrings) near your face. (See Photo 8.4.)

Because pure white acts like a bright color, *you may be able to wear a solid pure white outfit*—the all-one-color or monotone look—*provided* you take great care about your makeup. If you use pure white in this way, *your lip and cheek colors must be clear and vibrant to provide a color accent.* Your lip color also will act as a "color break," helping to keep your teeth—which rarely are pure white—from looking dull or yellowed.

Best shades of cream whites and off-whites may be used by all women with Contrast coloring. Off-whites do *not* act like bright colors, unless the off-white is your "best" white, so most of you will need to accent them with a bright or dark color to create the correct contrasting effect. Some of you will be able to wear off-white head to toe and look lovely.

Occasionally, a brown-haired woman with Contrast coloring finds herself more enhanced by a black and her best off-white combination than the stronger combination of black and pure white. The mixture of black and pure white creates too bright a white look for their coloring. But this is seldom, if ever, the case with women whose hair is black or a black-brown shade that's very close to black.

Do not try to use bone or beige shoes with an outfit that needs a white shoe. Remember, blended looks are not for you, so you must take care to be more explicit with your colors. If you don't like white shoes, show as little white on your feet as possible—wear a white strap sandal, for example, that has a neutral heel.

Here are two suggestions for wonderful white outfits:

- A white linen suit worn with a vibrant blue blouse, sheer bone hose, and black shoes, necklace, and handbag.
- White slacks combined with a light purple blouse and vibrant red jacket, pearls, bone hose, and red shoes and purse.

Beiges. Unlike white, your best beiges must always be coordinated with at least one bright or dark color to ensure the necessary level of contrast.

Never try to wear a monotone look in a beige shade, as beige does not have the bright quality of white. For this reason, they cannot stand by themselves on a woman with your extreme light–dark coloring (as in Photos 8.1 and 8.5).

Your beiges match your skin tones and thus make excellent shoe, belt, and purse colors for you. Here are suggestions for ways to wear beige:

- A beige suit with a black blouse, black belt with a gold buckle, gold earrings, black shoes and purse, and skin-toned hose.
- Vibrant green slacks and matching sweater, a beige jacket, shoes, and purse, skin-toned hosiery, and gold necklace and earrings.

Rust. For a Contrast color type, rust needs to be treated as a dark neutral, and you will always have to wear it with a light or a bright accent. For example, a lot of people, particularly in the fall and winter, try to do rust, blue, and brown combinations. Depending on the tone of those colors, that combination can look too blended on a woman with Contrast coloring. However, if the shades of those colors are exactly right for you and if the blue is bright enough and worn near the top of the outfit, you will have a fabulous fall and winter look.

Rust is a neutral that will mix with nearly every medium-toned bright or light color to form a wonderful contrast effect on you. Rust shoes could be worn whenever you are incorporating rust in your outfit.

Try these outfits when you crave rust in your wardrobe:

The companion photo (Photo 8.4) shows Helene in the same white suit, but this time she wears a bright red blouse and bold red, black, and white print scarf. This striking light–bright–dark combination looks just right. She has also intensified the colors on her eyes, cheeks, and lips to most telling effect.

- Rust slacks with a clear purple sweater, a scarf of purple, rust, and turquoise, turquoise earrings, and rust, camel, or brown shoes, purse, and hose.
- A brown skirt, a bright blue blouse, a rust blazer, a brown necklace of wooden beads, and brown or rust shoes, purse, and stockings.

Wine and Burgundy. If you've ever wondered why, all your life, you've instinctively shied away from burgundy, we're about to explain:

Helene Mills, a Contrast color type, should always wear medium to strong levels of contrast. In Photo 8.5, the blouse and suit are both in varying values of beige, which creates too soft or blended a look for Helene's coloring. Her makeup is also too pale.

By definition, wine and burgundy are a toned-down clarity. To demonstrate their muted quality, we want you to summon up the mental image of a wine or burgundy. Then picture a cranberry red. When compared to that burgundy shade, doesn't cranberry red have a clearer, brighter effect?

You require that clear quality in all the colors you wear, whether they're dark or light in value. This is why no Contrast color type will ever find the more typical shades of wine or burgundy on her color chart.

You do, however, have your own best versions of these colors on your chart. They are your bright plums, fuchsias, raspberries, and reds worn in their darkest incarnations. These are all dark but clear, vibrant shades that will look smashing on you.

Remember to treat your best dark values of plum, fuchsia, raspberry, and red as you would other dark neutrals. In short, always combine them with a light or bright color.

Here are a couple of great "burgundy" looks for you to try:

• Vibrant turquoise slacks with a deep, clear fuchsia sweater, turquoise earrings, shoes and purse the color of your hair, and sheer hair-colored hose.
• A deep clear red suit with a light gray blouse, sheer gray hose, gray or black shoes and purse, and silver jewelry.

Dark Green. Dark green seldom appears on a Contrast color type's chart because a vibrant medium-dark green—the darkest value of your best shade of green—is usually much more flattering.

Fabric Textures and Weights

Contrast and Muted color types have the widest latitude in their choice of fabric textures and weights.

"Texture" refers to the weave of a fabric. Nylon, for example, is a tightly woven fiber resulting in a cloth that is sleek and solid-looking. Nylon, of course, is a synthetic or manmade fiber. Of the natural fibers, there are two types: animal fibers (wool, silk, mohair, alpaca) and vegetable fibers (cotton, kapok, flax, hemp). These fibers are woven into fabrics with many different textures. Indeed, the same fiber can result in a material whose texture is smooth and almost nonexistent to one that is extremely rough and coarse.

For example, wool is used to make such fine, elegant material as French flannel as well as the more loosely woven tweeds. Cotton appears in tightly woven shirt material as often as you see it in textured knits. Silk comes in several incarnations, ranging from the delicate, diaphanous fabric most often used for evening wear to nubby textured raw silk cloth. The texture of the raw silk shirt in Photo 8.5 is lovely on Helene; it's just that she needs to increase the level of contrast in her clothing and makeup.

There is a further distinction to be made: The same fabric—velvet, herringbone wool, cotton knit—comes in different weights or thicknesses.

Your Contrast color type imposes no fabric weight restrictions on you, but your body weight and structure can. If you want certain parts of your body to look smaller or thinner, you should avoid bulky-looking materials in those areas.

The same rule applies to textures: For Contrast color types who wish to appear more slender, limit yourself to smooth and slightly textured garments. Otherwise, anything goes. You can wear garments that are as smooth as fine silk on the one extreme or as heavily textured as tapestry, brocade, and wide-wale corduroy at the other extreme.

Should you have narrow shoulders or wide hips that you want to disguise using fabric textures and weights, choose your blouses, jackets, and other tops in more heavily textured or weighty fabrics and your skirts and slacks in smoother and only slightly textured fabrics.

8.6

How much more exciting and vibrant Helene looks wearing the bright red and black lumberjack plaid jacket in Photo 8.6. Her blouse and skirt are solid black. The bright–dark combination is extremely effective on Contrast color types. Her makeup is also stronger, beautifully finishing her look.

Patterns, Prints, and Designs

Of the four major color types, only Contrast color types can seldom wear small patterns and prints. Indeed, a woman with Contrast coloring should never even attempt to wear a smaller print unless it meets two conditions: the print must have extreme dark–light contrast in

8.7

The tiny gold chain and pendant Helene Mills wears in Photo 8.7 is too small and therefore looks insignificant on a woman with her strong coloring. Medium- and large-scale jewelry is always preferable for Contrast color types. The only way they can get away with small-scale jewelry is if they wear several pieces together. Helene's makeup is also too lightly applied.

it, such as black with white; and the print must be accented with another solid splash of color—preferably an accent color that is bright. An example of this would be a small navy and white polka dot dress accented with a red belt, earrings, and shoes. Also effective is a solid-color accessory in one of the print's predominant colors, for example, a black and white small-print blouse, black skirt, and large black beads.

Conversely, Contrast color types are the only ones who always look enhanced in large, bold designs. Study Plate 36 (the wrong look) and Photo 8.2 and Plate 20 (the right look), as well as the fabric swatches in Plate 35 to see the truth of these statements.

Because they're short, a lot of women think they can't wear large prints regardless of their color type. This is not true. Even a five-foot-one-inch, dark-haired, ivory- or olive-skinned woman with Contrast coloring will look dynamite in a bold, strongly contrasting design. The moral here: Forevermore, stay away from the vast majority of prints that are small in scale. You'll look like a plain Jane in them. Your coloring—not your body type and height—determines your print and pattern sizes. Body weight and structure determine how you use large patterns.

The guidelines about levels of contrast are important to keep in mind when you are selecting prints. Confine yourself to prints whose colors create a strong or medium level of contrast.

Should you happen to own a garment with a print that is small in scale and whose colors do not create the extreme dark–light contrast you need to look your best, don't throw it out. There may be a way to salvage it *provided:* the print's background color is a good one for you; at least two of the other colors are among your best; and no "bad" colors predominate.

You can make it look better than it ever has before by adding a solid contrasting accent—a belt, scarf, or beads—in one of the strongest of your best colors already in the print to heighten the whole outfit's level of contrast.

Let's say you have a dress in a small paisley design. It's composed of light gray, white, and a small amount of black. Because of the small design, such colors, even at a short distance, create a soft contrast or blended effect. But wear a black vest or jacket over this dress and presto! You create the exciting illusion of a medium contrast outfit.

On the other hand, consider what would happen if you simply donned a white or gray vest or jacket over the dress. The effect of the outfit would remain that of a soft contrast.

Jewelry

Your visually powerful natural coloring allows you to wear the largest and heaviest-looking jewelry. Bold, innovative jewelry designs look handsome on you, while small, delicate pieces don't have enough impact. The moral: Only wear jewelry that makes a strong visual statement (see Photos 8.7 and 8.8).

Ethnic, antique, and contemporary jewelry are all fine as long as they are medium to large pieces. Smaller items such as gold or silver chains or lovely small pendants need to be combined so they have more impact. Wear several together or combine small pieces with medium and large pieces. If you have a long string of pearls or other beaded necklaces, you may double-wrap them or tie knots in them to create a larger-looking neck accent. Another way to create a stronger accent is to twist two or more necklaces together. Try this with a strand of pearls, a strand of colorful beads (turquoise, jade, or coral), and a gold or silver chain.

Be as extravagant as you want with jewelry. You can wear earrings, a necklace, a bracelet, and rings simultaneously without looking like a gypsy. Just take care that the different pieces all harmonize with each other and add to your outfit.

But before you add a piece of jewelry, make sure it meets these criteria:

Size. No matter what your height, you may wear large and medium-sized pieces. But small is out unless you combine them to create a stronger visual impact.

Remember, if you want to you can create the illusion of size and bulk simply by wearing more than one necklace or bracelet or ring at a time. Think in terms of showcasing a whole collection of jewelry pieces on your neck or wrist or hands. Do avoid, however, the looks of "a ring on every finger," and "I always wear all of my jewelry because I'm afraid to leave it home."

Metal Colors. Good metals on you are gold, shiny silver, a golden-toned (never greenish) brass, white gold,

8.8

In Photo 8.8 Helene wears the same bright yellow blouse, this time setting it off with a necklace of black onyx and silver. Her coloring needs substantial pieces of jewelry such as this. Her makeup is also done in medium and darker tones here, giving her a much more radiant look.

and platinum (if your skin is ivory). Darker-skinned Contrast color types should avoid the latter two metals. Shiny copper may be used but it's best worn with bright clarities and/or light colors to create needed contrast.

Metal Finishes. Shiny, highly polished metals are your best bet. Both smooth and textured metals are fine *provided* any textured metal has a bright, shiny finish or at least a subtle glow. Off limits to you are the dull, more toned-down metals that are so attractive on women with Muted and Gentle coloring.

Gems, Semi-Precious Stones, and Costume Jewelry. Your best colors are your guide in the selection of jewelry in these categories.

Often we've encountered clients who are startled when they compare the contents of their jewelry boxes with their color charts. With anguish, they realize that some of their most expensive jewelry items are in the wrong tones for them. After a desperate phone call to us, they're equally relieved to learn that these pieces can still be worn to telling effect.

How?

Pretend you own a strand of real pearls. Pearls, both real and simulated, come in many shades of white and off-white. What if your real pearls are a more golden ivory tone and, thus, look yellowish next to your skin? What should you do? The answer is don't wear them next to your skin. Instead, wear them *on top of* a blouse or sweater, provided the color of your top is anything but white, off-white, or beige.

Handbags and Attaché Cases

A handbag is an important accessory. People may not study your purse intently, but it is one part of a woman's total image that is always noticed if it's second-rate or beat-up but may not be noted specifically if it's of good quality and an appropriate style and color. Better to have people overlook your purse because it looks right than notice it because it's all wrong.

You may already be aware of handbag basics, such as the fact that smaller bags are dressier than larger bags and that purses made of natural materials are always preferable to those made of synthetics. It is far more important to own two good-quality handbags than an assortment of cheaper purses in all the colors of the rainbow. If you are a businesswoman, you will want the one attaché case you own to be in your hair color and to be of good quality.

We hope you long ago discarded the old-fashioned notion that your purse and shoes—or your attaché case, shoes, and purse—must match. True, your purse, shoes, and attaché case must coordinate with each other as well as with your clothing, but they do not have to match each other.

You will always want to own both dressy and casual purses in your hair color and your skin color. That way you'll always look coordinated because you are repeating a color that is eternally a part of your total look—the color on top of your head and the color of your skin. Your hair color is an excellent choice for your attaché case.

Other good colors for you to match in your handbags, and also possibilities for an attaché case, are all of the other neutrals on your chart. They will include the following: black, beige, brown, camel, white, gray, navy, and rust, all in your best shades.

Note that camel is a medium-toned shade you can wear year-round, which makes it particularly useful as a handbag and shoe color. Equally practical is a straw or wicker purse in your skin tone. It will serve you in spring, summer, and early fall.

Shoes

The points we stressed in the preceding section concerning natural materials and neutral go-with-everything colors apply equally to shoes.

Shoes in colors that you wear a lot will also get a great deal of wear. Build a wardrobe of neutral-colored shoes first, both dressy and casual shoes in shades that match your hair and skin tones. Then add shoes in your other neutral and most used colors.

As a Contrast color type, you are enhanced by pure white, and it's likely you own several summer outfits featuring a lot of white. Should you wear white shoes with these clothes?

We pose this question because many women do not like all-white shoes. They feel pure white shoes are attention-getters, and who wants to call attention to their feet? If you dislike white shoes, the trick is to make sure that the shoes you buy have a neutral heel and have very little white body to them like a lightweight-looking strapped sandal with as few thin white straps as possible.

Eyeglass Frames

Once again, it's an excellent idea to purchase your eyeglass frames in colors that match either your main hair color—the apparent overall color of your hair—or your skin tone. A tortoiseshell frame that combines your hair and skin colors seems an obvious choice. Unfortunately, this is a sporty frame that cannot be worn with formal evening clothes and some dressier daytime attire, thus it is limiting and should be considered only as a choice for a second pair of glasses. A black-haired woman could wear a solid black frame.

Any of your good metal colors and finishes are fine and very versatile. To make a brightly colored frame—a red frame, say—coordinate with an outfit, you must wear at least a touch of that color somewhere else in your outfit. This makes frames in your colors extremely limiting. If you want a colored frame, you'll need to own another pair of more neutral-framed glasses.

Finally, you might consider frameless glasses. They expose more of your face and eyes and look good with both dressy and casual clothing.

Evening Wear

Artificial lighting makes dressing for evening a major challenge.

Fortunately, it's less of a challenge for a Contrast color type. The clear, bright colors and strong-contrast outfits most enhancing to them during the daylight hours also happen to look good after dark. Very dark colors and very light colors (except black and white) become "noncolors" when lights are low. They wash out or fade out so they can't help you look radiant. Utilize your medium-toned brights for your most vibrant effects.

The night was made for shimmering fabrics. Bedazzle your escort in such deluxe materials as gold or silver lamé or colored sequined and beaded outfits. Metallic accessories—shoes and an evening bag in your best metal shades—coordinate well with many evening outfits. You may also match your clothing, your hair, or your skin tone.

A solid black or white dress may require an accent color near your face. If a black dress happens to be low-cut, your bare-skinned shoulders and neck can often provide the necessary light accent. Of course, black can be worn without an accent by most black-haired women.

Furs

Select your furs from your best white, off-white, beige, dark brown, black, and gray. Your rust will look sportier on you and for that reason may not be a terrific choice if you need a fur that can be worn on formal occasions.

There's another consideration: the length of the hair. If you have Contrast coloring and are five feet six inches or over, any length hair is fine. If you are shorter, consider short- and medium-haired furs, or try longer-haired furs that are styled to add height instead of bulk.

Finally, bear in mind that solid-colored furs are more versatile than multicolored furs such as raccoon and lynx. The solid-colored furs look good over any outfit whether it's sporty or dressy, patterned or plain. Multicolored furs, fabulous as they may be, will not work over many semi-formal and formal dresses.

Makeup and Hair Coloring Advice

Helene Mills, our Color 1 associate and model in the wrong-right makeup photos (Plates 44 and 45), has counseled a number of Contrast color types like herself. Many arrive on her Santa Monica, California, doorstep wearing little or no makeup. Each one of these women has tried using makeup at one time or another, but they claim they looked "painted" in it. Why?

After querying them about their makeup colors, Helene found out. All of them were wearing colors that were too brown or orange—in short, too muted—for their natural dark–light coloring. Helene convinced these women that they wouldn't look "painted" if they confined themselves to makeup colors chosen specifically for them. Wearing the right *clear* makeup colors, they'd look like they're supposed to look—and, at the same time, they'd be showcasing the extreme contrast between their hair color and skin tones.

A Contrast color type can wear more makeup without looking overly made-up than most of the other color types. Because the makeup is being applied to the stronger coloring of a woman with Contrast coloring, it takes more of it in order for her to look like she's wearing any at all. Indeed, a Contrast color type's strong visual appearance is most enhanced when it is set off with *clear, brighter makeup colors, mostly in medium to dark values.*

Makeup Colors

We've explained that muted, toned-down makeup clarities—that is, makeup with a lot of brown pigment in it—are not for you. Neither are pale colors. With your Contrast coloring, you need the strength that only medium to dark clear, bright makeup colors can provide.

Here are some specific pointers about appropriate foundation, lipstick, blush, nail polish, eye shadow, eye liner, and mascara colors:

Foundation. A Contrast color type has either ivory skin (see Plates 12 and 16) with little or no pink or golden tones in it, olive skin (see Plate 4), or—in the case of black Contrast coloring—light, medium, or dark skin that is *clear* and free from almost all pink or golden tones (see Plate 20). But no matter what the skin color, the base a woman with Contrast coloring wears should *match the skin tone on her neck exactly.* Nothing but disaster ensues when a woman tries to change her complexion by wearing an offsetting color in her foundation.

One client who instinctively wore the right clear, bright clothing colors to suit her Contrast coloring had not mastered her makeup. The result was jarring. She tended toward very toned-down, brownish colors in her cheek and lip colors. Her foundation color was even worse. By wearing a rose-beige base, she was trying to transform her lovely olive complexion to a rosy beige.

What this client failed to consider was her total look. Your makeup colors have to match the clear, bright clarity of your wardrobe colors. Otherwise, you'll look out of sync with yourself. If you've got an olive complexion, don't try to deny it by hiding it under the wrong makeup base.

It's unfortunate that the majority of makeup bases in the stores come in colors that are too pink, rosy, and peach for Contrast color types with their ivory and olive skin. Thus, you'll have to shop carefully, and even then you may have to mix two bases together to achieve the precise shade you require.

Blush. Blush should give you a healthy glow, as if you just got finished walking briskly around the block. You'll look this way if you stick with blush in your best red color, raspberry, fuchsia, and the vibrant plum shades. You will *not* look natural and glowing if you resort to rouge in coral or brown shades. Two good examples are Jennifer Ho wearing her red color blush in Plate 37 and Helene Mills wearing her plum blush in Plate 45.

Lipstick. Your strong Contrast coloring demands lipstick and nail polishes in your best clear shades of red, coral, raspberry, fuchsia, and vibrant plum.

Another option: By all means try combining your best lipstick and polish shades. Your best red, red-orange (that is, coral), or red-purple shades (raspberry, fuchsia, and plum) can be worn alone or mixed to create a new hybrid color. Be adventurous!

Eye Shadow. Eye makeup for Contrast color types can be as strong and dramatic as you wish. On the other hand, some women with Contrast coloring prefer a softer, more natural look. That's fine, too, as long as they don't end up with a washed-out instead of a subtle look (the problem in Plates 36 and 44). It's a matter of personal preference, how a woman is dressed, and where she is going.

All your best colors can be used for eye shadows, depending on the effect you are trying to achieve. Some good starter shades are your best blue, blue-green, green, at least one shade of purple, a creamy off-white for a highlighter, gray, and brown, if you like it. You may want both lighter and medium-dark tones of the colors so you can create many different looks.

For everyday business wear, eye shadows in your neutrals or those shades that pick up the colors of your eyes are basic. You will find that your purple eye shadows are also very basic in that they work well with all of your most enhancing colors and they compliment every eye color.

Your eye shadows' clarity must be clear or ever so slightly toned-down, never muddy, grayed, or muted-looking. The only women excepted from this stricture are those with Contrast/Muted coloring. Their eye shadows will be more toned-down because the colors on their charts are more toned-down than those of a straight Contrast color type.

As a Contrast color type, you can also wear intense colors on your eyes if you want to underscore a certain high fashion look.

A less conservative look is created when you repeat the colors of your clothing in your eye shadows. Helene Mills has done this in Plate 45. Helene's blue and plum shadows duplicate the shades in her outfit. Notice how this duplication tends to make you look in her eyes before you notice anything else about her. That's as it should be.

Eyeliner and Mascara. You are enhanced by black mascara as well as the other dark shades of navy and dark brown.

Eyeliners in all of your best colors can be effective. Your eye liner may or may not have to be smudged to diffuse the pronounced effect of the line. It depends on the look you want to achieve.

Darker vs. Lighter Color Values. Should you wish to create a less made-up look, we suggest lightening your best shades of lipstick and eye shadow. Substitute medium to medium-light clear colors for your regular medium to dark colors. But keep in mind that your lightest lip colors, in particular, are strictly for casual wear. Lipsticks in your medium tones give a finished and conservative look.

Of course, Contrast/Muted color types are always going to be making up their faces in colors that are ever so slightly toned-down. But Contrast/Muted coloring can sustain the same intensity of dark, medium, and light values as the other Contrast color types.

All Contrast color types can use lighter eye shadows as

highlighters to achieve a special effect or create a certain eye shape.

Blush can be purchased in medium or dark shades. Just vary the amount you apply depending on the occasion or the effect you are trying to achieve.

At night, a woman with Contrast coloring can pull out all the stops. When lights are low, she can wear stronger makeup in the clearest, most intense shades imaginable. Eye makeup especially can be emphasized.

Coordinating Your Makeup and Clothing Colors

This is the fun part—deciding which makeup colors to wear with which outfits. Only many women don't see it that way. Usually, it's because they're confused about what's permissible.

If you still find this process disconcerting rather than fun, we're about to change all that, for we're going to give you several examples that will enlighten you about how makeup color decisions are made. We'll describe an outfit and then suggest possible makeup colors that will enhance the overall look:

- You have on a pair of slacks with a black and white striped pattern and a white blouse. For jewelry, you've selected a silver bracelet and earrings. Your accessories are mostly red—red shoes and a belt, either a red or black purse, and sheer white hose.

What should you do about your makeup?

In terms of eye makeup, two of your many options are either to go for a more neutral look, on the one extreme, or a strong eye effect on the other.

With this ensemble, the neutral eye look is achieved with eye shadows of white or off-white, as a highlighter and light and dark gray as your main shadow colors. Wear a dark gray or black eyeliner and black mascara. The strong eye effect is achieved with purple eye shadows— a good basic color—the same light highlighters, and black mascara. This time, use both purple and black eyeliner.

On your lips, cheeks, and nails we suggest a red shade that matches the red of your accessories.

- Picture yourself wearing a yellow jumpsuit with a printed design of blue, purple, red, and white. Your earrings are shiny gold. At the waist, you don a blue belt. On your feet, you've got blue shoes with nude stockings, and you carry a blue purse.

Your colorful outfit cries out for an equally carefree and colorful feeling in your eye makeup. To do that, select eye shadows of purple and blue and a highlighter of soft white, and/or light yellow. Use purple and/or blue eyeliner and black mascara.

The red in the jumpsuit affords you the opportunity to match it in your lipstick, blush, and nail polish.

- Business is on your mind. You're wearing a navy suit with a white blouse. Your accessories are a lapis lazuli necklace, sheer skin-toned stockings, and navy shoes and a purse.

With conservative business attire such as this, you want your makeup to be strong enough to give your features definition, but not so strong that it calls attention to itself. Thus, you would choose eye shadows of dark blue and gray and a highlighter of off-white or light beige. You could use a navy eyeliner and black or dark navy mascara. (No bright navy mascara for business looks.)

To adorn your lips and cheeks you could wear a clear medium red or raspberry shade. If you select coral, though, remember that you can only wear it on your lips and as nail polish, never as blush unless you put just a touch of the coral on your cheeks and then blend it with your red blush. For blush with this business look stay with your red or raspberry shades. For nail polish, either match your lip color or remain with a neutral or "see-through" polish.

- This time you are dressed in an off-white skirt, a vibrant medium blue blouse, and a vibrant medium green jacket. These three separates are pulled together visually by a scarf of off-white, green, blue, and fuchsia. Your hosiery, shoes, and purse are off-white.

This ensemble mandates that you match its colors in your makeup. Your eye shadows could be a combination of blues and greens, or one or the other exclusively. Your highlighter will be off-white or light beige. Line your eyes with a green and/or blue eyeliner. And brush your lashes with black mascara.

The fuchsia in your neck scarf is the perfect color to repeat in your lipstick, blush, and nail polish.

Hair Coloring

You will lose part of your uniqueness and your contrast appearance if you highlight or streak your hair. Your dark hair is a vital component of the dark–light look that is so characteristic of your natural coloring.

Women with Contrast coloring who are unhappy that their hair is in the process of graying or whose hair is inadvertently being lightened by the chemicals used for permanents may want to reverse frost their hair to bring it back to its natural deeper shade. We describe the process in Chapter 4. If you're sure you don't want to keep your hair darker-looking and, at the same time, want to eliminate that medium graying stage, try a blond shade, one that would be enhancing with your skin tone. We suggest matching the beiges and the camel shades on your chart—usually champagne, honey, and wheat shades of blond—as light or dark as you like. Just make sure you get the shade right!

Contrast color types whose hair is salt-and-pepper or completely gray or white look striking and often prefer to do nothing to their hair (as in Plate 16). Obviously, this is a matter of personal preference.

One final word of advice: Women with gray or white hair should not put bluish rinses on their hair, but should endeavor to keep their hair shade as white and sparkling as possible. If you're going to use any rinse, use one that creates a clear, brighter gray or white tone, not one that adds even a hint of brown, blue, or yellow to your hair.

Your Contrast coloring is truly unique, and you now know how to use colors in their best shades, clarities, and levels of contrast to help you look terrific in your clothing and makeup. You are ready to begin Part III, where you can apply all of your new color knowledge and learn how to cast your most bewitching color spell!

Part III

Cast a Color Spell

Chapter 9

Color Chic

Over the years, we've noticed that our color concept tends to change people's outlook for the better in three major ways:

Knowing her own colors, a woman is *braver about wearing more colors*. She stops thinking of herself merely as a "blue person" or a "gray person" or a "beige person."

Also, most women find they end up *owning fewer clothes but wearing everything and enjoying them more*. In addition, they're *more adventurous in the way they combine colors*.

To help women think of colors as wardrobe building blocks, we developed the "capsule wardrobe concept." It's a system that helps solve the perennial mix-and-match quandary so many women find themselves in. And it is the core of a balanced wardrobe. Instituted by Color 1 in 1978, this concept works so well it has been imitated by department stores, fashion writers, and other image consultants.

Depending on your life style, your capsule wardrobe will be built with classic, high fashion, casual, or some other type of clothing. These clothes won't be the only ones you own, of course, but they will form the foundation upon which you build the most unique, enhancing, fun, and workable wardrobe you've ever had.

Our capsule wardrobe formula enables you to get the maximum mileage out of a minimum number of clothing items. The concept we've designed for the working woman, for example, requires that you have only two suits, five blouses, and two neck accessories. That's all. And here's the amazing part: Utilizing these nine items to their fullest, you can create thirty distinctive outfits—twenty suit looks and ten more looks without a jacket.

The capsule wardrobe concept is a godsend for any woman, but it is especially helpful for those who travel a lot or who have limited budgets. It's also useful for women who have another goal—to streamline their wardrobes, to create order where once there was nothing but chaos. "Chaotic" is, in fact, the best adjective to describe the average woman's wardrobe before she introduces some Color 1 organization into her life.

The Color 1 Capsule Wardrobe Concept

One woman became so adept at implementing our capsule working wardrobe system that one of her professional colleagues asked, "Did you inherit a lot of money or something? You have so many new outfits!"

All she had done was select *a few new items of clothing* to give her existing wardrobe more balance. The pieces she chose helped her to better coordinate the garments she already owned. And that's the only thing that was different about this woman's wardrobe.

Many women bemoan the fact that suits are so expensive. They claim they can't afford them. Meanwhile, they have a closet crammed with dresses and separates—blouses, skirts, jackets, sweaters, and slacks—most of which don't coordinate with each other.

You can approach your wardrobe overhaul modestly. You might, for example, start with one solid-color suit, giving yourself your first jacket to mix and match with other items in your closet. Then select a few new print scarves containing your best colors as well as some of the not-so-great colors you already have in your wardrobe.

With the minimal addition of a few items, you can give your old wardrobe a whole new lease on life. Suddenly, you can have a number of sharp, classy outfits to wear. And by continuing to experiment and combine the old as well as new items in your closet, you can eventually put together several more dynamite outfits.

This brings up an important point.

Unless your pre–color chart color choices are totally awry—which is seldom the case—you won't need to discard the contents of your closet and start afresh. Needless to say, that would be an incredibly expensive endeavor. Fortunately, there are certain "tricks" you can employ to make an item of clothing in an okay color look pretty terrific and to make a terrible color look, at the very least, okay. In Chapter 11 we will tell you how, by adding a few choice pieces to your wardrobe, you can extend the life of garments that may not be the optimum color for you.

However, for now let us assume you are assembling your capsule working wardrobe from scratch. Naturally, this is the ideal situation.

No matter what your color type, these are six fundamental rules to follow and in the order we're presenting them:

For the Color 1 Capsule Working Wardrobe:

• **Rule No. 1:** Purchase two solid-colored suits in colors that can be interchanged to make four suit looks. In lieu of suits, you can buy any four solid-colored pieces— two jackets, two skirts or slacks, or one of each—that interchange to make four suit looks.

Whether you select a skirted suit, a trouser suit, or one of each depends entirely on your preference. Take into consideration your occupation, your life-style, and what is deemed appropriate dress among your professional and social peers.

Suits are easier to work with if they are solid colors. But in choosing those solid colors, bear in mind that *when the suit pieces are worn together, they must always create your best level of contrast.*

In a more conservative capsule, the two suits would both be neutrals. If suits in colors are appropriate for your work or life style, one suit in a neutral and one in a color make a nice option.

Here are several examples of two solid suit colors that coordinate well: navy and camel, red and black, gray and camel, plum and navy, blue and beige, blue-green and purple, navy and gray, off-white and red.

You can also make one of your suit choices a tweed *provided* it works well with several solid colors.

Suit pieces in tweeds, patterns, and plaids are a possibility, but they make the mixing and matching of your capsule wardrobe pieces much more complicated. With patterned and plaid jackets, skirts, and pants in your capsule wardrobe, you must limit yourself to solid-colored blouses and tops in the colors that exist in the tweed pattern or plaid. Granted, there are ways to tie in an "outside" color, just as there are ways to mix patterns. But you must have a trained eye for color as well as a good sense of scale in order to pull it off.

Your capsule working wardrobe will last several seasons only if you choose suit pieces that are classic in style. Thus, you should avoid highly stylized jackets, very narrow or very wide lapels, very full skirts, slit skirts, or very wide-legged or very skinny-legged slacks. In short, avoid this season's fad.

There is a compromise position. You might select one suit in a less than classic style, knowing you'll get one, possibly two seasons' wear out of it, and the other suit in a classic style, expecting it to last several years. Remember, the suit pieces must be interchangeable; the style of the jackets must look great with the style of the skirts and slacks.

What suit fabrics do we recommend?

Depending on the climate in your region, you may need both a winter and a summer capsule. For women living in most parts of North America and Europe, we suggest suit fabrics of lightweight wool gabardine, wool crepe, or other lightweight wool blends that have the look of gabardine. These fabrics will work for most of you in all but the hottest months of the year.

If your climate is strictly warm going on hot, linen and silk, or blends of these with cotton and other fibers, are your best bet. But hot or cold, always choose suits in natural fibers such as wool, silk, cotton, and linen—or fabrics that are a blend of natural and manmade fibers.

Because you will be interchanging your suit pieces, the fabrics need to be alike or compatible. This is a matter of weight and texture as well as fiber. All different weights and textures of wools can be combined: wool flannel with wool crepe; wool gabardine with wool tweed, etc. In combining wool and silk, you must consider both weave and weight. For instance, a lightweight wool gabardine or wool crepe jacket can be worn over a silk garment, but heavier wools will not work. Silk and linen can be combined, as can linen and cotton, as well as the finest, dressiest cottons and silk.

- **Rule No. 2:** Acquire two neck accessories—scarves and/ or necklaces—that *match the color of your skirt and/or slacks.*

These neck accessories should, most often, be solid in color, and they must create the impression that you are repeating the skirt or slack color near your face.

- **Rule No. 3:** Your five tops must be in *colors complimentary to all your suit pieces.* These tops can be blouses, man-tailored shirts, or sweater tops. Make your style choices according to how formal or casual you want your wardrobe to be.

Your tops can be plain or patterned. But if a top is a print, it must contain the colors of your suit pieces. To make certain the patterned top has enough of your suit colors in it to look well coordinated, study the combination from a distance of five feet or more. If your suit colors are still apparent in the top, it is an excellent addition to your capsule.

Blouse fabric can be silk, cotton, linen, or blends of any natural and manmade fibers.

Tops made of 100 percent synthetic fibers are only an option if they look like a natural fabric. For instance, today many polyester blouses are an excellent imitation of silk. We must warn you, though, that 100 percent synthetic tops don't "breathe" the way natural fabrics do. For this reason alone, they are a poor choice for warm climates.

When choosing appropriate tops, style is the one final consideration. You've selected your suit pieces first. Choose your tops in *styles that compliment all your suit pieces.* In other words, if one of your suit jackets is very dressy-looking, don't include in your capsule wardrobe a strictly casual plaid blouse or casual sweater. Other tops to avoid are blouses with very full sleeves, very wide collars, and a super-abundance of ruffles.

- **Rule No. 4:** If the two suit pieces you are wearing are in two different colors—a navy skirt and a camel jacket is one example of this mixed suit look—a neck accessory in the color of the skirt is necessary to balance the outfit.

   In our example, a navy scarf or navy bead necklace would bring the bottom color (skirt or pants color) up to the top (your neck area), affording a visual balance to the whole outfit.
   On the other hand, a traditional solid-colored suit look where both the jacket and skirt or pants are the same color does not require a neck accessory to create balance. The suit itself is balanced because the same color appears both on the bottom and top half of your body. When you're wearing a matched suit, a neck accessory in the bottom color is optional as long as you keep your jacket on.

- **Rule No. 5:** In choosing shoe, belt, and purse colors for your capsule working wardrobe, you have several options: Match them either to your suit colors, your hair colors, or your skin tones. Generally you will want to use medium- and dark-toned shoes with medium- and dark-toned suits; light-, medium-, or dark-toned shoes with medium-toned suits; and medium- or light-toned shoes with light-toned suits.

- **Rule No. 6:** When you want to add clothing items to your capsule, keep this in mind: With the addition of just one skirt or pair of slacks, one blouse, and one neck accessory (in the color of the new skirt or slacks), you can create twenty-four more looks. Obviously, the additions must coordinate with the existing capsule pieces to make a total of fifty-four outfits. But even if the new pieces only coordinate with half of your existing capsule, you've still been incredibly efficient at wardrobe building.

To help you visualize the rules we've just laid out, we've compiled three suggested capsule working wardrobes for each of our color types in the charts below. Since you can combine nearly all of your best colors, these more conservative color combinations are merely to teach you the process of creating a capsule. Depending on your needs, you may prefer less conservative suit colors.

Capsule Wardrobes for Muted Color Types

Suggestion #1	Suggestion #2	Suggestion #3
2 Suits	**2 Suits**	**2 Suits**
Rust jacket and skirt	Brown jacket and pants	Gray jacket and skirt
Beige jacket and skirt	Camel jacket and skirt	Green jacket and skirt
5 Tops	**5 Tops**	**5 Tops**
Blue blouse	Beige blouse	Pink blouse
Green blouse	Red blouse	Gray blouse
Purple blouse	Coral blouse	Beige blouse
Gray blouse	Blue-green blouse	Yellow blouse
Peach, rust, and beige print blouse	Purple blouse	Green and Gray patterned blouse
2 Neck Accessories	**2 Neck Accessories**	**2 Neck Accessories**
Rust beads or scarf	Brown beads or scarf	Gray beads or scarf
Beige scarf or beads	Camel scarf or beads	Green scarf or beads
Shoes	**Shoes**	**Shoes**
Beige and rust	Brown and camel	Gray and hair color

The beige color mentioned in this chart should always match or be a lighter or darker version of your skin tone or, in the case of a light-haired Muted color type, your hair color. If you are a brunette, the brown color should match your main hair color; if you are light-haired, it will be a darker value of your hair color. All the colors mentioned must be in your best shades and clarities of colors.

Capsule Wardrobes for Gentle Color Types

Suggestion #1	Suggestion #2	Suggestion #3
2 Suits Navy jacket and skirt Medium gray jacket and skirt	**2 Suits** Beige jacket and pants Camel jacket and medium blue skirt	**2 Suits** Red jacket and skirt Off-white jacket and skirt
5 Tops Light gray blouse Soft coral blouse Beige, navy, and gray print blouse Green blouse Purple blouse	**5 Tops** Pink blouse Yellow blouse Brown blouse Blue, beige, and camel print blouse Off-white blouse	**5 Tops** Pink (i.e. a lighter shade of the suit's red) blouse Blue blouse Purple blouse Light gray blouse Blue-green blouse
2 Neck Accessories Navy beads or scarf Medium gray scarf or beads	**2 Neck Accessories** Beige beads or scarf Blue scarf or beads (match skirt color)	**2 Neck Accessories** Red beads or scarf Off-white scarf or beads
Shoes Navy and gray	**Shoes** Beige, camel, or your main hair color	**Shoes** Beige or off-white and red

The beige color mentioned in this chart should match or be a lighter or darker version of your skin tone or hair color. The camel should match either your skin tone or your hair color. All of the colors mentioned must be in your best shades and clarities of colors.

Capsule Wardrobes for Light-Bright Color Types

Suggestion #1	Suggestion #2	Suggestion #3
2 Suits	**2 Suits**	**2 Suits**
Light camel jacket and skirt	Medium-toned blue jacket and pants	Off-white jacket and skirt
Navy jacket and skirt	Beige jacket and light gray skirt	Light red jacket and skirt
5 Tops	**5 Tops**	**5 Tops**
Light coral blouse	Light yellow blouse	Light gray blouse
Light green blouse	Light raspberry blouse	Light blue blouse
Light gray blouse	Light coral blouse	Light yellow blouse
Off-white blouse	Blue-beige-gray patterned blouse	Off-white and red print blouse
Light purple blouse	White blouse	Light purple blouse
2 Neck Accessories	**2 Neck Accessories**	**2 Neck Accessories**
Navy beads or scarf	Blue beads or scarf	Off-white beads or scarf
Camel scarf or beads	Gray scarf or beads	Light red scarf or beads
Shoes	**Shoes**	**Shoes**
Navy and camel	Camel and gray	Off-white or light beige and red

The beige color mentioned in this chart should match or be lighter or darker version of your skin tone or, in the case of light-haired Light-Bright color types, your hair color. The camel color should match either your skin tone or hair color. All colors mentioned must be in your best shades and clarities of colors.

Capsule Wardrobes for Contrast Color Types

Suggestion #1	Suggestion #2	Suggestion #3
2 Suits Beige jacket and skirt Navy jacket and skirt	**2 Suits** Off-white jacket and skirt Brown jacket and blue-green pants	**2 Suits** Black jacket and skirt Red jacket and skirt
5 Tops Medium coral blouse Navy and beige patterned blouse Medium purple blouse Emerald green blouse Beige blouse with navy and red pinstripe	**5 Tops** Red blouse Medium purple blouse Off-white blouse Off-white, brown and blue-green print blouse Rust blouse	**5 Tops** White blouse Red blouse Medium blue-green blouse Light gray blouse Medium blue blouse
2 Neck Accessories Beige beads or scarf Navy scarf or beads	**2 Neck Accessories** Blue-green beads or scarf Off-white scarf or beads	**2 Neck Accessories** Black beads or scarf Red scarf or beads
Shoes Navy and beige	**Shoes** Brown and off-white (only wear off-white shoes when wearing either the off-white jacket or skirt)	**Shoes** Black and red

The beige color mentioned in this chart should match or be a lighter or darker version of your skin tone. If you're a brunette, the brown should match your hair color. All the colors mentioned must be in your best shades and clarities of colors.

Perhaps the most exciting thing about your capsule is that, by utilizing your best shades and clarities of colors combined in your best levels of contrast, you have built a wardrobe that is uniquely enhancing to *you*!

Alice—A Case Study

Alice is a petite woman with olive skin, a Contrast color type. She is a good example because she wanted a lot of help in putting together her ideal capsule working wardrobe.

Alice is a real estate agent who also sells cosmetics. It is important that she look her best at all times because both of her occupations are concerned with image.

Alice began to transform her look by changing the color of her hair, getting it closer to its original, very dark brown color.

To eliminate the gray, Alice had been coloring her hair a medium brown. The color was the wrong shade for her olive complexion. She changed it to a different shade, a flattering black-brown color. It looked terrific! The darker shade did not make Alice look hard or give her hair an artificial appearance because it was a very natural-looking shade for a woman with her coloring.

Next, Alice had to change some of her other wrong-headed notions. For years, she had been wearing small prints and accessories and avoiding strong contrast outfits. Why? Because she was petite and all the wardrobe books and magazine articles she read told her to. (Plate 36 illustrates this problem clearly.)

But using the Color 1 concept Alice learned she needed to do just the opposite. As a Contrast color type, Alice needs to wear clear colors and medium- to large-scale patterns and jewelry in order to look her best. In addition, she should wear strong and medium contrast color combinations.

Because Alice felt that all-one-color looks made her appear taller and slimmer, she learned to create her necessary level of contrast on the top half of her body near her face. How? By combining a matching dark jacket and skirt with a light or bright blouse rather than by combining a dark jacket and light skirt, or vice versa. Alice can wear her all-one-color looks in her best medium-toned bright colors. Plate 37 shows another way to create needed contrast near the face.

Alice can wear a contrasting jacket and skirt or slacks: (1) if the garments are styled right to create the long, lean illusion she seeks; and (2) if she wears skirts or slacks with a matching-colored blouse under that contrasting jacket. In the latter case, Alice must also keep that contrasting-colored jacket open at all times, allowing the matched bottom and top color to create a vertical line.

Then Alice wondered what to do about all the dainty jewelry she owned. She learned to wear several of her chains, bracelets, and rings together to create a stronger visual accent. Alice did go out and immediately buy one large shiny metal neck accessory as a psychological booster, however. It helped her set her course in a different direction for the future.

Creating a capsule work wardrobe for Alice was equally challenging. Alice had recently purchased two new suits. One was off-white and the other dark rust. Knowing what she now did about contrast levels, Alice was puzzled how to choose five tops that matched both suits and still created the right level of contrast for her. If she bought light-colored blouses in order to create a light–dark contrast with the rust suit, then those blouses created a blended light-on-light look when worn with the off-white suit.

By following the Color 1 rules, Alice learned that five tops that were medium values of bright colors would create good medium levels of contrast with both suits. Alice could also wear light or dark values of her best colors if she added the necessary accent to create her best level of contrast—for example, a black blouse with the rust suit and a medium to large necklace and matching earrings of turquoise, or a light gray blouse with the off-white suit and a medium- to large-scale print scarf sporting the colors off-white, light gray, and black. The end result was pleasing and enhancing to Alice's dramatic Contrast coloring.

The Color 1 Capsule Coat Wardrobe

Millions of women have had the experience. They get dressed up in an exciting outfit, their escort is enchanted with the effect, but just as they prepare to leave it happens. The coat these women are forced to wear because of the weather doesn't relate to their outfit in any way. Suddenly all that effort to look terrific seems ruined. How do these women feel? Probably not terrific.

Many women are confused about coats—how many to own in which colors and styles to cover all occasions and seasons. Fortunately, there is a way out of this dilemma. The capsule coat wardrobe calls for three coats in specified colors and suggested styles. It is designed for women with an active business as well as social life who live in climates that have four seasons.

There are three rules for putting together a capsule coat wardrobe:

- **Rule No. 1:** First and foremost, you need a raincoat or a lightweight all-weather coat. You must select this coat with the idea that it will be worn with daytime attire as well as with nonformal but dressy evening attire.

Since this coat will be a staple in your wardrobe, it should be as basic as possible. That means *a coat in a solid color whose style is neither too casual nor too formal but somewhere in between.* You must avoid any coat that has sporty-looking buttons, or a coat with sporty stitching, including stitching in a color that contrasts with the coat fabric, or a coat with tabs, epaulets, or large pockets, particularly flap pockets, or a coat in a sporty fabric such as a coarse poplin, a rubberized material, or denim, or a quilted, down-filled coat. None of these styles or fabrics passes muster as all-around coats suitable for many occasions, rain or shine.

What details should you look for in such a coat?

First of all, choose a go-with-everything color. Good choices are a beige that matches your skin tone, white, off-white, the dark neutrals on Your Color 1 Color Chart, or your main hair color or a prominent highlight hair color.

Next, select a smooth fabric that does not appear casual. Some possibilities are a waterproofed smooth or polished cotton, silk, or a lightweight leather or suede. Also take a look at some of the new natural fiber and synthetic blends. Many are quite handsome and fulfill the requirements for the all-purpose coat we are describing.

By all means consider the purchase of an all-weather coat with a zip-out lining *provided* it meets the other criteria we've given you. These coats are a godsend in climates with very cold winters and hot summers. Just make sure the lining is as plain as possible. Wild plaids, checks, stripes, or printed linings won't do because they signal that the coat is for casual wear only. Some dressy-looking reversible coats are also options.

Fit is very important in any coat that you may wear over a heavy sweater, blazer/jacket, or suit. In fact, we suggest you wear a suit on your shopping expedition so you can try the coat on over it. Make sure the coat sleeves and chest area are ample enough to accommodate the extra bulk of your suit jacket or a sweater. We can't tell you how many women follow our advice to the letter but forget this one vital requirement. They end up with a coat so tight around the top half of their body when they wear it over a suit that they could swear they were wearing a straightjacket instead of a versatile all-weather coat.

Finally, make sure the coat is long enough to cover the longest street-length dress or skirt you own. A mid-calf-length coat is an excellent choice. Should the fads and fashions dictate shorter hem lengths, our advice is *not* to shorten your coat. Coats are intended to last many seasons. If you shorten them, you'll only have to buy yourself a new coat when the hem lengths drop again—as they always do eventually. It is far better to wear a coat that's longer than your skirt than one that's even a smidgeon too short.

• *Rule No. 2:* The second coat in your wardrobe should be a woollen one. It's to be worn when it's too cool for a raincoat.

Your wool coat's style should be classic, and the color solid. In fact, all of the pros and cons concerning rain/all-weather coats—including our suggestions about color—apply here.

One of our recommended styles is a classic wrap-style coat with the self-fabric belt because it goes with everything with the exception of a formal evening dress. Other recommended styles are dressy-looking buttoned coats with matching-colored buttons. Most double-breasted coat styles are too sporty-looking to wear over dressy evening attire.

Even with wool coats, fabric remains an important consideration. After all, wool comes in a myriad of weights and textures. Definitely avoid sporty-looking wools like tweeds and herringbones. Instead, select something approximating a smooth, fine-textured wool, or maybe a cashmere or a mohair.

- *Rule No. 3:* Your third multipurpose outerwear garment should be a jacket. *A jacket made of fur, velvet, satin, silk, or a dressy wool* such as mohair or crepe are your best choices.

Since this jacket is the coat you will wear over long and short formal and semiformal evening attire, its style and fabric must be dressy. Depending on the jacket material and current fashion, your jacket might even work over suits, jeans, or slacks.

Again, opt for a solid color—a beige, white, off-white, one of the dark neutrals on Your Color 1 Color Chart, or your predominant hair color. If you are purchasing a fur jacket, you should keep in mind that solid-colored furs are dressier than multicolored furs. Good fur jacket colors are the white or light beige on your color chart, an off-white, black (if it's on your chart), or your exact hair color.

For more information on furs and the length of hairs that are best for you, consult the section on the subject in the wardrobe chapter devoted to your color type.

The length and fit of your jacket is crucial.

Your jacket should skim or hug the hip area. The jacket length that works best for most body types is one that stops halfway between the lower part of your buttocks and waist—mid-hip in other words. This is inches *above* the fullest part of your hips. A jacket this length gives a longer-legged look. In addition, it augments and enhances the lines of a variety of different skirt and dress lengths, even floor-length gowns.

Some of you will find that a jacket worn with a fairly short skirt can create a balance problem unless you are wearing boots or opaque or textured stockings, which add weight to the lower half of your body. With shorter skirts, check the balance carefully in a full-length mirror. If you look top-heavy, add visual weight to your bottom half or wear a lighter-looking jacket or a coat.

We are not precluding somewhat longer-length jackets for taller women. In a visual sense, just be careful not to cut yourself in half. Mid-calf-length furs are not as appropriate and don't look as balanced as a jacket when worn over floor-length evening wear. Jackets shorter than mid-hip length can be worn, but be careful. Most have a tendency to look boxy.

The Color 1 Capsule Casual Wardrobe

The capsule wardrobe concept is adaptable to any type of wardrobe to suit any life-style. For example, the same capsule wardrobe formula—$2+2+5=30$—applies equally well to a casual wardrobe. The principles are the same.

A casual capsule wardrobe might include:

- 2 jackets—a tweed blazer and a solid-colored sweater jacket
- 2 pants/skirts—corduroy, denim, wool, etc.
- 5 tops—blouses and sweaters

Two neck accessories, scarves or strands of beads in the color of the skirt/slacks, will add the necessary finishing touch and balance to the minimum of thirty different outfits you can create with these nine items of clothing. If you add one more bottom, one more top, and one more accessory (in the color of the bottom), believe it or not, they actually enable you to create twenty-four more outfits beyond the thirty you've already got!

Chapter 10

Color Charisma

Red is stimulating. Bright yellow is cheery. Blue is cool.

How many times have you heard people say these things? Such notions are so widespread they've become clichés.

But cliché or not, it's certainly accurate to say that color is a mood inducer. Psychologists have been studying this aspect of color for years. They've discovered that different colors can have a profound, physiological impact on people, to the point where they even affect people's behavior.

The effect generated by colors is often subliminal. In fact, it's generally so subliminal that, in most cases, a person neither comprehends nor realizes what's happening—that he or she is under the influence of such a seemingly innocuous intangible as color.

Without going into detail about the clinical discoveries made by color researchers, we want to acquaint you with some of the desirable effects you can create on others by the judicious use of color. We will teach you to think of color as a psychological weapon to use in your quest to achieve your career or personal objectives. After all, when you wear a certain color, either alone or coordinated with other colors in unusual and exciting ways, you are making a statement. We want to make sure you understand that statement—and all its ramifications.

Color—the Great Self-Motivator

Before we talk about the effect your clothing colors have on others, let's talk a little about the positive effect they can have on you.

Face it: The colors you wear affect your own mood at least as much as they do that of the observer. For this reason we say be kind to yourself. Dress in colors that please *you*, first and foremost, and, while you are pleasing yourself, you will present a very pleasing vision of yourself to others in the colors you've selected.

It is a truism that when a woman looks in the mirror in the morning and likes what she sees she automatically feels more confident and exudes that confidence in her behavior throughout the day.

One of our associates advises her clients to get up in the morning and ask themselves what color they want near their face that day. That means choosing a blouse, sweater, necklace, or scarf first. Once her clients decide that, the rest of their outfit falls into place. She says her clients feel good all day because they started out by focusing on the area of the body that's most crucial to all of us in our everyday dealings.

Color—Its Impact on Others

Every woman has goals she wants to achieve. To achieve those goals, she has to bring the right people around to her way of thinking. Color can help any woman succeed where otherwise she might fail.

Don't misunderstand us. It's unrealistic to depend too heavily on color to make all your dreams come true. We hope it goes without saying that it takes appreciably more than the right-colored dress or a closet full of dress-for-success suits to get your boss to recommend you for a promotion. How you do your job will have far more to do with the final outcome. Nevertheless, over a period of time your wardrobe and how you utilize color in your wardrobe do give your boss and your colleagues a powerful subliminal message about you. That message can either help or hinder you in your quest for advancement.

The important point here is that you must remain goal-oriented in choosing colors and planning your wardrobe. You must assemble a wardrobe that not only meets your long-term goals for success but makes allowances for any contradictory short-term goals as well. If that seems confusing, keep in mind that your short-term goals won't always parallel exactly your overarching long-term ones.

What do we mean by this? Take a case where you want to leave the strangers you meet at an important event with an impression of you that's totally at odds with the real you, for whatever the reason. If that's your goal, make sure you're fully aware of it and understand color well enough to deploy it to create the desired image.

Here's a series of examples:

Perhaps you want to go unnoticed for a day. Every woman has days when she'd like to transmogrify into the proverbial fly on the wall. On the other hand, she doesn't want to appear as an unattractive fly. Unfortunately, reducing yourself to nonentity size may be hard to do if you have a larger-than-life quality about you. But it can be done and color can help.

Just suppose you have a strong, assertive personality that serves you well in your occupation as a saleswoman. However, at a forthcoming luncheon meeting with a group of powerful, elderly male clients, your boss has warned you it may do your company great harm if you act like your usual garrulous, liberated self. Before the luncheon, your boss pleads with you to behave in a way that makes these men think you're simply "a nice lady," one who is soft and quietly intelligent.

Or suppose you're a celebrity and you want to travel incognito but without looking like a complete frump. Or maybe you're going to an intimate dinner party and you want to make sure you don't threaten or outshine your shy hostess, who also happens to be your best friend.

Indeed, dressing down while still looking good is an art that most women would do well to master. Here's how you do it:

If you are a Muted or Gentle color type, you can create a subtle, unobtrusive look by dressing in all one color head to toe. One of your best neutral colors with no second accent color near the face is your best camouflage. Select an outfit with a simple silhouette—no avant-garde styles, please—and wear little or no jewelry or other distinguishing accessories. Your shoes should be classic styles and neutral in tone.

Wear very natural-looking makeup—medium-toned lipstick, a touch of eye shadow, mascara, and blush, clear or soft-toned nail polish, and a classic hair style, nothing elaborate.

If you are a Light-Bright or Contrast color type, you can create an unobtrusive image by bending the rules for women with your coloring. Put together an outfit in your best colors, but combine them in such a way that they create a softer contrast than you would ordinarily wear. Blended looks, as you'll recall, are not your best level of contrast.

For women with Light-Bright or Contrast coloring, another option is to create a monotone look using one of the dark neutrals or light colors on Your Color 1 Color Chart—but don't choose white or black. Stark white and jet black are hardly forgettable colors on you. Do not add a second accent color to your monotone outfit or wear much jewelry.

The same makeup and hair style advice we gave Muted and Gentle color types applies to you. Keep it simple. Wear a slightly toned-down lip color and blush and less eye makeup.

By this time, you must see our point. In choosing the outfit you're going to wear for a particular event, decide up front the effect you want to have on others. Then be highly selective about the colors and color combinations you wear to achieve that effect.

Mood Dressing and Other Special Effects

We do not agree with those who claim that a woman's coloring dictates her personality type. The idea that coloring and personality bear any relation whatsoever to each other strikes us as utter nonsense.

A woman with Gentle coloring does not necessarily have an ethereal, romantic outlook on life. Nor is a woman with Muted coloring automatically some sort of earth mother. Contrast color types are not all exotic-looking women with dramatic, extroverted personalities. Nor are all those with Light-Bright coloring heaven-sent golden girls with halos around their heads.

There is some merit, however, in trying to create ethereal, earthy, or showstopper looks no matter what color type you are.

The Ethereal or Fragile Look

You might also call this a romantic look. It's a soft, ultra-feminine kind of beauty. (We've illustrated this in Plates 1–4.)

To create this effect, you must choose a garment in a style and fabric that connotes femininity. Ruffles, lace, and sheer, smooth, lightweight fabrics are ideal. Any pattern in the fabric must also further the cause of this starry-eyed romantic vision of loveliness you seek to become.

Here are the color rules to follow depending on your color type:

Muted. Several color combinations will help you evoke an utterly feminine softness. Combine your best off-white with one or several of your best pastels (e.g., off-white, light purple, and pink), or combine your best pastels with some other good medium-light values (e.g., light yellow and coral), or combine the same color in both a medium and light value (e.g., light blue-green and medium blue-green), which creates a duo-monotone look. No small patterns in these blended combinations, please. An all-one-color look in off-white, light beige, or one of your pastels can also create a "romantic" look.

Women with Muted and Muted/Contrast coloring may have to add a medium or dark accent—a belt, piece of jewelry, or scarf—to complete these rather light-looking outfits.

Gentle. Because of your natural coloring, this is the easiest effect in the world for you to create. You were born with a more softened, ethereal look to your coloring, even though you may belie that image every time you open your mouth.

For you, the look of romance is fostered by blended levels of contrast and all-one-color looks in your white, light beige, and pastels. For example, combine a light and medium-light value of one of your best colors, such as light blue and medium-light blue, to create a blended, duo-monotone look, or combine several of your light colors with different medium-light colors, such as yellow, medium-light purple, light pink, and a touch of pure white, or combine two or more of your best pastels, such as light green and light coral.

Light-Bright and Contrast. Because of their coloring, Light-Bright and Contrast color types must create at least a medium level of contrast with the following combinations. No blended looks, please:

Using your best colors, mix the light values of one color with the medium values of a different color, such as a clear light pink with a medium-value bright purple, or wear pure white with a medium-value bright color such as white and medium-value blue-green, or wear head-to-toe pure white, or a medium-value bright, such as a medium-value coral.

Light-haired Light-Bright color types may use the same color combinations listed for Gentle color types, but they must use their own best *clear* pastels and *clear* medium-light values.

Earthy Looks

People associate the word "earthy" with autumn. They're not far off since browns, camels, beiges, orange-corals, yellows, golds, greens, and rusts are the colors we recommend to summon up this effect. They also happen to be the colors of the falling leaves. Plums, purples, and teal blues are also shades that create this look, especially when you combine them with the "earthy" tones we just listed.

There is no one style associated with earthy looks. Casual knockaround clothes, tailored suits, high fashion outfits, even formal evening gowns can be given an autumnal ambiance by the studied use of "earth colors."

Besides the use of certain colors, there's something else about this look that's evocative of autumn: texture. Every color type can wear textured fabrics and jewelry effectively. Gentle and Light-Bright color types must simply avoid the coarsest, roughest textures. And those with Light-Bright and Contrast coloring must make sure their textured metals are not dull.

A fabulous "textured" fall look can be evoked by coordinating two or more patterns with each other in the same outfit. Be really daring and experiment with this pattern-on-pattern effect.

In addition, ethnic, antique, handcrafted, and primitive jewelry lend a nice finishing touch to any earthy style of dress.

Muted. You were born to this look by dint of your natural coloring. You wear texture exquisitely, and muted colors look lovely on you.

The different autumn looks you put together are limited only by your imagination. So combine your best browns, beiges, camels, corals, yellows, golds, greens, and rusts in any innovative way that suits your fancy. And don't overlook your plums, purples, and teals.

Gentle. You can simulate a fall look by creating soft and medium levels of contrast with various combinations of your best toned-down, even subdued shades of browns, corals, camels, beiges, yellows, greens, and rusts. Don't forget to add your best shades of plums, purples, and teal blues.

Light-Bright and Contrast. These color types can create earthy looks by using medium levels of contrast to assemble outfits that utilize their best shades of browns, clear corals, camels, beiges, clear yellows, clear greens, rusts, clear vibrant plums and purples and clear teal blues. Just be careful not to create blended looks. In short, avoid medium-dark and dark ensembles unless you add a light or bright accent. And remember that your best colors are *clear* colors.

As we've said earlier, the use of texture, pattern-on-pattern effects, as well as antique, ethnic, primitive, and handcrafted jewelry enhance this earthy image for all color types.

Showstopper Looks

What do we mean by a "showstopper look"? It's a look so striking yet tasteful that heads turn in admiration when you walk into a room.

Granted, not all women want the spotlight thrown on them in this way. The attention is too intense, or their ego is not sufficiently developed to handle all the ooohs and aaahs with grace and decorum. For many women, it's more comfortable to maintain a lower visibility level.

We should add that many a conservative employer won't appreciate this image either, especially if you're an up-and-coming executive at a staid, old investment banking house, for instance. On the other hand, if you're an up-and-coming promotion assistant at a major department store, your employer may love it.

It's up to you. If the notion of a Wow! image appeals to you, here's how you do it:

First of all, the showstopper look doesn't have to be a high fashion one. It can be created by combining classic clothing in unusual or strong mixes of color such as red and purple, blue-green and red, or any two medium tones of colors on your chart. (Attention Light-Bright color types: Either combine the medium-light values of your best colors or accent your best medium tones with a light color.)

Other types of showstopper outfits can be dazzling and incorporate the latest styles. If a certain type of jewelry or accessory is part of the "in" look, by all means wear that too—but make sure the jewelry is in the right scale and metal finish for a woman with your coloring.

Sometimes a high fashion style dictates a special makeup effect and a more contemporary hair style. If you're working to achieve that look, your makeup and hair must be altered accordingly. Otherwise, you'll appear to be playing "dress up." This does *not* mean you should ignore the makeup color rules we gave you in the chapters devoted to the subject earlier in this book.

Some high fashion styles are accompanied by specific colors. The "in" colors for an Art Deco clothing renaissance would certainly include an electric royal blue, for instance. A throwback to turn-of-the-century styles would dictate a plentiful use of mauve.

Many times the popular colors for a particular season seem to emerge by some mysterious and unspoken consensus among the better-known fashion designers. Usually, they're colors due for a comeback because they've been overlooked for several of the preceding seasons.

Because you can wear every color in the spectrum—provided, of course, they are in your best shades and clarities—you'll always be able to put together an outfit in your shades of the latest fashion colors. Fortunately, clothing designers and manufacturers make the current styles in that season's colors in a range of shades and clarities. Thus, you'll always find something you love that enhances you, too!

Just remember, *under no circumstances must you ever succumb to haute couture pressure to conform to unflattering colors.* Be resourceful and put together the latest fashion look in shades of color you wear well.

Muted. Since a showstopper look is an eye-catching one, you will want to wear the *medium* tones of colors on your chart in the brightest clarity you can handle. That means making sure that those brighter colors don't ever make you look washed-out or garish. Aim for unusual color combinations.

Some head-turning combinations for you might be:

a toned-down red suit worn with a toned-down bluish purple blouse and red beads

blue-green slacks worn with a coral sweater and capped off with a multicolored scarf of blue-green, coral, and yellow

red silk pants and a matching camisole worn with a yellow kimono jacket and yellow-amber chunky beads

a plum skirt, ruffled along the hemline, worn with a ruffled plum blouse and a turquoise and silver studded belt a silk medium-scale geometric-patterned dress in green, purple, rust, and cream with a necklace of soft gold metal and rust beads, a soft gold metal bracelet, and matching hoop earrings

Of course, all of the above colors will have a toned-down clarity.

Gentle. Showstopper combos for Gentle color types involve the strongest, boldest colors in *medium* values that you can wear. Just make sure any colors you choose aren't so strong they overpower your coloring.

What level of contrast underscores the look? For you, a medium level of contrast.

Try mixing and matching some of the following:

a purple suit with a green blouse and amethyst beads

coral slacks with a blue sweater and coral beads

blue-green silk slacks and camisole worn with a raspberry silk overshirt and raspberry-toned jewelry

a "la belle France" floral print dress with medium and light tones of blue, pink, yellow, and white

All of the above colors will have a toned-down clarity.

Light-Bright. Warning! You have delicate coloring that is easily overpowered by strong mixes of colors. So make certain you always add a *light* color when you create your showstopper *bright* looks.

To emulate that showstopper look, aim for more dramatic and unusual color combinations than you might ordinarily wear.

For you, there are two levels of contrast appropriate to the showstopper look: your strongest level of contrast as well as a medium level of contrast.

Experiment with combinations like these:

a clear medium-toned red suit worn with a clear light yellow blouse and a red beaded necklace twisted around a gold chain

clear medium-light green slacks coordinated with a clear medium-light coral sweater and a small- to medium-scale patterned scarf of coral, green, and white vibrant medium purple silk pants worn with a bright but light-looking pink tunic

a white dress with navy dots accessorized with a clear red belt, shoes, and earrings

Contrast. Since you must always create strong or medium levels of contrast with your best clear colors, you are wearing your showstopper looks anytime you wear unusual mixes of your strongest and brightest colors.

Here are a few suggestions:

a clear red suit worn with a vibrant purple blouse and shiny silver accessories

bright blue-green slacks and a sweater in your best hot pink, finished off with a turquoise necklace, bracelet, and earrings

vibrant yellow silk slacks and camisole coordinated with a vibrant blue silk jacket and vivid blue and gold beads worn with gold earrings

a dress of black and pure white in a bold design worn with bold black and white earrings.

Power Dressing

This is the look that says, "I'm a person of authority." It says several other things, too, such as "You can trust me implicitly. I'm a capable, well-educated, streetwise professional. Put me on your team and you'll never regret it."

You can attain this look by wearing your best dark and light neutrals together in the strongest appropriate level of contrast for your coloring. You may add touches of other colors if you like.

Over the last ten years, a lot has been written about this mode of dress for women. Much of it we couldn't disagree with more.

First of all, too many women have been brainwashed to equate career dressing with man-style dressing. This is not necessary. Business attire for ambitious women does not have to be severe or imitate men's clothing to be effective. In fact, in the right style and color, a dress can foster an authority image just as well as a tailored skirted suit look.

Moreover, the often-suggested "uniform" of a dark suit worn with stark white blouse creates too strong a level of contrast for more than half of you. In such a uniform, instead of looking powerful, you can end up looking weak and overwhelmed—as if your suit, not you, is the controlling factor in your look. (Photos 5.3, 5.4, 6.3, and 6.4 show just how this happens.)

But if suits are your preference, today you have many different suit styles to choose from, some of them quite feminine in terms of both their lines and fabric. This broad range of styles enables you to find suits in colors and neutrals that look superb on you and also fit any and all of your career dress requirements. (Plate 31 offers a good example.)

Fortunately, the mass entry of women into responsible jobs over the last decade has forced fashion designers to recast their thinking on the subject of suits and to create more dresses appropriate for career dressing. Thus, working women are no longer limited to the conservative tailored suit look.

If you haven't been wearing many dresses, we suggest you take a look at what's available. Give special consideration to dresses that can be worn with a jacket, blazer, or beautifully tailored cardigan sweater jacket. Just make sure they are well-made dresses in appropriate styles and handsome fabrics. (See Photo 6.2 and Plate 37.) For business wear, print dresses, particularly if the design has stronger contrast or is a bit busy-looking, may need a solid-colored jacket to mitigate the print's overall effect.

Are there certain colors associated with power dressing?

Unfortunately, there are. For men, they are the dark neutral colors of navy and medium to dark gray. For women, too, they are darker colors, but the range is somewhat wider. In addition to the two colors just mentioned, there are deep greens, burgundy, wine, deep plum, deep teal blue, browns, and black. Beige, camel, and lighter grays are also very businesslike colors, but because of their lighter value, you cannot create as strong a level of contrast. Therefore you get less of the so-called power look.

We are happy to report that such color stereotypes in business are gradually evaporating. Color 1 Associates is in the vanguard of forces leading the revolution in female professional dress. We're eager for the day when a tasteful, understated outfit *in any color that looks good on the wearer* is deemed appropriate business dress.

But to be realistic about it, that day hasn't arrived yet. That 180-degree turnabout we seek is still a few years off. So until the business color millennium is reached, here are the color rules for each color type. They will help you create the look of a woman with one foot already placed on the next step of the career ladder:

Muted. No navy suits with pure white blouses for you, please. This is far too strong a level of contrast for a woman with your Muted coloring.

But don't despair. If you want a dark–light powerful look, a light beige blouse worn with that same navy suit will create the same effect and look enhancing. You may also wear light gray or any of your pastels in blouses with any of your dark neutral suits. Experiment with a medium to dark gray suit worn with an off-white blouse or a navy suit worn with a light coral blouse. Such outfits represent the ideal way for a woman with Muted coloring to approximate a traditional power look. Also, dark-haired Muted color types can wear their dark brown with *their* white.

Maybe a less buttoned-down image is your goal. Then try mixing and matching the following muted colors in dresses and less tailored suits:

Wear the darkest toned-down clarities on your color chart—for example, dark blue, dark blue-green, or dark red—with your lightest neutrals (i.e., pale grays, beiges, and your whites). Or try various combinations utilizing the darker values of green, blue-green, plum, purple, wine, burgundy, rust, and brown coordinated with your best pastel shades.

For example, wear a silk print dress that has a subtle stripe or geometric pattern of blue and gray on a rust background. Add a blue jacket that matches the blue in the dress. Or how about combining a dark purple skirt with a medium gray jacket, an off-white blouse, and purple beads, or your darkest brown skirt with a camel blouse and a subtle coral, camel, and brown tweed jacket.

Gentle. Like Muted color types, you must avoid the strong contrast of black, navy, or dark brown combined with white. You can get that same "powerful" look, however, by combining your best dark neutrals with all of your other light neutrals and pastels. Because of your natural coloring, these combinations look as strong on you as black and white or navy and white look on a woman with Contrast or Light-Bright coloring.

For a high authority look, try wearing a dark gray suit with a light coral-pink or off-white blouse and gray pearls, or a navy suit coordinated with a pale beige or light blue blouse and a delicate gold chain and earrings.

For a businesslike but slightly less powerful look, combine your light neutrals in suits with the light, medium, or dark values of your colors, a light gray suit combined with a medium blue blouse, for example. Or wear your darker colors in suits with the light and medium tones of your neutrals, say, a dark plum suit worn with an off-white or camel blouse. Very dark-haired Gentle color types may combine their dark brown with their white.

Light-Bright and Contrast. Because strong levels of contrast are enhancing to them, women with Light-Bright and Contrast coloring have an easier time creating an authoritative appearance.

Any color combinations that create a dark–light effect are good. Try combining your best navy in a suit with a white blouse or a clear light pink blouse, or a black suit (if black appears on your chart) with a white, light beige, or light pearl gray blouse.

For a businesslike but slightly less high authority look, you might wear your darkest clear blue-green in a suit with several of your best clear pastels or light neutrals, or combine your dark gray with a clear medium shade of red (and, if you are a Light-Bright color type, accent the outfit with pearls), or try your best dark brown with your best clear light blue.

There is one distinction to be made between Light-Bright and Contrast color types. To look businesslike and influential, women with Light-Bright coloring should avoid mixing their dark colors and dark neutrals with their bright colors unless they add a significant amount of lightness to the outfit. Lighter-haired Light-Bright color types can wear light neutrals with clear light pastels or with other light neutrals, but Contrast color types need to add a bright or dark accent to such combinations, otherwise they are too soft or blended a level of contrast for their coloring.

A Final Note About Your Get-Ahead Wardrobe

We hope you understand that you must take your industry into account in deciding how to put together a career image. This is vitally important. An aspiring banker cannot be equated with a striving advertising copywriter or an ambitious dietitian for a major food company.

In 1982, *Savvy* magazine surveyed their readership on the subject of executive dress, emphasizing style, *not* color, in its questionnaire. The findings were reported in the March 1983 issue. The *Savvy* editors discovered that:

Women who work in the Northeastern United States are the most liberated fashionwise and consider a wider range of styles appropriate for business wear.

Women who work for manufacturing companies and financial institutions, surprisingly enough, feel less restrained about what they can wear than women who work in old-line, client-service industries such as the law.

To no one's surprise, women in the creative industries—advertising, publishing, and communications—feel the least constraints of all about their working wardrobe.

Do not conclude from these results that in the "creative industries" anything goes. Like their counterparts in the more conservative sectors of the economy, "creative women" also find that classic styles form the core of their wardrobes. It's just that they feel freer to wear more avant-garde color combos (as in Plate 45) and unusual accessories (see Photo 5.6) and to incorporate some of the high fashion looks that are in for one season and out the next.

Chapter 11

Color Budgeting

Now that you're almost at the end of this book, we've got a hunch about what you're thinking.

All this advice is terrific. For the first time, I know what clarities of color and levels of contrast to wear. I understand how to select prints, jewelry, and makeup colors that enhance my natural coloring. I know how to dress to create a desired effect.

"But," that inner voice of yours is wailing, "what am I supposed to do about all the costly mistakes in my closet and drawers? Dump them out and spend a mint replacing everything?"

No, that is not what you're supposed to do—unless, of course, you're an heiress or a self-made millionairess and can afford such extravagance. Most women are neither. So it is to the woman on a budget or the woman who simply abhors waste that this chapter is dedicated.

Wardrobe Errata

Over the years, we've noticed that our clients tend to fall into one of six general categories in terms of their pre–Color 1 wardrobe mistakes.

To help you assess your own wardrobe situation, we're going to describe these six universal garment collection goofs. As you read through the list, ask yourself, Which capsule profile sounds like me? Or other women I know?

The Conglomeration Collection

Women in this category are always complaining, "I have nothing to wear," despite their several closets filled with clothes. They're right. They don't have anything to wear—that is, nothing that coordinates into even one dynamite-looking outfit.

So what's in all those closets?

A thorough examination usually reveals a mish-mash of items in every style and color imaginable ("Isn't variety the spice of life?") and often several sizes as well ("Oh that! I bought it to wear when I lose ten pounds").

In those closets and drawers you'll also find clothes so dated that they remind you of Judy Garland in the 1954 remake of *A Star Is Born* ("Full skirts and crinolines have to come back sooner or later, don't they?"). Then there's the rag-bag notables with the broken zippers, missing buttons, grease spots, and cigarette holes ("Well, I just haven't had time to repair them yet").

Perhaps saddest of all are the clothes that bear no relationship whatsoever to the woman's life-style ("Who knows? I may turn into Cinderella and get invited to a fairy-tale ball someday. I can dream, can't I?").

Excuses aside, the conglomeration collection is a wardrobe with no balance, unity, or direction. Plowing through these closets to come up with just one passable outfit every day is an enormous waste of time and energy, not to mention the enormous waste of money the whole kit and caboodle represents.

Bargain Bare

Instead of amassing a closet full of mistakes for the reasons above, this woman is a slave to "a good buy." In choosing clothes, she has one prime motivation: to save money.

"I bought it on sale. Maybe it's not the greatest but at $10.98, how could I resist?"

Or . . .

"This blouse was marked down *five times*, and I know I'll be able to find just the perfect skirt for it!"

This woman's wardrobe is probably the worst hodge-podge you've come across since you left the environs of the conglomeration collector. A different cause, the same end results.

The Neutral Niche

Next to the conglomeration collector and the bargain hunter, who at least get some joy out of the sheer act of shopping and collecting, the woman who has backed herself into a neutral niche lives on short rations, indeed. She's afraid of color, afraid of making a mistake, afraid of attracting too much attention. Somewhere along the line she got it into her head that neutral colors are "more tasteful and expensive-looking." So she plays it safe by confining herself to these nonthreatening neutral shades she thinks "go with everything."

Regardless of her natural coloring, this woman's closet displays a tidy assortment of almost every neutral imaginable—off-whites, beiges, browns, taupes, grays, camels, navy, black, burgundy, wine, maybe even a rust piece here and there.

What she fails to realize is that the *wrong* shades of any color, including neutral colors, are not safe. They're simply not enhancing. The wrong shade of beige can sallow or gray a person's skin. The wrong shade of brown can make your hair look dull and drab and cast gruesome shadows on your face. The wrong shade of navy, or one that's too dark for your coloring, can give the illusion you've got dark circles under your eyes.

Another less obvious problem is that different shades of the same color cannot be combined. For example, you cannot wear a taupe-beige with a golden beige, a pink-beige with a golden camel, or a golden camel with a reddish brown. This means that many garments in the "neutral niche" cannot be worn together.

Whereas a journey through the first two closets gave you a headache, this one makes you want to curl up and go to sleep. Faced with such a closet, we sometimes wish we could just wave a magic wand and zap some color in between all those neutrals.

The Uniform Dresser

Some people are the visual equivalent of a broken record. Every time you see them, they are dressed in the same colors and style. The preppy look is one example.

Maybe you first hit upon this image in college and haven't changed it since. If that was ten or fifteen years ago, consider how dated you look. Or you simply don't care much about clothes and you've been too lazy to learn. Or you're afraid and don't know how to go about developing other styles. Or you think—accurately or inaccurately—that your singular look is the only acceptable one at your place of work or for your life-style.

We hope this book will give you the knowledge and courage to add a little more variety to your wardrobe, to create some of those special effects we talked about in the previous chapter.

Think of your wardrobe as a medium of expression. Not only do clothes serve the practical purpose of covering your body, they're also a kind of resumé that tells other people who you are—where you are coming from and where you are headed. Viewed that way, ask yourself: "Am I really as one-dimensional as my wardrobe suggests?"

The Headless Person

Remember the headless horseman who scared Ichabod Crane out of his wits in *The Legend of Sleepy Hollow*? Well, if you're inadvertently affecting this look, your clothing could be giving people a real jolt too.

Washington Irving's headless horseman wore black.

You, on the other hand, wear a rainbow of glorious colors, all of them too clear and bright to suit your natural coloring. You appear "headless" in your clothes because, when people look at you, all your outfits have a more pronounced visual impact than your soft or toned-down natural coloring. People keep scanning your attire when they should be looking at your face and listening to what you're saying. (Plates 27, 30, and 40 illustrate this best.)

Now don't misunderstand us. The bright colors you wear might look great on a different color type. But on you they're simply overpowering. Not only are your wardrobe colors too bright, you also may be combining them in a way that creates too strong a level of contrast.

You guessed it. Women with Gentle and Muted coloring are the typical offenders here. But a Light–Bright color type, too, could be at fault if she tends to wear dark colors with bright colors two overly bright colors together, or two dark colors together.

What about Contrast color types?

It would be hard for them to err in this direction unless they consistently wear shades of colors that are far more intense or glowing than those on their color charts. Or if they wear bright clarities that are not in their best shades.

Ms. Insignificant

This is the opposite mistake from the one being made by the headless person. This woman has assembled a wardrobe guaranteed to make her the most forgettable character anybody ever met.

Why? Because the colors and contrast levels she wears are too toned-down, muted, or blended-looking for her natural coloring. (Study Plates 36 and 38 to see what we mean.)

Any woman, regardless of her color type, could fall prey to this offense. Contrast and Light–Bright color types will look insignificant, washed-out, even "mousey," if they wear blended looks and clarities that are more toned-down than those on their color charts. Gentle and Muted color types will look this way if they dress in colors that are far more subdued than their best toned-down clarities.

Salvaging Some of the Clothes You Already Own

Notice we used the word "some."

If you own an item of clothing in a color that's "just okay" for you—not great, but not bad either—we don't expect you to throw it out just because your color consciousness has been raised. Not at all. Read on, for we're about to explain how to make this middling color look almost terrific. Utilizing our *trompe l'oeil* effect called a "color break," you can keep wearing all the clothes in this category until they are ready to be discarded through the normal process of attrition.

On the other hand, if you own garments in shades or clarities of color that are diametrically opposed to those you should be wearing, those items will have to be weeded out of your closet immediately. The sooner the better.

For example, suppose you're a Muted color type and hanging in your closet is an intense lemon yellow dress that makes you look washed-out and ill every time you've tried to wear it. The color is beautiful, though. You love it!

Forget the beautiful color. It's not right for you, that's all. Unfortunately, there's no way we know of to make a color like that look even remotely acceptable on you. In all likelihood, you haven't been wearing that dress much anyway because "There's always been *something* about that dress. . . ."

Sorry, the dress—and anything else in such disaster shades for your personal coloring—has got to go. With luck there won't be too many garments in this extreme category in your wardrobe.

Deploying the "Color Break" as a Salvage Tool

A "color break" is a blouse, sweater, other type of top, or neck accessory in a shade that looks gorgeous on you.

This gorgeously colored garment also happens to coordinate well—and in the right level of contrast—with the not-so-great color of the garment you are trying to rescue.

The principle of the color break is this:

Since the face is the predominant area of focus on the body, it's imperative that you wear enhancing colors near your face. If you do, people will notice how radiant the color break garment makes you look and take less notice of the rest of your outfit.

For instance, suppose you own a beautiful cashmere sweater in a shade that is too somber for you. Don't despair. There's no reason why you can't continue to wear that luxurious cashmere *provided* you accessorize it with a color near your face that looks terrific on you. In Plate 33, Jeanne is wearing a dress that is not flattering to her Light-Bright coloring; additionally, her makeup is too browned and too strong. The addition of a scarf (solid color or patterned) in her best colors, as well as a change of makeup, would create a much more becoming look. If your color break takes the form of a patterned scarf, the scarf must contain the less than perfect color, admittedly, but its predominant colors should make your eyes sparkle and your complexion glow. If you can wear the sweater over a blouse, the collar of the blouse becomes the color break. At the very least, a strand of beads in an enhancing color must be worn.

On the other hand, suppose the garment you are trying to save is a suit, skirt, or pair of slacks. Then a correctly colored blouse or sweater will do the trick. If it's a blouse or sweater (crew or V-neck) that's at fault, be innovative. Wear a jacket, another blouse, or a cardigan sweater as your color break, and perhaps add a scarf or a handsome, eye-catching piece of jewelry.

If your problem presents itself in the form of a turtleneck or cowl sweater, frankly, rescue attempts may be difficult. High-necked garments are the hardest to "save." But here's a suggestion: Try rolling the necks down so they are as small and as far away from your face as possible; then wear a wonderful scarf or piece of jewelry as close to your face as possible. Or try tying the scarf around the turtleneck and covering it completely.

In deciding how to deploy a color break, always bear in mind its purpose: to deflect attention away from the blah or harmful colors you're wearing and throw the spotlight where it belongs—on your face.

Not every garment or outfit that needs help to make it work needs a color break—some just need a *color accent* to bring up the level of contrast. In Plate 36, for example, there is no offending color involved, just too soft a contrast level for Jennifer's Contrast coloring. If she added red accessories and a touch more makeup, the dress would look much more flattering. To bring up the level of contrast illustrated in Plate 38, Betty could add a neck accessory in the strongest color that appears in her print blouse—the purple.

The Cost of Your Wardrobe Salvage Operation

It shouldn't cost you much provided your pre–Color 1 wardrobe isn't too far off course.

What you should spend your money on first are color-perfect lipsticks, blush, foundation, and eye makeup and color break and color accent garments—blouses and other tops, scarves and necklaces that look expensive and are as visually arresting as possible. When you choose those color break clothing items, remember that seizing the viewer's attention is the whole idea of a color break.

Before you know it, the not-so-great colors in your closet will gradually begin to wear out. The minute they do, you can replace them with color-perfect garments that, we predict, will bring you more pleasure than you ever could imagine!

Shopping with a Color Chart

At first blush, you might feel that shopping for specific shades of colors in a specific clarity will take more time. Just the opposite is true. Once your eye gets attuned to your best colors, you can stand in the middle of a boutique or a section of a department store and note whether your colors are hanging on the racks. If they aren't, you can check another department or store. Unless you are an inveterate browser, there's no sane reason for you to bother sorting through the garments on those racks, none of which contain your colors—especially since you may find yourself tempted by an item in a smashing style but the wrong color for you.

After you've been collecting clothes in your best colors for a while, you'll discover something wonderful. All your new purchases will coordinate with the things back home in your closet because they're in your best colors, too. That's one of the life-saving aspects of the Color 1 Associates concept: *Nearly all your best colors coordinate with each other in some exciting way.*

You'll also discover you can afford to purchase more expensive clothing, if you have the desire, because (1) you know the color is ideal for you; and (2) you won't need as many individual items of clothing because nearly everything you own mixes and matches, creating the loveliest-looking outfits you've ever worn.

If you don't believe us, start counting the number of daily compliments you get wearing *your* best makeup colors with *your* best clothing colors.

Glossary

BLACKING OUT—A color is said to be "blacking out" when it is so dark in value that it looks almost black against the skin. For example, an extremely dark purple that is blacking out will no longer look purple but like a purple-toned black. Each individual has her own level at which a color will start to black out.

BODY COLORING—Those colors that exist on the body: the natural color of the skin, hair, and eyes as well as the red color of the lips, palms, and fingertips. See *complimentary colors*

CLARITY—A color's brightness, on a scale from very bright to extremely subdued. Each color shade and color value (see *shade* and *value*) can come in the full range of clarities. The same shade of red, for example, could be bright on the one extreme or subdued at the other. Color 1 divides clarity into four categories: *intense, bright, toned-down,* and *subdued.*

CLARITY, BRIGHT—A color that contains a fairly strong saturation of pigment with a little white added. The touch of white lightens the color just a bit, taking the edge off its glowing intensity, yet keeping the color bright.

CLARITY, INTENSE—A color that is strong and electric-looking because it, of all the clarities, has the greatest saturation of pigment. It is the most vivid, powerful clarity.

CLARITY, SUBDUED—A color that appears quiet-looking because it has an obvious gray or brown pigment added to it. Next to a color that is toned-down, a subdued color has a dusty overlay and looks far more muted.

CLARITY, TONED-DOWN—A color that has a slight softness to its clarity. Such a color may have a touch of brown or gray pigment in it to create this softening effect.

COLOR ACCENT—A touch of color worn near the face or at the waist—a scarf, tie, necklace, pin, earrings, blouse, shirt, sweater, or jacket. This item of color is used to brighten, lighten, create contrast, or otherwise balance a person's outfit.

COLOR BREAK—A *necessary* color accent worn near the face. Its purpose is to keep an unflattering color from appearing right next to the skin. For example, a woman who wears a suit in a color that's less than enhancing for her would add a color break in the form of a blouse. To act as a color break, the blouse must be in a color that is ideal for her. In another instance, a sweater in an unflattering color requires a color break. In this case, it might be a scarf, tie, necklace, or jacket in a good color.

COLOR FAMILY—Light, medium, and dark values of the same shade of a color.

COLOR TYPE—A Color 1 category, based on a person's skin and hair colors and most enhancing levels of contrast in color combinations.

COMPLIMENTARY COLORS—All of the shades of colors, other than a person's body colors, that are most enhancing to her, and complete her personal color spectrum. The shades are always in the best clarity for that individual. See *body coloring*

CONTRAST, LEVEL OF—Color combinations that create one of three effects: *soft (or blended) contrast; medium contrast;* or *strong contrast.*

CONTRAST, MEDIUM—A combination of colors that is neither severely contrasting nor extremely blended-looking. The visual effect is one of moderation. Examples are a medium blue worn with cream, or red worn with navy.

CONTRAST, SOFT (or BLENDED)—A combination of colors that gives the impression the colors are running together, as when the colors are: (1) all close in the color spectrum, such as blue and blue-green; (2) all light values, such as beige, light pink, and light gray; or (3) all from the same color family, such as a light value of periwinkle blue worn with a medium value of the same periwinkle blue.

CONTRAST, STRONG—A combination of colors that creates the strongest contrasting visual effect: black and white, navy and white, and dark brown and white. All other color combinations create either medium or soft contrast.

OVERPOWERING—An adjective used to describe colors —or color combinations—that are too bright or strong for a person's coloring. For instance, if a person is wearing too strong a level of contrast, her clothing will visually "overpower" her. See *underpowering*.

SHADE—Every color and every neutral comes in many different shades, e.g., rose red, fire-engine red, and brick red; kelly green, lime green, emerald green, moss green, and sea green; golden brown, red-brown, chocolate brown, and ash brown.

UNDERPOWERING (or DULL, DRAB)—Adjectives used to describe colors—or color combinations—that are too toned-down for a person's coloring. If a person is wearing too soft a level of contrast, for example, her outfit could be said to look "underpowering." Such an outfit will make her look dull and drab. See *overpowering*.

VALUE—Value refers to a color's darkness or lightness. The lightest values of a color are often called pastels. The deepest values are termed dark colors. Those in between are medium-value colors.

WHITE, PURE—The brightest, starkest white there is. It is sometimes referred to as a "bright white" or "blue-white."

WHITE, "YOUR"—The shade of white that looks like white on you. It is not so white that it appears to "jump off" your skin, or so off-white that it looks like a cream color.

Color 1 Associates in the United States and Abroad

This list represents all the Color 1 associates trained through September 1985. The list grows every two months as another group of men and women leave the Color 1 Associates training program to begin color-charting in their area.

If you do not find an associate listed for your area, you may contact either Color 1 Associates' corporate headquarters in Southern California or our Eastern office in Washington, D.C.:

Color 1 Associates
3176 Pullman Street, Suite 122
Costa Mesa, CA 92626
(714) 545-4517

Color 1 Associates
2211 Washington Circle
Washington, D.C. 20037
(202) 293-9175

Asterisk indicates larger city nearby.

Alabama

Joyce Edwards, Enterprise
(205) 347-2529
*Dothan
Sarah Haynie, Birmingham
(205) 870-1624
Noretta Jones, Mobile
(205) 476-0457
Suzanne Kloess, Tuscaloosa
(205) 556-1579
Rosemary McKenzie, Selma
(205) 872-9477
Ali Padlo, Montgomery
(205) 264-0463
Darlene Real, Birmingham
(205) 823-3607
Yolanda Trahan, Birmingham
(205) 823-3666
Betty Wyatt, Decatur
(205) 350-4208
*Huntsville

Alaska

Jolene Larson, Anchorage
(907) 337-7944
Pamela Libby, Anchorage
(907) 338-3358

Arizona

Pamela McNair, Tucson
(602) 299-4661
Marilyn Butler Subach, Phoenix
(602) 992-7441

Arkansas

Donna Bradshaw, Hamburg
(501) 835-5421
Sudie Henderson, Fayetteville
(501) 443-0599
Kay McKoy, Little Rock
(501) 664-2094
Elizabeth Moffett, Fort Smith
(918) 427-5366
Mary Frances Stonecipher,
Hot Springs
(501) 624-2194
*Little Rock
Linda Sulcer, Marion
(501) 739-3556

California (Northern)

Myrt Arthur, San Mateo
(415) 349-8409
Betty Banner, Gilroy
(408) 842-2236
Sharon Bird, San Francisco
(415) 585-8478

Usha Burns, Belvedere
(415) 435-4720
*San Francisco
Susan Conrardy, Santa Rosa
(707) 578-5415
JoAnn Grose, Tiburon
(415) 435-3899
*San Francisco
Kathy Hasley, Gilroy
(408) 847-1517
Jennifer Ho, San Francisco
(415) 349-8409/342-3797
Kathryn Jones, Sacramento
(916) 924-1252/447-8677
Meredith Ketscher, Waterford
(209) 874-1591
*Modesto
Chris Lynch, Mill Valley
(415) 383-0521
Julie Midili, Kentfield
(415) 461-3750
*San Francisco
Sheri Pfitzer, Los Banos
(209) 826-1130
*Fresno
Jacqueline Pidge, Pacifica
(415) 355-7858
*San Francisco
Rosanne Polidora, Davis
(916) 753-7331
Lynne Reinhardt, Redding
(916) 221-2942
Tamara Shaff, Palo Alto
(415) 424-1120

Rosemary Snider, Pacific Grove
(408) 649-4537
*Monterey
Elizabeth Soblin,
Castro Valley
(415) 886-0970
*Oakland

California (Southern)

Carol Benton, Ridgecrest
(619) 375-8550
Dolly Boyd, Calabasas
(818) 880-5793
*Woodland Hills
Jamie Byrne, El Toro
(714) 859-3262
Susan Corbett, Laguna Niguel
(714) 495-6565
Ginger Crallé, Laguna Beach
(714) 494-8978/499-3795
Barbara Dellinger,
Palm Springs
(619) 323-7739
Penny Eversole, Lake Forest
(714) 768-4150
*Irvine
Joanne Franklin, Ramona
(619) 789-2518
Karen Frazier,
Carbon Canyon
(714) 528-5155
Mary Gadway, Riverside
(714) 781-6468
Evelyn Georghiou, Ventura
(805) 643-2822
Vicki Goodman,
Santa Monica
(213) 393-8564
Nancy Harrer, Bakersfield
(805) 323-5562
Vembra Esra Holnagel,
Long Beach
(213) 438-5857
Marjorie Howe, San Diego
(619) 460-1438
Susan King, Northridge
(818) 885-9957/886-8887
*Los Angeles
Betil Kunzler, Whittier
(213) 693-7424
Lona Larsen, Westchester
(213) 645-4469
*Los Angeles
Judy Lewis-Crum,
Corona del Mar
(714) 545-4517/640-0317
Janet McCann, Santa Barbara
(805) 966-9785
Helene Mills, Santa Monica
(213) 394-2282

Marjorie Mitchiner, Arcadia
(818) 447-4970
*Los Angeles
Ellen Nichols, Glendale
(818) 248-7296
Julie Nyquist, South Pasadena
(818) 799-3468
*Los Angeles
Melanie Pankow, Sherman Oaks
(818) 501-0677
*Los Angeles
Regina McMahon Purtzer, Redlands
(714) 792-0488
Lisa Rakers, Harbor City
(213) 539-5871
Ruth Richter, Montrose
(818) 957-0024
Jeanne Schoenfeld, La Jolla
(619) 456-2688
Patti Sparks, Newport Beach
(714) 545-4517
Jill Sprengel, Torrance
(213) 373-8048
Beverly Stephens, Pasadena
(818) 792-2656
Peggy Szameitat, Riverside
(714) 369-0372
Catherine Tastor-Little, Roseville
(916) 791-2757
Suzanne Terry, Bel-Air
(213) 472-3487
*Los Angeles
Bonnie Thornburg, De Garcia, Brea
(714) 956-5747
*Anaheim
Pat Weaver, Marina del Rey
(213) 306-2396
Edee Wolfenberger, Santa Ana
(714) 662-2348
Marie Wright, Santa Barbara
(805) 966-2417

Colorado

Cassie Andrews, Durango
(303) 247-0750
Ann Crawford, Denver
(303) 333-9111
Katherine Frost, Denver
(303) 778-1045
Gail Ann Jones, Littleton
(303) 973-8331
Mary V. Lawson, Aurora
(303) 699-7002
Merdith McBride, Durango
(303) 247-3211
Edie Pepper, Englewood
(303) 758-5375/2920
*Denver
LuAnn Schell, Steamboat Springs
(303) 879-4091

Marietta Smit, Littleton
(303) 797-3881
Janet Thornton, Ft. Collins
(303) 493-7309
Persis Wood, Colorado Springs
(303) 635-8091

Connecticut

Else Chapman, Wilton
(203) 762-0780
*Bridgeport
Stephanie Hall, Darien
(203) 655-0340
*Stamford
Martha Roberts, Andover
(203) 742-8904
Gayle Tainter, Fairfield
(203) 259-3508
*Bridgeport

Delaware

Marcia Loschiavo, Wilmington
(302) 478-0523
M. Lorraine Nelson, Wilmington
(302) 652-3580

Florida

Sidney Radinger Bayne, Clearwater
(813) 726-0386
*Tampa
Marlene Culler, Tequesta
(305) 746-0506
*West Palm Beach
Barbara Decker, Boca Raton
(305) 391-7760
Ava Fluty, Ft. Myers
(813) 936-6500
Dorothy Foley, Indialantic
(305) 723-6634
*Melbourne
Mattie Fraser, Jacksonville
(904) 751-0500
Sandra Galloway, Plantation
(305) 472-9585
*Keys
Gloria Gant, Tallahassee
(904) 386-5957
Dwan Green, Longwood
(305) 862-8524
*Orlando
Sonya Griffin, Ocala
(904) 237-3011
Nancy Loose, Shalimar
(904) 651-8289
*Ft. Walton Beach
Nancy Marin, Palm City
(305) 283-4550

*Ft. Pierce
Paula Miller, Plantation
(305) 472-2338
*Keys
Michele Mingoia, Orlando
(305) 876-4758
Mabel Jean Morrison, Laurel Hill
(904) 652-4519
*Ft. Walton Beach
Linda Pate, Pensacola
(904) 476-5129
Donna Patrick, Sanford
(305) 321-0872
*Orlando
LuAnn Powers, Longwood
(305) 788-0324
*Orlando
Malvarie Severance,
Lake City
(904) 752-3822
Ellen Todd, Ft. Walton Beach
(904) 243-1881
Susan Votaw, Ft. Myers
(813) 955-5531
*Sarasota
W. O. Whittle, Winter Haven
(813) 324-4936
Mary Zimmerman,
Jacksonville
(904) 739-3332

Georgia

Jane Avera, Thomaston
(404) 467-9402
Pamela Elkins, Valdosta
(912) 244-3775
Dot Nixon, Macon
(912) 474-9527
Diane Schultz, Atlanta
(404) 458-2838
Evelyn Thompson, Smyrna
(404) 436-2883
*Atlanta

Hawaii

Greta Jones, Honolulu
(808) 422-6175

Idaho

Mavis Hagberg, Boise
(208) 376-7848

Illinois

Debra Blackman, Naperville
(312) 355-6781

Jean Blazekovich, Lockport
(815) 838-7977
*Joliet
Barbara Disse, Crystal Lake
(815) 459-0144
Jane Hinze, Rock Island
(309) 788-1488/5479
Marilyn Tyler Hughes,
Western Springs
(312) 246-7918
*Chicago
Jerene Pankow, Park Ridge
(312) 692-7275
Melanie Pankow, Chicago
(312) 698-1111
June Woodcock, Manhattan
(815) 478-3709
*Joliet

Indiana

Cindy Baum, Wakarusa
(219) 862-4424
Sherry Boram, Pendleton
(317) 778-2745
*Indianapolis
Lolita Crouse, Greenwood
(317) 882-9772
*Indianapolis
Dorothy Garber, Greenwood
(317) 881-8992
*Indianapolis
Judee Gartland, La Porte
(219) 324-2305
Jenene Goodfellow,
Indianapolis
(317) 257-9090
Carolyn Lahrman, Ft. Wayne
(219) 432-5087

Iowa

Nancy Baker, Spirit Lake
(712) 336-3392
Jane Bauer, Marshalltown
(515) 753-3126
*Des Moines
Marcia Buising, West Des Moines
(515) 225-2187
Peggy Fergeman, Waterloo
(319) 233-7599
Marcia Lippold, Des Moines
(515) 255-2315
Rebecca McDowell, Fairfield
(515) 472-8276
Marilyn McGrew,
West Des Moines
(515) 225-8966
Deborah Otto, Dubuque
(319) 556-7807

Sherrie Rossiter, Sioux City
(712) 276-2055
Della Staples, Shenandoah
(712) 246-3244
*S.W. Iowa
Jan Swinton, Iowa City
(319) 351-2832

Kansas

Mary Athey, Overland Park
(913) 381-4945
*Kansas City
Sara Curran, Shawnee Mission
(913) 831-2265
Mary Ann McDonald, Wichita
(316) 685-3113
Jeannine Shadwick, Salina
(913) 827-6761
Ginny Sloo, Salina
(913) 825-6523

Kentucky

Teri Cruse, Lexington
(606) 277-4289
Marna Zalla, Burlington
(606) 586-7168
*Cincinnati

Louisiana

Trudy Breithaupt, Shreveport
(318) 868-6333
Carolyn Caillouet, Opelousas
(318) 942-5723
*Lafayette
Faye Guidry, Baton Rouge
(504) 766-4858
Charlotte Haslam, New Orleans
(504) 282-1038
JoAnn Hebert, Houma
(504) 872-6255
*S.E. Louisiana
Mary Ann Janss, Slidell
(504) 641-9639
Sherry Landry, New Iberia
(318) 369-3777
*Lafayette
Nancy W. Morrison, Shreveport
(318) 868-2163
Candy Nichols, DeRidder
(318) 463-8878
Debra Norton, New Orleans
(504) 891-4330
Ali Padlo, New Orleans
(504) 288-7237

Maine

Tilly Atkins, Hampden
(207) 862-3614
*Bangor
Lindley Harmon, Hancock
(207) 422-3084

Maryland

Marcia Behlert, Baltimore
(301) 296-0239
Dee Bibeau, Annapolis
(301) 268-0020
Lynne Lashlee, Laurel
(301) 776-1549
(202) 576-3345/3133
Tina Saddler, Easton
(301) 822-6440
Lissa Townsend, Severna Park
(301) 544-1524

Massachusetts

Susan DeSanna, Northampton
(413) 586-2622
Barbara Doty, Barnstable
(617) 362-9666
Lucinda Goldhill, Boston
(617) 723-6165
Marcia Mee Lee, Newtonville
(617) 965-3785
*Boston
Barrie Miller, Weston
(617) 891-8294
*Boston
Judith Shea, North Andover
(617) 683-5599
*Lawrence

Michigan

Marjorie Andreae, Pt. Huron
(313) 385-4631
Ilene Berger, Milford
(313) 685-8519
Barbara Bogart, Delton
(616) 721-8880
Irene Bushaw, Ann Arbor
(313) 761-2210
Sue Forrest, Midland
(517) 839-0269
*Saginaw
Tina Franco, Birmingham
(313) 649-3828
*Detroit
Sandra Lowden,
Grosse Pointe Park
(313) 886-0169

*Detroit
Jode MacMartin, Sawyer
(616) 469-0580
*S.W. Michigan
Lynn Meagher Pettyjohn,
Traverse City
(616) 941-4468

Minnesota

Kathie Behrens, Marietta
(612) 668-2556
Marlene Breu, Duluth
(218) 722-0619
Patricia Falls, Minneapolis
(612) 922-1044
Leslie Hilliard, St. Paul
(612) 698-7966
Susan Jacobsen, Minneapolis
(612) 938-9141
Sheila Lapp, Bemidji
(218) 751-1964
Rae Morgan, Maple Grove
(612) 425-7275
*Minneapolis
Joanne Reinertson, Chanhassen
(612) 474-5769
*Minneapolis
Patricia Shough, Bemidji
(218) 751-8841/8716
Pat Tarara, St. Paul
(612) 293-1637

Mississippi

Mary Ann Frugě, Oxford
(601) 234-6357
Anne Kellum, Ridgeland
(601) 856-4301
*Jackson
Maxine Sanders, Jackson
(601) 922-2413

Missouri

LuAnn White Ellis, Seneca
(417) 776-8357
Carol Henry, Richmond
(816) 776-6366
Colleen Kliethermes, Columbia
(314) 449-0473
Martha Wilson, Hazelwood
(314) 739-6724
*St. Louis
Mary Ellen Worlledge, Clayton
(314) 725-3972

Montana

Carla Dean, Billings
(406) 656-0539

Miriam Underwood, Billings
(406) 252-5826

Nebraska

Susan Olsen, Omaha
(402) 493-6598
Lynda Pepin, Omaha
(402) 734-1172

Nevada

Vernell Cocanour,
Carson City
(702) 882-3808/246-3569
Jana Leavitt, Las Vegas
(702) 452-4918
Janie Wilson, Reno
(702) 827-6354

New Jersey

Elaine Arpin, Robbinsville
(609) 259-3458
Elaine Brower, Pennington
(609) 737-9467
*Trenton
Sandra Criscuolo,
West Orange
(201) 736-1705
*Newark
Thelma Gold, South Orange
(201) 762-1237
*Newark
Ruth Mechur, Ft. Lee
(201) 592-0352
Marilyn Scherfen, Atlantic Highlands
(201) 291-3779
Jaquelin Schluter, Rumson
(201) 842-4120
Martha Weinstein, Parsippany
(201) 335-7081
*Morristown

New Mexico

Peggy Balcomb, Albuquerque
(505) 344-7867
Carla Beasley, Alto
(505) 336-4352
Judi Lujan, Las Cruces
(505) 522-8476
Lesley Tucker, Albuquerque
(505) 821-1144

New York

Sonya Bonnett, Baldwinsville
(315) 638-8431
*Syracuse
Susan Demme, Orchard Park
(716) 674-5013
*Buffalo
Joyce Grillo, New York
(212) 686-6484
Kathy Halbower, New York
(212) 254-2151
Anne Runyon, New York
(212) 355-4143
Deborah Sottile, Port Ewen
(914) 331-0099
Cathy Stevens, Corning
(607) 936-8369
Ellen Storey, New York
(212) 570-6865
Katherine Wood, Poughkeepsie
(914) 454-2625

North Carolina

Linda Cooper, Winston-Salem
(919) 748-0140
Nancy Everhart, New Bern
(919) 638-2786
Martha Koljonen, Charlotte
(704) 568-5551
Jein-Paul Newland, Raleigh
(919) 787-8644/6643
Betsy Powers, Charlotte
(704) 365-0998
Sharon Wells, Morehead City
(919) 247-2557/726-9089

North Dakota

Roberta Herr, Williston
(701) 572-6477
Beth Lapp, Fargo
(701) 232-0082

Ohio

Bil Fox, Akron
(216) 644-1823
Sandra Freedle,
Maple Heights
(216) 475-6211
Maggie Hurd,
Cleveland Heights
(216) 321-5366
Lyra Lalosh, Cincinnati
(513) 381-2938
Jane Rogers, Dayton
(513) 433-3674

Jan Sylvester, Worthington
(614) 888-6610
Marna Zalla, Cincinnati
(606) 586-7168

Oklahoma

Sue Andrews, Norman
(405) 360-7788
Rebecca Caves,
Oklahoma City
(405) 632-7318
Jo Dunham, Guymon
(405) 338-3232
Margaret Ghostbear, Tulsa
(918) 749-5997
Gerri Hutchinson, Thomas
(405) 661-2665
*Weatherford
Arlene Maguire Johnson, Moore
(405) 799-7329
*Oklahoma City
Kaaren Kelly,
Oklahoma City
(405) 632-1888
Janelle Neely, Edmond
(405) 348-7677
*Oklahoma City
Judy Yancer, Duncan
(405) 252-9325
*Lawton

Oregon

Ann B. Holland, Portland
(503) 245-2813
Alice Marie Livingston, Pendleton
(503) 276-5722
Lin Marie, Portland
(503) 228-9246
Mary Martin, Corvallis
(503) 752-5210/753-2555
Sigrid Ozyp, West Linn
(503) 635-7681
*Portland
Jo Reimer, Portland
(503) 645-4175
Edith Smith, Portland
(503) 297-6706
Louise Wicks, Eugene
(503) 686-9780

Pennsylvania

Rebecca Alexy, Washington
(412) 222-0616/225-4553
*Pittsburgh
Deborah Caruso, Washington
(412) 228-2408

Stephanie Garbon, Du Bois
(814) 375-9558
*W. Central PA
Ellen Grossman, Merion
(215) 664-6445
*Philadelphia
Sally Horner, Erie
(814) 838-1756
Barbara Koch, Pittsburgh
(412) 766-8008
Helen Kuberik, Murrysville
(412) 327-7832
*Pittsburgh
Janet Larkey, Pittsburgh
(412) 731-8558
M. Lorraine Nelson,
Kennett Square
(215) 444-0131
Marcy O'Brien, Warren
(814) 726-3314
*N.W. PA
Judy Peltz, Holland
(215) 968-9422
*Philadelphia
Jill Pettit, Meadville
(814) 724-2411
*Erie
Roberta Revness, Holland
(215) 860-0370
Susan Williams, Somerset
(412) 593-2926
Peter Willms, Camp Hill
(717) 761-6826
*Harrisburg

South Carolina

Sara Patterson, Columbia
(803) 776-2795

South Dakota

Vicki Donovan, Spearfish
(605) 642-4075
Anne Hughes, Sioux Falls
(605) 339-0689

Tennessee

Barbara Bogart, Memphis
(901) 276-2179
Mary Beth Johnson, Clarksville
(615) 647-2132
Judy McLellan, Germantown
(901) 754-4358
*Memphis
Linda Sulcer, Marion, AR
(901) 276-2179
*Memphis

Fay Wilson, Johnson City
(615) 929-1933
*E. Border

Texas (Northeastern)

Janna Beatty, Waco
(817) 776-5369
Lenore Bransford, Hurst
(817) 267-1761
*Ft. Worth
Kathryn Bryan, Ft. Worth
(817) 732-2170
Dorothy Campbell, Texarkana
(214) 792-0657
Keiko Couch, Ft. Worth
(817) 923-9837
Leslie Hill, Arlington
(817) 483-2299
*Ft. Worth–Dallas
Tisha Knudson, Gainesville
(817) 665-1019
Dorothy Lane, Graham
(817) 549-1428
Marilyn Murphy, Dallas
(214) 553-9658
Marsha Newman, Mineola
(214) 569-9643
*Tyler
Julianne Parazo, Carrollton
(214) 245-2688
*Dallas
Marsha Rawlins, Dallas
(214) 526-6813
Lou Robbins, Plano
(214) 867-8444
*Dallas
Ruth Rutchik-Pack, Dallas
(214) 661-8353
Donna Smith,
Highland Village
(214) 436-0950
*Dallas
Marcy Weil, Dallas
(214) 361-4085
Sally Wilder, Ft. Worth
(817) 738-8324

Texas (Southeastern)

Shirley Anslinger, Corpus Christi
(512) 241-6788
Jo Ellyn Bernardin, Houston
(713) 988-2835
Linda Best, The Woodlands
(713) 367-2965
*Houston
Jeannine Cassell, Houston
(713) 977-2022
Ann Connelly, Houston
(713) 370-0218/739-0005

Ruth Constant, Victoria
(512) 578-1801
Terry Davis, San Antonio
(512) 826-3233/0939
Judi Doherty, San Antonio
(512) 684-2421
Sandi Doolan, San Antonio
(512) 657-3827
Ann Hudson, Victoria
(512) 575-5664
Deborah Huff, Katy
(713) 578-5918
Mary Beth Ince, Mason
(915) 258-4484
*Austin
Kelly Lindsey, Austin
(512) 339-7902
Gwen McMurry, Carrizo Springs
(512) 875-3388
Robin Pascal, Houston
(713) 988-1179
Carol Van Pelt, Houston
(713) 465-6076
Sandra Williams, Houston
(713) 973-6320

Texas (Western)

JoAnn Attaway, Quanah
(817) 663-2527
Velm Barton, Canadian
(806) 658-4481
Shirlyn Christian, Odessa
(915) 362-9678
Diane Cole, Abilene
(915) 698-7510
Lynne Griffith, Lubbock
(806) 797-2422
J. J. Love, Midland
(915) 697-0838
*Odessa
Annette McCloy, Morse
(806) 878-3474
Mary Mathieson, Abilene
(915) 698-2831
Victoria Moser, Amarillo
(806) 353-6567
Wynell Noelke, San Angelo
(915) 653-3856

Utah

Brenda Alcorn, Salt Lake City
(801) 968-6181
Toni Bahen, Orem
(801) 225-9692
*Salt Lake City
Cheryl Crowley, Farmington
(801) 451-5353
*Salt Lake City

Darlene Gregersen,
North Salt Lake
(801) 292-5530
Faye Washburn, Alpine
(801) 756-5732
*Provo

Virginia

Rebecca Banis, Chesapeake
(804) 465-0646
*Norfolk
Mary Jane Barnes, Virginia Beach
(804) 425-0926
*Norfolk
Renee Benton, Bena
(804) 877-9666/642-6257
*Hampton
Susan Cook, Reston
(703) 860-0910
*Arlington
Jackie Dye, Ft. Lee
(804) 733-5763
Linda Gobbi, Richmond
(804) 285-8129
Sherri Benton Hargis, Blacksburg
(703) 953-2021
Marilyn Hearn, Virginia Beach
(804) 425-7868
Caryl Krannich, Manassas
(703) 361-7300
*Arlington
Claudine Lee, Richmond
(804) 262-6292
Bonnie Dean Miller, Berryville
(703) 955-2676
Carrie Rehberg, Fredericksburg
(703) 786-4251
Petsy Rudacille, Front Royal
(703) 636-6327
Kathleen Skretvedt, Richmond
(804) 358-4141
*Richmond
Susan Straight, Vienna
(703) 938-4445
*Arlington

Washington, D.C.

Nancy Bagley
(202) 822-9195
Trina Duncan
(202) 362-0800
JoAnne Nicholson
(202) 293-9175
Mimi Wolford
(202) 362-0532

Washington

Daphne Lindsay, Bellingham
(206) 676-1535
Colleen Marie, Bellingham
(206) 734-0404
Shannon O'Leary, Seattle
(206) 325-2904
Linda Scarvie, Auburn
(206) 833-6384
Kay Stewart, Issaquah
(206) 641-1483
Janice Van Eaton,
Woodinville
(206) 483-2660
Paula Wilson, Seattle
(206) 643-5168

West Virginia

See Neighboring States

Wisconsin

Elaine Feder, Oconomowoc
(414) 567-4963
Ardith Lawson-Cipar, Verona
(608) 836-8401
*Madison
Rosemary Lloyd, Neenah
(414) 725-8854
Susan Kaul Moeschberger,
Milwaukee
(414) 442-3551
Yvonne Staacke, North Lake
(414) 966-2381
*Milwaukee
Joan Stone, Dousman
(414) 392-9604
*Milwaukee
Debbie Young, Clintonville
(715) 823-5390

Wyoming

Lynne Applegate, Cheyenne
(307) 638-9498
Cherry Manion, Jackson
(307) 733-4792
Daphene Minter, Riverton
(307) 856-2581
*Casper

Australia

Jacqueline Ainsworth
Sydney, N.S.W.
231-6500
Nancy Uchytil Annett,
Port Hedland, W.A.
(091) 73 1197
Diane Humphreys
Canberra, A.C.T.
(062) 81 2460
Yvonne McMahon,
Westleigh, N.S.W.
875-1032

Canada

Paula L. Boer, Vancouver
British Columbia
(604) 266-6833
Carolyn Correia,
Manotick, Ontario
(613) 692-4473
Gail Johnson,
Ottawa, Ontario
(613) 236-2777
Deborah Kerfoot
Edmonton, Alberta
(403) 429-3498
Rosalind Logue,
Toronto, Ontario
(416) 485-7799

England

Phyllis Quasha, London
(01) 235-5677

France

Mary Beth Behrent, Paris
(01) 527-6816

Indonesia

Barbara Rucker, Jakarta
715-280

Israel

Nina Tronstein, Jerusalem
(02) 719-691/240-077

Japan

Elaine Barron, Okinawa
09893-5-2534
Debbi Krafft,
Yokota Air Base
(0425) 52-2511, Ext. 4898

Philippines

Backie Celdran, Makati
817-1005
Patricia Dale Eyre, Manila
842-3486

Singapore

Joanna Haak
468-0392
Gisel Potts
469-86056

Index

A

All-one-color looks, *see* Monotone looks
All-weather coats, 171–72
Attaché cases
  for Contrast color type, 146–47
  for Gentle color type, 97–98
  for Light-Bright color type, 122–23
  for Muted color type, 73–74

B

Balanced look, 41, 44
Bargains, 192
Basic color types, 3, 6, 22
  determination of, 16–21
  See also Contrast color type; Gentle
    color type; Light-Bright color
    type; Muted color type
Beige, 40
  for Contrast color type, 140–41
  for Gentle color type, 92
  for Light-Bright color type, 117–18
  for Muted color type, 62, 68
Best color families, 24
Black, 31–32
  for Contrast color type, 136–37
  for Gentle color type, 88–89
  for Light-Bright color type, 113–14
  for Muted color type, 63–64
Black skin tones, 12
Blacking out, 199
Blended look, 36–37
Blonds, 4, 15, 54–55
Blouses, 5, 163–64
Blush, 52
  for Contrast color type, 151
  for Gentle color type, 102
  for Light-Bright color type, 126–27
  for Muted color type, 77

Body color, 3, 7, 12, 24, 199
  determination of, 26–28
Bright clarity, 34, 199
  for Contrast color type, 133
  for Light-Bright color type, 109
Brown hair, 16
Browns
  for Contrast color type, 137–38
  for Gentle color type, 91
  for Light-Bright color type, 116–17
  for Muted color type, 67
Brunettes, 4, 16
Burgundy, 40
  for Contrast color type, 141–42
  for Gentle color type, 93–94
  for Light-Bright color type, 119–20
  for Muted color type, 69–70

C

Camel
  for Contrast color type, 138
  for Gentle color type, 89–90
  for Light-Bright color type, 114–15
  for Muted color type, 64–65
Camouflaging figure faults, 40–41
Capsule wardrobe, 159–74
  case study, 169–70
  casual, 174
  coats in, 171–74
  for Contrast color type, 168
  for Gentle color type, 166
  for Light-Bright color type, 167
  for Muted color type, 165
  for working, 161–65
Casual wardrobe, 174
Caucasian skin tones, 12
Cheeks, color for, *see* Blush
Children, 50
Clarities, 19, 25–26, 34, 199–200
  for Contrast color type, 133–34

for Gentle color type, 85
for Light-Bright color type, 109–10
for Muted color type, 60–61
Coats, 171–74
  See also Furs
Color
  impact on others of, 176–78
  as self-motivator, 176
Color accents, 197, 200
Color breaks, 195–97, 200
Color families, 200
Color types, 200
  See also Basic color types
Complimentary colors, 28–29, 200–201
Conglomeration collection, 191
Contrast color type, 6, 11, 132–55
  capsule wardrobe for, 168
  clarities for, 34, 35, 133–34
  color accents for, 197
  contrast levels for, 134–36
  determination of, 17–20
  dressing down by, 178
  earthy looks for, 181–82
  ethereal look for, 179–80
  evening wear for, 148–49
  fabric colors and weights for, 142–43
  full-figured, 42–44
  furs for, 149
  glasses for, 148
  hair color for, 54, 155
  handbags and attaché cases for, 146–47
  as headless person, 194
  insignificant look on, 194
  jewelry for, 145–46
  makeup for, 149–55
  neutrals for, 136–42
  patterns for, 143–44
  power dressing for, 188
  shoes for, 147–48
  showstopper look for, 184
  universally enhancing colors and, 39

Contrast levels, 36–38, 200–201
  for Contrast color type, 134–36
  for Gentle color type, 85–87
  for Light-Bright color type, 110–12
  for Muted color type, 61–62
  universally enhancing, 39
Cross-color types, 3, 21

D

Dark neutrals, 31–32
Dark values, 35
Designs, *see* Patterns
"Dress for success" theory, 4–5
Dressing down, 177–78

E

Earthy looks, 180–82
Ethereal looks, 179–80
Evening wear
  for Contrast color type, 148–49
  for Gentle color type, 99–100
  for Light-Bright color type, 124
  for Muted color type, 75–76
Eye color, 12, 27–28
Eye makeup
  for Contrast color type, 151–52
  for Gentle color type, 103
  for Light-Bright color type, 127–28
  for Muted color type, 78–79
Eyeglass frames, *see* Glasses

F

Fabric textures and weights
  for Contrast color type, 142–43
  for Gentle color type, 94–95
  for Light-Bright color type, 120
  for Muted color type, 70–71
  for suits, 162–63
Figure faults, camouflaging, 40–41
Foundation, 45–49
  for Contrast color type, 150–51
  for Gentle color type, 102
  for Light-Bright color type, 126
  for Muted color type, 77
  for sun tan, 48–49
  toner under, 47–48
Fragile looks, 179–80
Full-figured women, 41–44
Furs
  for Contrast color type, 149
  for Gentle color type, 100
  for Light-Bright color type, 124–25
  for Muted color type, 76

G

Gentle color type, 6, 11, 84–107
  capsule wardrobe for, 166
  clarities for, 34, 35, 85
  contrast levels for, 85–87
  determination of, 17–21
  dressing down by, 178
  earthy looks for, 181
  ethereal look for, 179–80
  evening wear for, 99–100
  fabric textures and weights for, 94–95
  full-figured, 42

furs for, 100
glasses for, 98–99
hair coloring for, 106–7
handbags and attaché cases for, 97–98
as headless person, 194
insignificant look on, 194
jewelry for, 95–96
makeup for, 100–105
neutrals for, 87–94
patterns for, 95
power dressing for, 187–88
shoes for, 98
showstopper look for, 184
universally enhancing colors and, 39
Gentle/Light-Bright color type, 21, 34
Gentle-Muted color type, 21
Glasses
  for Contrast color type, 148
  for Gentle color type, 98–99
  for Light-Bright color type, 123–24
  makeup and, 53
  for Muted color type, 75
Gray, 30–31
  for Contrast color type, 138–39
  for Gentle color type, 90
  for Light-Bright color type, 116
  for Muted color type, 65–66
Gray hair, 4, 16
  coloring, 56
Green
  for Contrast color type, 142
  for Gentle color type, 94
  for Light-Bright color type, 120
  for Muted color type, 70
  universally enhancing, 39

H

Hair color, 4, 11, 12
  changing, 53–56
  of children, 50
  for Contrast color type, 155
  determination of, 15–16
  for Gentle color type, 106–7
  for Light-Bright color type, 131
  for Muted color type, 81–82
Handbags
  for Contrast color type, 146–47
  for Gentle color type, 97–98
  for Light-Bright color type, 122–23
  for Muted color type, 73–74
Headless person look, 193–94
Heavier women, 41–44
Highlights, 15–16

I

Image consultants, 5
Insignificant look, 194
Intense clarity, 34, 199
  for Contrast color type, 133

J

Jackets, 173–74
Jewelery
  for Contrast color type, 145–46
  for Gentle color type, 95–96
  for Light-Bright color type, 121–22
  for Muted color type, 71–72

L

Light-Bright color type, 6, 11, 108–31
  capsule wardrobe for, 167
  clarities for, 34, 35, 109–10
  color breaks for, 196
  contrast levels for, 110–12
  determination of, 17–21
  dressing down by, 178
  earthy look for, 181–82
  ethereal look for, 179–80
  evening wear for, 124
  fabric textures and weights for, 120
  full-figured, 42–43
  furs for, 124–25
  glasses for, 123–24
  hair coloring for, 131
  handbags and attaché cases for, 122–23
  as headless person, 194
  insignificant look on, 194
  jewelry for, 121–22
  makeup for, 125–30
  neutrals for, 112–20
  patterns for, 120–21
  power dressing for, 188
  shoes for, 123
  showstopper look for, 182, 184–85
  universally enhancing colors and, 39
Light-Bright/Contrast color type, 34
Light values, 35
Lip color, 12, 26, 50–51
  for Contrast color type, 151
  for Gentle color type, 102–3
  for Light-Bright color type, 126–27
  for Muted color type, 78

M

Makeup, 45–53
  for cheeks, 52
  for Contrast color type, 149–55
  foundation, 45–49
  for Gentle color type, 100–105
  glasses and, 53
  for Light-Bright color type, 125–30
  for lips, 50–52
  for Muted color type, 76–81
Medium contrast, 37–38
Monotone looks, 42
  for Contrast color type, 135–36
  for dressing down, 178
  for Muted color type, 62
Mood dressing, 179–88
Muted color type, 6, 11, 59–83
  capsule wardrobe for, 165
  clarity for, 34, 35, 60–61
  contrast levels for, 61–62
  determination of, 17–20
  dressing down by, 178
  earthy look for, 181
  ethereal look for, 179–80
  evening wear for, 75–76
  fabric textures and weights for, 70–71
  full-figured, 42
  furs for, 76
  glasses for, 75
  hair coloring and, 54
  as headless person, 194
  insignificant look on, 194
  jewelry for, 71–72

Muted color type (continued)
  makeup for, 76–81
  neutrals for, 62–70
  patterns for, 71
  power dressing for, 187
  shoes for, 74–75
  showstopper look for, 183–84
  universally enhancing colors and, 39, 40
Muted/Contrast color type, 21, 34

N

Navy
  for Contrast color type, 139
  for Gentle color type, 90–91
  for Light-Bright color type, 115–16
  for Muted color type, 66
  universally enhancing, 39
Neck accessories, 163, 164
  for color breaks, 195–96
Neutrals, 192–93
  for Contrast color type, 136–42
  dark, 31–32
  for Gentle color type, 87–94
  gray, 31–32
  for Light-Bright color type, 112–20
  for Muted color type, 62–70
  for power dressing, 186

O

Off-whites, 30, 39
  for Muted color type, 62
Orange, 28–29
Overpowering colors, 201

P

Pastels, 35
  contrasts with, 36–37
Patterns
  for Contrast color type, 143–44
  for Gentle color type, 95
  for Light-Bright color type, 120–21
  for Muted color type, 71
  size of, 43–44
  for suits, 162
Personal Color Harmony Chart, 25
Personal color spectrum, 3

Power dressing, 185–88
Prints, see Patterns
Pure pigment colors, 34
Pure White Test, 17
Purple
  shades of, 28
  universally enhancing, 39

R

Raincoats, 171–72
Redheads, 4, 15
Reds
  body color and, 26–27
  for lip color, 50–52
  shades of, 33
Reverse frosting, 56
Rust
  for Contrast color type, 141
  for Gentle color type, 91–92
  for Light-Bright color type, 117
  for Muted color type, 67–68

S

Seasonal colors, 4
Shades, 25–26, 33–34, 201
Shoes
  for Contrast color type, 147–48
  for Gentle color type, 98
  for Light-Bright color type, 123
  for Muted color type, 74–75
  for working wardrobe, 164
Shopping, 197–98
Showstopper looks, 182–85
Skin tone, 3, 11–12
  aging and, 49–50
  determination of, 12–15
  foundation and, 45–49
Soft contrast, 36–37
Stripes, vertical, 43
Strong contrast, 36
Subdued clarity, 34, 200
  for Gentle color type, 85
  for Muted color type, 60
Suits, 4–5, 161–63
  for power dressing, 186
  tops to wear with, 163–64
Sun tan, 48–49

T

Tan, makeup and, 48–49
Toned-down clarity, 34, 200
  for Gentle color type, 85
  for Light-Bright color type, 109
  for Muted color type, 60
Toners, 47–48
Tops
  for color breaks, 195–96
  to wear with suits, 163–64

U

Underpowering colors, 201
Uniform dressing, 193
Universal color principles, 33–35
Universal Skin-Tone Chart, 13, 14
Universally enhancing colors, 38–40

V

Value of colors, 35, 201
  contrast of, 36–38
Vertical stripes, 43

W

Wardrobe mistakes, 191–94
  salvaging, 195–98
Wardrobe planning, see Capsule wardrobe
White, 29–30, 201
  for Contrast color type, 139–40
  for Gentle color type, 93
  for Light-Bright color type, 118–19
  for Muted color type, 60, 69
  universally enhancing, 39–40
Wine
  for Contrast color type, 141–42
  for Gentle color type, 93–94
  for Light-Bright color type, 119–20
  for Muted color type, 69–70
Woman-Across-the-Room Test, 17–20
Wool coats, 172–73
Working wardrobe, 161–65

Y

Yellow, eye color and, 28